PHILADELPHIA

Y L V A N I A

R Y L A

WITHDRAWN

N E W

D E L A W A R E

WASHINGTON

BELLE
GROVE

9'

COLES HILL

LITTLE BYRD CREEK
PLANTATION

C H E S A P E A K E   B A Y

GLAMOROUS DOLLY MADISON

Books by

ALICE CURTIS DESMOND

FAR HORIZONS

SOUTH AMERICAN ADVENTURES

LUCKY LLAMA

FEATHERS

JORGE'S JOURNEY

SOLDIER OF THE SUN

FOR CROSS AND KING

MARTHA WASHINGTON, OUR FIRST LADY

THE SEA CATS

GLAMOROUS DOLLY MADISON

ALICE CURTIS DESMOND

Glamorous Dolly Madison

Dodd, Mead & Company
New York   1948

Published April, 1946
Second printing, November, 1946
Third printing, October, 1947
Fourth printing, January, 1948

Contents

Contents

GLAMOROUS DOLLY MADISON

Prologue

THE FEBRUARY DAY WAS BRIGHT AND CLEAR, WITH A PROMISE of Virginia spring in the air. Across the rolling hills of Hanover County, the clay road curled ahead like a long, rust-colored ribbon.

The driver of the two-wheeled chaise guided his weary horse along this muddy highway that ran from the North Carolina border to his plantation above Richmond. John Payne was twenty-nine that year of 1769. But his thin face under the broad-brimmed Quaker hat was so stern that no look of youth remained. His cold gray eyes mirrored the intense absorption of a man who knew his duty and never swerved from it.

"John, it's good to be going home."

Slender in her drab cape, Mary Payne (Molly to her family) lifted her sweet face, framed in a Quaker scoop bonnet, to smile at her grave husband. Molly's body was bone-tired from the long journey from her uncle's home in Guilford County, North Carolina. But a light of happy anticipation gleamed in her eyes.

At the sight of his wife's brunette beauty, John Payne's heart beat the faster. Molly's crimson cheeks were not quite proper for a prim Quaker wife. But they were her natural inheritance as one of the women of the handsome Winston family. And besides, there was no more industrious wife in Hanover County, no wiser mother.

John's eyes rested on his two little boys, one on his lap,

1

the other nodding beside him in the carriage. Grasping the reins more firmly, he agreed, "Home will be good."

Molly scarcely heard her husband's reply. There was a low whimper from the bundle cradled in her arms. Pushing back the white shawl, the young mother kissed her baby's rose-leaf cheek. The little girl slept again, lulled by the swaying of the vehicle.

A short year ago, when the Payne family drove southward along this road to North Carolina, there had been no baby daughter, only the two boys. Sturdy, brunette Walter, six then; and his sandy-haired brother, two-year-old William Temple. The twentieth of last May, down in Guilford County, in the home of Molly's uncle, not far from the New Garden Meeting House, this dear little mite had opened her blue eyes for the first time.

Enjoying the hospitality of the North Carolina plantation, the Paynes had stayed on as guests of their relatives all through the summer and fall. But Friend John Payne, the sober-faced head of the family, was worried. England had passed the Townshend Acts that levied heavy duties on tea, glass, lead and other necessities imported into her American colonies. In the Virginia House of Burgesses, George Washington and Patrick Henry urged the boycott of these taxed goods.

Would there be a revolution? John asked himself. The September before, two British regiments had landed in Boston to enforce the Townshend Acts. If the haughty troops turned and fired on the crowds, would it lead to war? And if war came to Massachusetts, might it spread to Virginia?

Sorely troubled, Friend Payne bundled his little family into the two-wheeled chaise and turned his horse's head toward home. If war came, he must be in Virginia to protect Little Byrd Creek plantation. He was the squire of four hundred acres, the gift of his father, another John Payne, a gentleman of English birth, who had settled westward in Goochland County.

The carriage lurched through the red mud. A grove of chestnut trees loomed ahead. At the sight among them of two red brick chimneys above a slate-gray roof, Molly's heart warmed.

"Thy Negroes will be glad to see thee, John," she said eagerly. "I hope thee finds everything all right. The baby's nurse—"

"Niles wrote he had found a good woman, named Amy. Her child has died. Thee will find her waiting," replied John, as he turned the chaise up the drive to the house.

It was not a stately Virginia mansion; merely a square white farm house, slate-roofed and flanked by twin brick chimneys. But with its faded blinds and small, pillared porch, the place had a friendly, welcoming look.

John Payne drove past the stables, the kitchen garden and the slaves' quarters—tiny log cabins. At the white door, he pulled the horse to a stop. With a shout of welcome, a half dozen Negroes sprang from behind the house. A smiling brown urchin caught the horse's bridle.

Acknowledging their greeting with grave dignity, the master of Little Byrd Creek plantation descended from the carriage, lifted out the sleepy boys, and held up his hand to his wife.

Molly Payne stepped out with the ease of a child. As she stood before her home, tears of joy sparkled in her eyes. The parting of a curtain drew her glance to a window at which a woman stood, staring out intently. Her brown, haggard face was framed by a red calico turban.

The child in Molly's arm squirmed. From beneath the shawl came a loud cry.

"All dat noise, honey, and you'se so small." At the soft-voiced sound, Molly jumped. The gaunt-faced Negro woman had opened the front door.

"Molly, this is Amy—thy new nurse," the master said.

The woman's face was as light as well-creamed coffee. In her stiff white dress, she seemed neither young nor old. Her dark, melancholy eyes held Molly.

"Of course, I knew," she answered slowly. "She's starved for a baby," she told herself. "She has lost her own child."

Behind Amy, other household servants had gathered, grinning and bowing. Everyone wanted to see the new baby.

A red-haired man in work clothes pushed his way through the crowd. "Glad to have you back, sir. Things are upset," he sighed.

John Payne glanced at his wife. "Come and tell me about it, Niles." Taking the overseer's arm, he drew him into his study.

Amy had not taken her hungry eyes from the shawl-wrapped bundle in Molly's arms. "Shall I take the baby now?" She held out her large, capable brown hands.

The woman's fierce expression frightened Molly a little. But her natural kindness and common sense conquered her fear. "Yes, please," she said, and turned her child over to the new nurse.

Immediately, the infant let out a series of piercing screams. As Molly tried to comfort her, the study door was flung open. John Payne frowned out at the group.

"What's the trouble?" he asked sharply. He was tired from the long journey. And Niles's brief comments on serious unrest in Virginia had borne out his worst fears. "Give the child to me," he said sternly. "I'll quiet her."

Instead of calming down, the baby screamed crossly. Her red, indignant little face seemed all open mouth. Her tiny hands beat the air. Tremendous energy was focused in the small, tense body.

As unreasonable anger surged over him, Friend Payne lifted his hand and slapped his daughter's plump rear.

"Oh, John, don't," Molly said in an agonized whisper. It had been right to punish the two boys with whippings when they misbehaved. But this baby, this little girl . . .

The squalling ceased abruptly. The child's mouth was still open, but no sound came. Then the white lids over the blue eyes fluttered. The lips parted in a winning smile.

"Look, Molly, thy child is quiet again," said her father triumphantly.

The young mother stretched out her hands. "Let me have her, John." How different her third babe was from the others! Fat, stolid Walter had never cried. Neither had William Temple, although a sensitive, mouse-like little boy. But this girl-child needed special treatment, not spankings. Molly's pretty face wore a critical, accusing mask.

Friend Payne was keenly aware of his wife's displeasure. "She will need discipline, Molly," he reminded her. He stroked the child's cheek. "Look, she is happy now. With that smile, she will make her own way in life, without money or high connections. She has a great asset—the whole world will love her."

The baby's beguiling smile wrung Molly's heart. "Go to sleep, my sweet, my Dorothea . . ." she crooned.

John caught the strange name. "Who is that, Dorothea?"

"It's the child's name," said his wife stoutly. During the whole nine months of their daughter's life, this was the first time they had discussed a name.

"Dorothea," repeated her husband. "What sort of name is that? Comfort, Temperance, Charity—or even Patience, if thee wishes. Faith, Submit, Silence; those good Quaker names are better. But never *Dorothea*."

"Her name is Dorothea," Molly insisted with a rare stubbornness that surprised and shocked John Payne. "I want my daughter named after Dorothea Dandridge."

John flushed. He was always angered at the mention of the Nathaniel West Dandridges of Williamsburg, wealthy friends of his wife's first cousin, Patrick Henry.

It was not that John was less well born than pretty, dark-haired Mary Coles Payne. True, her father, William, had come from Enniscorthy, on the River Slaney in County Wexford, Ireland, and her mother, a Winston, was the aunt of Virginia's famous orator, Patrick Henry.

But the Paynes themselves were well-connected, fairly prosperous Virginia planters. John's father, a man of some wealth and education, had represented Goochland County in the House of Burgesses for over fifteen years. His mother was Anna Fleming, granddaughter of Sir Thomas Fleming, who claimed to be a second son of the Scottish Earl of Wigton. Landing with the early settlers at Jamestown, Fleming had established his family in Kent County.

The root of the annoyance was simply that, as a strict Quaker, Friend John Payne disapproved of the fashionable Nathaniel West Dandridges and their freer way of living.

Nathaniel was first cousin to Mrs. George Washington of Mount Vernon, and a captain in the Royal Navy, retired because of a leg wound. His wife was a daughter of the royal governor of Virginia, Alexander Spotswood. The four Dandridge girls, Elizabeth, Anna Katharine, Mary Clairbourne and Dorothea, formed a troop of dashing horsewomen, each with her own mount, who, so John Payne had heard, galloped gaily along the Duke of Gloucester Street to the admiration of the cocked-hat Williamsburg gentry.

"I thought—Mother thought—" Molly faced her husband

bravely, "that if I had a daughter and named her Dorothea, the Dandridge family would like it."

"Does thee imagine those high-nosed aristocrats will feel honored to have a Quaker child named after one of theirs?" thundered John Payne. "Come to thy senses, Molly. We Friends cling to our own names—Deliverance, Peace, Endurance, Truegrace. Thee has many to choose from."

At the sound of these formidable names, the baby gave a cry of protest. "Please, Massa, give me the chile." Nurse Amy stepped between the parents, her hands outstretched.

Molly's mouth was set in a firm line. "I felt a concern, John. I prayed to God. That was the name that came—Dorothea—it means 'gift of God.'"

John Payne's gray-clad shoulders stiffened. He stared curiously at his wife. "If thee had a concern, Molly, I cannot oppose it," he said at last. "Our babe's name is Dorothea. But I do not like it. It has a worldly sound. With that name, she may stray far from the Friends—far from us—"

He looked pale and defeated. Turning abruptly, he stepped into his study and closed the door.

Quaker babies have no christening in church with consecrated water. A name is simply selected and bestowed on the child. So then and there, the third child of John and Mary Payne became Dorothea.

As Mammy Amy carried the baby up the stairs, Molly followed. For nine months down in North Carolina, the little one had been her own, to feed and cherish. Now she must share her with this strange, possessive woman. But for a moment, the sense of triumph over the baby's naming dulled Molly's motherly envy.

Dorothea! The picturesque name colored the whole future of the sleeping child. She would be no quiet, acquiescent little girl, her tiny feet set in the straight path of Quakerdom. She would know how wide and golden could be the road that leads to fame and wealth.

Even in her sleep, little Dorothea's baby face seemed determined. Hidden within the tiny body were the qualities that her new name represented—valiant courage, fierce loyalty, and warm generosity—traits that were to be a very real part of the nature of an older Dorothea Payne.

Upstairs, Molly bent over the wooden cradle in which Mammy Amy had placed her child. "Don't stray too far from me, little Dorothea," she whispered.

1 Hard to Be Good

*I*T WAS STIFLING HOT THAT JULY DAY IN THE CEDAR CREEK Meeting House. For over an hour, the members of the Quaker congregation had remained in heat and silence, waiting for the Spirit to move someone to speak.

On one side of the bare hall, on narrow, uncomfortable benches, were the gray-clad men. The boys were beside them. On the other side were the women and girls in drab bonnets and plain, dun-colored dresses.

One small girl sat like a tiny statue, her mittened hands folded in her lap. She must keep perfectly still, she knew. She must not so much as peek around her scoop bonnet at her brothers, Walter and William Temple. It was First Day, as the Friends call their Sunday. On this, of all days, Quaker children must be quiet and good.

The blue-eyed girl stifled a yawn. It was hard for a seven-year-old to sit still so long—doubly hard for Dorothea Payne, a restless child, and talkative by nature.

Her feet, just showing below the long gray dress, were numb; her shoulders ached. A fly lighted on her straight little nose. She lifted her hand to swat it, and missed. Her reticule fell with a thud that echoed through the hall. Everyone jumped.

A wave of shame dyed Dorothea Payne's cheeks to the roots of her curly black hair. Miserably, she lifted her big eyes to where Mother and Father sat with the elders on the raised benches that faced the congregation.

9

John and Molly Payne were clerks of the Cedar Creek Meeting, and very important. Why did their daughter always have to disgrace them? Why was she "naturally naughty," as her father often said. Why couldn't she be "good" like her brothers? Especially pious Walter, who always behaved in meeting.

"Dolly, *quiet!*" Mother's pained look from the facing-bench seemed to admonish her. Dorothea, the worldly name that so offended John Payne, had long ago been shortened by the family to "Dolly."

Sure of a scolding, the child settled herself rigidly on the bench and listened intently for the Inner Voice.

"If thee keep perfectly still in meeting, thee will hear the Inner Voice," John Payne had explained to his children, "just as the boy, George Fox, heard it."

It seemed that when James I was King of England, the first Quaker—George Fox, a weaver's son—had lived in the village of Fenny Drayton, near London.

The boy used to sit for hours in the village church, watching the hourglass on the preacher's pulpit. He hated the long, threatening sermons mouthed by certain of the clergy in "steepled" churches. He dreamed of a different religion; one based on love of God, not fear.

The weaver's son became a shepherd. One day as he guarded his flocks on a Yorkshire hilltop, Pendle Hill, a revelation came to George Fox. In a blinding flash he knew that Jesus, Who had died on the cross 1,600 years before, was still living. Ordinary mortals could not see Him. But if they would listen and believe, He would speak to them and show them how to live.

George became a preacher. He traveled about England, spreading his gospel that God would speak directly to the souls of men. But some English churchmen believed all God

would ever say was in the Bible, and only they should inter-
pret His will. So for his sermons, George Fox and his followers were persecuted and put in prison.

Even then, Fox continued to teach the religion of the
Inner Light in every soul, and a Voice, through which God
tells men how to live. That was why the Quakers sat silent in
meeting and waited for God to speak to them. They are
called Friends because Jesus said, "I have called you friends."

But the Inner Voice moved no one to preach that hot July
day of 1775, in the Cedar Creek Meeting. At last two elders
rose from the facing-bench and shook hands—the signal that
the meeting was over.

Dolly Payne walked out of the building with her mother.
On the steps, Father and the boys were waiting. Walter and
William Temple wore the same gray coats, the same broad-
brimmed hats as their father, just as Dolly was dressed in the
straight basque, meekly folded kerchief, and long full skirt
of her mother.

The men and boys had kept on their hats in meeting. This
was a Quaker custom, except when praying aloud. George
Fox believed hat-removing to be a mark of servility. He had
refused to take his off, even before Oliver Cromwell. He
removed his hat only to God.

Standing beside Father was Henry Bull from North Carolina, the Payne's guest today. Because John and Molly were
clerks of the congregation, visiting preachers usually stayed
at Little Byrd Creek plantation. If Dolly were lucky, her
father might be so absorbed with Friend Bull that he would
overlook punishing his daughter for dropping her reticule in
meeting.

To her surprise, she was not even scolded. That day in the
Payne's keeping-room, Dolly and her brothers sat in rapt attention at the feet of the gaunt, white-haired preacher, as he

told of seriously disturbed conditions in the outside world.

Month by month, the breach between America and England had widened. That March of 1775, Benjamin Franklin, agent for several of the colonies in London, had returned home with the conviction that further diplomacy was useless. In April came the battle of Lexington. Last May, the second Continental Congress had met in Philadelphia; Ethan Allen and his Green Mountain Boys had captured Fort Ticonderoga. In June, Gage's army stormed the Americans on Bunker Hill. This very July, George Washington had taken command of the Continental army which besieged Gage in Boston.

Henry Bull had been present on the April night when Gage sent troops to seize the powder stored at Concord and to arrest the "traitors," John Hancock and Samuel Adams, hiding in Lexington.

"Did thee see Paul Revere?" Walter asked eagerly.

The elderly preacher nodded. From Revere's own lips, he had heard how he had galloped ahead of the British troops, roused the farmers on the way and warned the refugees.

Dolly's face was pink with excitement. Her father was tense and anxious; there was worry in her mother's eyes. But these events in far-off Boston seemed no more real to the seven-year-old girl than the tales visiting preachers told of their escapes from Indians.

Yet war was closer to Virginia than she knew. The March before, Dolly's own cousin, Patrick Henry, had risen in St. John's Church, Richmond, and pleaded with his state to join Massachusetts in resisting English oppression. "Is life so dear, or peace so sweet, as to be purchased at the price of chains and slavery?" Patrick Henry cried to those who still hoped for peace. "I know not what course others may take, but as for me, give me liberty or give me death."

Molly Payne repeated these stirring words to her children. Young Dolly had not quite understood. But she was proud that Patrick Henry was her second cousin, although she had never met him. John Payne did not approve of the liberal ways of his wife's relative.

Indeed, no visitors lifted the brass knocker on the Payne's white door except the Quaker preachers. The family lived quietly, and very much within themselves.

Days at Little Byrd Creek began before dawn. At daylight, John and Molly gathered with their children for breakfast, a plain but hearty meal—plenty of porridge, rye bread and corn pone; but none of the hot popovers, cold meats, jams and marmalades found on non-Quaker tables. Each child must eat every scrap of food on his plate. Not a crumb must be wasted. George Fox, who lived simply, had left his example to his followers.

And each child must do his share of work. Before going to the school run by the Cedar Creek Meeting, Dolly had to make her bed and tidy her room. The two boys split kindling wood and hauled water.

Evenings it was the same, not an idle moment for John Payne's children. It was Dolly's duty to slip out while the others were at supper, stir up the keeping-room fire, and place the chairs about in a circle. Later the household all gathered there. Even Mammy Amy.

Always the aging colored woman sat close to her "chile," on her face the look of possessive love that Molly had feared when the baby had first been laid in her arms. All evening she hardly took her eyes from the pretty little girl seated by the keeping-room fire, industriously knitting.

Until bedtime, which came early, the boys studied their lessons. Mother worked on her quilt—Job's Trouble was the design, all hexagon pieces. Sometimes the children quarreled.

Or Walter pulled Dolly's yarn and teased her. Then Father packed them off to bed with a rousing scolding.

Punishments were frequent in Dolly's life. She had been told countless times that her high-spirited ways would bring shame to her Quaker family. She dreaded a scolding, especially from her nervous, quick-moving father, whose eye spoke severity and censure. His voice was stern and forbidding, not musical and sweet like Molly Payne's.

Dolly feared Father least in the garden among his flowers. There the pale, earnest man seemed kind and loving. There his daughter spoke to him freely and without fear.

It had been John Payne who taught his children the names of the flowers—the blue hyacinths, the tiny forget-me-nots, and the sweet-smelling lilacs. The Puritans were not the only flower lovers to come to the new land. Quakers were quick to plant gardens, to raise blossoms as well as fruit. Father had shown them what fascinating curls could be made by splitting the dandelion stems and sucking them. But he flew into a temper when Dolly made the yellow dandelions into necklaces and bracelets, and decked her plain gray gown with glowing color.

"Quakers do not wear vain ornaments!" John flushed with anger. "My child, thee are not too young to be made to understand what it means to be a Friend. Go to thy room at once. Stay there without supper. Some way must be found to teach thee to be less worldly and sinful."

Love of flowers might have brought father and daughter closer—in his strict way, John Payne was a devoted parent. But the garden was the source of many of their quarrels. For in Dolly the longing for bright colors grew and grew.

Other Colonial girls played with rag or china dolls. Dolly made her dolls from the flaming poppies, whose petals formed gay scarlet petticoats. Hollyhocks, she found, could be tied into dolls with shining satin gowns. The lungworts' bells made blue dancing ladies. If pins were stuck upright in a piece of wood, the blue silken frocks could be hung over them. The green calyx looked like a tiny hat.

Forbidden all amusement on First Day, Dolly was allowed to gather lungwort bells in the garden on the holy day. Later Father discovered to his horror that his daughter had arranged her pink and blue ladies in colorful rows, and was happily playing "dancing party" to pass the long, weary afternoon.

"Child, give me those sinful things at once!" His voice quivered with anger.

The little girl's eyes filled. When Father crushed the dolls in his big hands, Dolly sobbed as though her heart would break. So father and daughter grew apart.

How was the child to know that John Payne's severity was partly due to anxieties she was too young to understand? In 1777, one of the darkest years of the Revolution, Dolly was only nine years old. Americans, tense with the greatest crisis since the battle of Lexington, were enlisting by the hundreds—even the gentle Quakers whom George Fox had taught to hate war and deeds of violence. Intensely patriotic, but true to the principles of his sect, Friend Payne was torn with doubts. Should he remain at home? Or should he enlist to defend his country? This self questioning made him cross and irritable.

Dolly, particularly, was the object of her father's wrath. No matter how much John Payne prayed, the love of "vain things" could not be killed in his daughter.

At nine, the pretty, rosy-cheeked child detested the drab gray gowns she was forced to wear. She longed for red and blue and green silk dresses, with hoops beneath to sway as she walked. She hated her plain, ugly bonnets, that pinched her ears and were very hot.

One day as Molly Payne tried in vain to arrange Dolly's thick black curls into sleek braids proper for a Quaker child, her daughter burst out: "I wish I had pretty clothes . . . a bright silk frock . . . a bonnet with flowers on it."

Molly's face paled. What had John Payne predicted? "With that name, she may stray far from the Friends—far from us—"

"Sometimes thee troubles me, Dolly," her mother said gently. "And thy father is troubled, too."

"Why can't we have flowered bonnets and colored dresses, Mother?" the child insisted.

"Because we're Friends. The simplicity of gray is part of our religion. We believe ornaments to be worldly and wicked."

Her daughter pouted. So many lovely things were forbidden to strict Quakers. It seemed as though they feared their natural love of beauty, believed it to be a sin.

Even the singing and dancing down at the slave quarters went on secretly. Dolly did not think her parents knew. They would have forbidden it. Nor did solemn-faced Walter guess; if he had, he would have told Father. But shy, poetic William Temple and his sister knew, and they guarded their secret well. It was on moonlight nights that the slaves danced and sang down behind their cabins, too far from the master's house for the sound to reach John Payne's ears.

On such an evening, in October, 1777, Dolly tossed in her bed. The slaves were dancing, she was sure. All day in the kitchen, there had been suppressed excitement. Poppy and the other maids giggled continuously. Old Sue, the cook, crooned over her dishpan. In the garden, Banjo, Amy's little nephew, had tapped out the news with his feet as he raked the leaves.

Dolly rolled over, gave her pillow a thump. Then she

bounded upright and strained her ears. Faintly, off in the night, she heard the sound of music.

In one leap she was out of bed and hurried into her long gray dress. Forgetting her cap in her excitement, she threw a shawl around her shoulders and groped her way from the room.

At the top of the stairs, Dolly crept quickly across the moonlit path below the fan-shaped window in the hall. The bottom step on the stair creaked loudly. She held her breath and waited. But no door opened. No voice called.

Crossing the lower hall, she tugged at the latch until the front door swung open. She slipped out, pulled it shut behind her. Then she ran down the steps and out across the dewy lawn.

❧   ❧   ❧   ❧   ❧

Back in the house, Mammy Amy woke in a cold sweat. Her "chile" was in trouble and needed her, she knew. Painfully, because her rheumatism was bad, the faithful mammy clambered from her bed and hurried into her clothes. Then she groped her way downstairs to the second floor, and opened the door of Dolly's room. The bed was empty!

A moment later there was a frantic knocking at John Payne's door. Aroused, he faced his daughter's trembling nurse.

"De little missie, she ain't there," Amy gasped. "Her bed's empty. I'm tellin' you—she's been *stolen*."

"Wait for me." The door shut. When it opened again, John rushed out fully dressed. His face pale, he followed the frightened mammy down the hall to Dolly's room. At the sight of the empty bed, his jaw grew as tense as Amy's.

"Come, we must find her," he snapped.

Fear for "little missie" made Mammy Amy forget the pains of her rheumatism. Outside the house, she followed the master as fast as her gnarled limbs would let her.

"I'll never forgive myself, if I've lost dat chile," she moaned.

"Don't cry, Amy." Friend Payne tried to calm her. "Miss Dolly—" he stopped short. They were some distance from the house now, and he could catch the sound of music drifting up from the slave quarters.

"Here, this way. Perhaps they've seen her." Thinking only of finding his child, John hardly realized what this distant music meant. He ran toward the slaves' cabins.

It was too late to stop him. The frightened mammy hobbled after him, groaning with terror.

Breathless, they came to a hedge that screened the rows of white-washed houses. A shout of laughter from the other side greeted them. John Payne stooped down to peer through a hole in the shrubbery. Amy looked, too. One glimpse and she began to moan, "Mercy! Mercy!"

The open space in front of the cabins was lighted by pine knots stuck in the ground to make torches. On this grassy plot, under the full moon, a group of laughing Negroes capered and pranced. A big young man, Jasper, scraped his fiddle, while the others sang, keeping time by clapping their hands, or danced. Poppy and the maids from the house were dancing, too. Even old Sue and Timothy, her husband, were there.

Suddenly the circle of dancers thinned. There was left, one small boy—Banjo.

As he threw back his head, his white teeth flashed. His bare feet moved in time to the music; his hands flapped as loosely at his sides as those of a scarecrow. Jasper hunched his shoulders over his violin. His bow moved swifter still.

But Banjo kept right with the music, his nimble feet making the dust fly.

The jig finished, the crowd drifted apart. Suddenly, in the moonlight, the figure of a small gray-shawled girl was revealed. She was swaying with the music. Her long curls flew as her head tossed to and fro.

"Little missie!" cried Mammy Amy, rapturously.

Now that he knew his daughter was safe, John Payne felt only anger. "Come, we must get her." He pushed his way through the hedge.

As a tall shadow fell suddenly across the moonlit clearing, the startled Negroes turned in horror.

There was the master, a Quaker, who forbade all singing and dancing. He was coming toward them—

With one shriek, the slaves scattered in all directions. Big fat Mammy Sue lifted her great bundle of skirts in both hands and actually kept up with young Poppy and the kitchen maids. Banjo flashed around the corner of a cabin like a swallow. But Dolly was even faster. Scrambling up a bank, the frightened little girl began to run toward a shed to hide. Father's head appeared above the bank just behind her.

"Dolly, come here!" His voice was terrible.

On she ran. Once she tripped over her long shawl and fell, but was up again. Now her father was gaining. It would be only a moment more, and then—

Dolly felt a sharp stitch in her side. She gasped. Then she tumbled over in a heap.

Father ran up, panting. *"Dorothea!"* he thundered. He never called her that unless he was terribly angry. He leaned over and clutched her arm. His grasp hurt.

*H*URT TEARS IN HER BIG EYES, DOLLY WATCHED THE SUN rise over the tobacco fields. It was the morning after the slaves' celebration down in their quarters. Dragging his erring daughter home, John Payne had spanked her soundly and locked her in her room to repent.

Dolly had wept most of the night. At dawn she slept a little, only to be awakened by Mammy Amy with her bread-and-water breakfast. The child had sobbed, expecting sympathy. But the nurse left without a word, her brown face stern. The slaves had been punished, too, by John Payne. If the headstrong girl had not run out into the night, their innocent celebration would have gone undiscovered.

Hungry for any sign of life, Dolly spent the lonely day at the window. She saw Hannah bring out the iron kettles for the autumn soap boiling. Dolly hated to make soap, but she would willingly have helped Hannah that morning—anything to get out of the locked room.

Niles rode in from the tobacco fields. Jasper raked leaves. Banjo went by—a sad-looking boy, not a jig left in him. Poppy came to hang clothes on the line . . . one of Dolly's despised gray dresses . . . a row of white kerchiefs.

The grandfather clock in the hall boomed out the hours. How long would Father keep her here? A week? Two weeks? Perhaps forever? Dolly began to cry, feeling very sorry for herself.

At sunset a carriage drove up. She saw old Doctor White enter the house, satchel in hand. Mother was ill, and Dolly couldn't get to her. She sank into a heap, sobbing wildly. In her heart grew a mounting anger against Father—he kept her from Mother, who was dying.

Weeping her heart out, the little girl crept into bed and fell into a troubled sleep.

At dawn the next morning, someone entered the room. Dolly hid her face in the pillow.

"Dorothea—" It was her father's voice. He stood before her, stern and forbidding.

The child's heart leaped with fright. "I—I'll be good, Father," she stammered. "Please forgive me."

"Dorothea," he repeated, "does thee not know, after all my teaching, it is not whether I forgive thee or thy mother? Only the Lord can pardon thy sin, if thee will enter into the Silence."

The little girl shrank back. She could find no answer to this thundering question.

"My daughter, has thee prayed to God for forgiveness?" John Payne put it more simply.

Dolly shut her lips tight and shook her head.

Not to pray—how lost, how wicked! Father's eyes darkened to the blackest anger. But before he could speak, Mammy Amy appeared at the door. "Missus says it's time for de chile to be dressed," she said. "Timothy must be off, if he's to git Miss Dolly and Massa Willie to dey Granny's by nightfall."

Dolly's face lightened. She was going to her Grandmother Coles' for a visit. She was not forgiven. But at least she was to be freed from the locked room. And surely Mother was getting well, or she would not be sent away.

Father's eyes were unrelenting. "Dress her, Amy," he said, and left the room.

Dolly leaped from the bed, her unhappiness vanished. As when a baby, her expressive face could change swiftly from sadness to merriment. "I won't be a minute," she told her mammy. While she said it, she was putting on her gray dress. Then she slipped on her cape, and tied the strings of her gray bonnet. From the driveway outside came the crunch of wheels, the clatter of horses' hoofs, and William Temple's voice talking to Timothy.

Dolly knelt beside her mother's bed to kiss her good-bye. Molly Payne's face was as white as the pillow; her eyes large and dark. Dolly knew she had caused her sick mother grief. Her heart ached.

"Mind thee is industrious at Granny's," Molly admonished. "Take thy knitting. Finish thy stocking before thee return."

Dolly kissed her mother and promised, "I'll knit on my stocking, even on the ride over."

Everything forgiven, Dolly gave her mammy a hug. Her bonnet was hot and pinched her ears. But how good any hat felt, exulted the repentent little girl, as she bounded down the stairs into the outdoors and freedom.

※   ※   ※   ※   ※

At nightfall, Timothy turned the carriage through an open gate and stopped before the high, pillared porch at Coles Hill.

The Payne children jumped out and raced up the steps. There stood dear, darling Grandmother Coles—a tiny old lady, her arms outstretched to hug them.

"Rose, just look at Miss Dolly. Isn't she Miss Molly all over again?" An arm around each, Granny led her grandchildren into a wide hall that ran through the center of the big white house. "And this tall young man—would you believe it was William Temple?"

"Both of 'em starved, I reckon," replied a smiling Negro woman in an orange turban. "Hurry, childums, before my supper gets cold."

In the dining room, candles on the mahogany table shed their soft light on broiled ham and chicken, pitchers of creamy milk, red plum preserves, chocolate cake and gingerbread. Grandmother Coles presided at the head of the table, white curls showing beneath her sheer lacy cap.

Grace was a short spoken prayer, not a long silence. Granny was not a Quaker. In a moment she looked up briskly. "Rose, fetch the hot waffles." She laughed. "You'll have two weeks to admire my grandchildren."

Two weeks! Dolly and her brother exchanged happy smiles.

The next morning the excited children rose before sun-up. Breakfast over, a young slave, little Moses, solemnly bore a big Bible across the room and laid it on Mrs. Coles' lap. A dozen house servants came into the parlor and took seats. As Granny read the chapter aloud, the sunshine made a halo over her white head. Then everyone knelt for the Lord's Prayer.

Soon it was time for Dolly to accompany her grandmother on her household rounds. "Fine weather for exploring, child. Wouldn't you rather run about and have fun?" Lucy Coles asked.

"Fun" was a word the Payne children seldom heard at home. "Granny, may I really do anything I please?" Dolly asked.

"Anything, dear." Mrs. Coles smiled, rattling her keys.

There were no rules at Coles Hill. No "don'ts." No household chores; no tiresome lessons. Dolly ran joyfully out of the house, omitting to put on her bonnet.

❧   ❧   ❧   ❧   ❧

The first week at Coles Hill went all too quickly. Dolly and her brother romped contentedly over the plantation. Each morning William Temple practiced riding along the country lanes. Later there was apple picking, or roaming the woods to gather nuts. The happy children helped an old Negro, Uncle Rufus, feed the chickens. Each chose a pigeon to tame.

At the end of the week, a slave from Little Byrd Creek arrived with a message from John Payne. There was a new baby in the Payne household. A little girl named Lucy, after Granny. She was plump and healthy, and her mother, too, was well.

Dolly and William Temple were enchanted. In her delight over the news, Dolly forgot to be jealous of a second little daughter in the Payne family.

One morning the Coles Hill house was wakened by music. Leaping out of bed, Dolly quickly dressed and ran down stairs.

In the hall she met Granny. The music drew them toward the parlor, where a tall, red-haired man stooped over the flute he was playing.

"Patrick Henry! What are you doing here?" Delighted as a girl, Lucy Coles rushed over to kiss her sister Sarah's son.

"I'm on my way from Scotchtown to Williamsburg," he explained.

Scotchtown, off in a remote section of Hanover County, had been Patrick Henry's home. He had recently sold it to Colonel Wilson Miles Cary, for Patrick Henry, as Virginia's governor, now lived in Williamsburg.

He smiled at flushed, pretty Dolly. "Who's this?" he asked.

"Molly Payne's daughter," replied Granny.

"The one Molly named after Dorothea Dandridge?" Governor Henry stared at Dolly thoughtfully. "Your namesake is a beautiful girl, my child. I think you'll grow to be like her."

Mrs. Coles looked into her nephew's blue eyes. "Pat, are you in love with Dorothea?" she demanded.

The tall Governor reddened and was silent.

"Then why don't you marry her?"

"What would she want of a forty-one year old widower with six children? A girl of twenty-one, ex-Governor Spotswood's granddaughter, with all Williamsburg at her feet."

"Fiddlesticks! Don't let Dorothea's mother frighten you off with her Spotswood ancestry, Pat. You're a governor of Virginia, too, aren't you?"

Patrick Henry beamed like a boy. "Aunty, you're a wonder. Now how about giving a hungry governor some breakfast?"

❧   ❧   ❧   ❧   ❧

Wonderful days followed for the young Paynes. By day, Patrick Henry roamed with them through the forest. When they came to a brook, the Governor of Virginia pulled off his shoes and stockings. They all went in wading.

Later, drying in the sun on the bank, he told the children, "I always did enjoy roaming the woods, lying on my back, and listening to the song of the birds, better than studying." They loved him for it.

Evenings, a merry group gathered around the fire in Granny's parlor. Patrick Henry poured hot melted butter over bowls of fluffy white popcorn. They had a candy pull. They raked toasted chestnuts from the fire.

Each time the Governor suggested leaving, his aunt begged him to remain. Ben, the coachman, had been sent to Williamsburg on a mysterious errand. "Please stay until Ben comes back," she pleaded. "We need a responsible man on the place."

Sitting with her grandmother by the fire one afternoon, Dolly asked wistfully, "Granny, did Mother wear bright colors and jewelry, before she married Father and became a Quaker?"

"Indeed she did, dear—"

Mrs. Coles looked up at the portrait that hung over the mantel. The smiling, dark-haired little girl in it wore a blue satin gown. Around her throat was a gold chain. It was hard to believe that Mother had ever been like that, Dolly thought. Life had changed the radiant child into a sober, quiet-voiced matron.

But as a young girl, pretty Molly Coles had been a belle. Fascinated, Dolly listened while Granny told how her daughter, on visits to her cousin, Colonel John Coles, in Albemarle County, Virginia, had danced and hunted with the young blades of the neighborhood—Patrick Henry, James Monroe, and Thomas Jefferson. Everyone had been surprised when she married the serious-minded Quaker, John Payne.

"Tom Jefferson was once in love with your mother, Dolly," her grandmother said proudly.

It made Dolly proud, too. Of course she knew of Thomas Jefferson from Albemarle County, who had written the Declaration of Independence the year before.

"You look like your mother did, honey." Lucy Coles gazed into her granddaughter's blue eyes, roguish behind long black

SCOTCHTOWN, VIRGINIA

*Two views of the girlhood home of Dolly Payne where Patrick
Henry, her cousin, had previously lived. Still standing outside
Ashland, twenty-five miles north of Richmond*

HAREWOOD

Home of Lucy and George Steptoe Washington, still standing three miles out of Charles Town, West Virginia

ROOM AT HAREWOOD WHERE DOLLY TODD MARRIED JAMES MADISON

D.P. Madison

DOLLY MADISON: AGE TWENTY-SIX

Miniature by James Peale, painted in 1794, after Dolly's second marriage

THOMAS JEFFERSON: AGE SIXTY-TWO

By Rembrandt Peale

lashes. "You've Scotch and Irish blood in you. But I think you're mostly Irish. Your Grandfather Coles gave you that gay smile, your warm heart and soft tongue—" She rose and put away her knitting. "Come with me to the attic, Dolly. I think I can find that blue dress your mother wore when her portrait was painted."

It was cosy up in the dusty attic. Spider webs hung everywhere. A broken spinning wheel occupied one corner. A big chest another.

Opening the chest, Granny brought forth a little box. "Hold out your hand, dear," she said, and placed a dainty gold chain in her granddaughter's outstretched fingers.

"Your mother wore it while she was being painted," she explained. "I want you to have it, honey."

Dolly's eyes gleamed. "Father wouldn't let me wear it."

"He needn't know. Or your mother either." Granny fastened the fragile chain around her granddaughter's neck. "When you get home, hide it under your dress. No one will notice it."

Dolly fingered the chain lovingly. A Quaker child, she had never expected to own a "vain ornament." She would wear it, hidden beneath the kerchief of her demure gray dress.

The little girl was roused by a sweet scent, the thrilling swish of heavy silk. The dark attic seemed bathed in color reflected from a blue satin gown flung over the chest lid.

Granny held up the dress. "You must be about your mother's size when she wore this, dear. Try it on."

The dress was blue—a "worldly color," Father called blue. Dolly reached out, almost afraid to touch the gleaming satin.

"Miss Lucy! There's company comin'."

It was Rose's voice from below. Through the attic window came the noise of wheels on the drive, the echo of horses' hoofs.

Mrs. Coles replaced the blue dress in the chest. They hurried down, just as Thomas opened the front door to a lame gentleman, his dignified lady, and a young girl in a red cape.

"Mistress Coles, here we are." The gentleman limped over to kiss her hand. "Your Ben insisted on bringing us back with him."

"When Ben arrived, we were just leaving for Mount Vernon to visit Mrs. Washington," explained his wife. "We're delighted to stop with you overnight."

Dolly was introduced. When she learned that the visitors were the Nathaniel West Dandridges and their daughter, she knew why Ben had been sent to Williamsburg, why Granny had not allowed Patrick Henry to leave Coles Hill.

Weak with admiration, the younger girl looked at Dorothea Dandridge. Dorothea was equally pleased with her pretty namesake. "Your *thee's* and *thy's* sound like a page from the Bible, Dolly," she said and kissed her.

A jubilant voice caused them to turn. There in the doorway stood Patrick Henry. "Can it be the Dandridge coach I see at the door?" he exclaimed.

Captain Dandridge warmly greeted his friend. His wife allowed the Governor to kiss her hand. Their daughter, pink-cheeked and starry-eyed, motioned him to a place close to her on the sofa.

Later, when the Dandridges were shown to their rooms, Patrick hugged his laughing aunt. "You little matchmaker!" he said huskily.

"The rest is up to you, Pat," she warned.

Governor Henry had only until the next morning to woo Dorothea and win her parents. Wisely, he spent part of the afternoon talking politics with Captain Dandridge and flattering his wife. He merely contented himself with looking adoringly at his sweetheart. It was her parents—especially her mother—he must win first.

Dorothea Spotswood Dandridge was a great lady. Perhaps too proud of her Spotswood ancestry; but an aristocrat in the finest sense. Patrick Henry, the rawboned backwoods lawyer, had never met anyone like her. In the course of his siege it was not only Mistress Dandridge who capitulated, but the suitor who lost his heart to his hoped-for mother-in-law.

Only then did Patrick suggest to Dorothea a stroll in the garden. In a billowing pink gown, a brown bonnet with a matching muff, she seemed prettier than ever to her admiring namesake. As for Cousin Pat, happiness made him almost handsome, despite his rumpled red hair and careless dress.

A half hour later, the ringing tones of an orator were heard at the door. "With that voice, Patrick could make love in a corner or call hounds a mile away," laughed Captain Dandridge.

"I hope he's been doing the former," Granny retorted.

Dorothea came in, her eyes alight with joy. Patrick Henry walked as erect as a lord, a new look on his gaunt face.

Mrs. Dandridge called her daughter to her. "Have you something to tell me, dear?"

"Oh, Mother, I'm so happy!"

There was no need to explain why. Even Dolly and William Temple knew.

Granny's cheeks were pink with excitement. "We'll have a party tonight to celebrate the engagement!" she exclaimed.

Feeling forlorn and left out, Dolly watched her grandmother dress for dinner. What a picture she made in a ruffled black dress, lace at her neck, a bit of it perched upon her curly white hair! Dolly fingered her golden chain. If only she had something to wear to the party other than her dull gray dress!

Granny saw the little girl's dejected expression. "Rose, go up to the attic." She turned to her maid. "You know that big chest—"

At dinnertime, when Mistress Coles appeared, the gentlemen bowed over her hand. Then all turned to stare at the doorway, where Dolly stood in her mother's blue satin frock. A rose the color of her kerchief was tucked in her dark hair. On her bare throat gleamed the gold chain.

"My dear child!" As gallantly as though she were Granny, Captain Dandridge kissed her little hand.

Only William Temple gasped in astonishment at his sister's radiance.

Then Thomas announced dinner. Tall tapers in branched candlesticks shed their soft light on the mahogany table, set with gleaming silver and Granny's best china. The old butler, in blue livery with brass buttons, served a long procession of dishes from Flora's kitchen—turkey, venison pie, chicken, hams, a small roasted pig. There were a dozen vegetables, tarts, and custards.

Presently Captain Dandridge stood up and raised his glass. "Ladies and gentlemen, I give you a toast. To the Governor of Virginia and his future lady!"

After dinner, they went into the parlor where Uncle Rufus stood waiting, violin in hand.

Captain Dandridge bowed before his hostess. "May I have the honor?"

Patrick Henry led his future mother-in-law to the head of the line. "Dorothea, show the children how to dance," he called.

As Quakers, the young Paynes had never danced.

"Don't be afraid." Granny smiled encouragement.

Uncle Rufus played a lilting tune. Mrs. Dandridge and Granny stepped as lightly as girls. Dorothea's slippers twinkled. Only William Temple could not make his feet follow his bidding.

Dolly took to dancing with natural grace. As she bobbed back and forth like a flower in the wind, she smiled happily. With her eyes fastened on Dorothea, she imitated the older girl's every action.

In the midst of the minuet, Patrick Henry smiled down at the bright-eyed child. "You're quite the belle," he teased, "only a little less charming than your lovely grandmother."

Dolly smiled back. She, a Quaker girl, was dancing to music. Instead of feeling wicked, she was very happy. Then, in the candle gleam, her father's stern face seemed to appear before her. What would John Payne say if he saw his daughter now?

GLOOM HUNG OVER THE WHITE FARMHOUSE AT LITTLE BYRD Creek plantation. To Dolly and William Temple, home from Granny Coles', the joyless atmosphere seemed doubly depressing.

John Payne spent most of his time in his study. When he emerged for meals, his face was drawn and haggard. Molly Payne, usually bustling and cheerful, seemed to share her husband's strange anxiety. When they were together, the children heard snatches of war talk and hints that Friend Payne would not long be able to withstand the pressure of his own desire to fight for his rights.

Even Mammy Amy seemed too absorbed in nursery cares to pay much attention to her beloved charge. The new baby, a fat, pink-cheeked dumpling of a child, needed attention. To relieve Molly Payne, still white and thin from her long illness, the faithful Negro woman cared for the infant night and day.

Dolly was soon back at her task of helping with the family spinning, weaving and sewing. Back at making butter and cheese, stuffing sausages, salting meat and preserving. The carefree times at Coles Hill seemed far away.

Every day now there was school. Trudging across the fields to the log schoolhouse, the Payne children sniffed the sharp December air with its vigor and challenge. To keep warm, Walter and William Temple played running games. Dolly moved more sedately. Her long, flowing gray gown reached to her shoes. Her boned stays held her girlish body erect as in armor.

No ray of the sun could penetrate the broad-brimmed Quaker hood, the muslin complexion mask sewed to it, or the long finger mitts that covered her white arms. Seeing her daughter growing into a beauty, Molly Payne was worldly enough to wish to protect Dolly's lovely complexion from the harmful rays of the sun.

One December day Walter stayed home with a cold. With her favorite brother, William Temple, Dolly hurried to school, her books under her arm. Hidden beneath her kerchief nestled Granny's secret gift, the golden chain.

The thought of her "vain ornament" made the long hours at school pass more swiftly, for Dolly was not a student. She would always like people better than books. Master Tobey, the teacher, knew her thoughts were not on her lessons. Each time she looked up, he was watching her sternly.

Spelling was taught aloud, as were most of the lessons. Master Tobey gave out the word—a signal for the roomful of children to spell out the word in syllables in chorus. His keen ear could catch any mistake.

"Dolly Payne!" She had spelt clatter with a k; syllabarium with one l. For that, Master Tobey rapped her knuckles smartly.

Dolly was better at writing. Even Father, who wrote a fine regular hand, complimented his daughter on her clear, uniform penmanship.

After writing came "cyphering"—a period of torture, while Dolly puzzled over intricate sumbooks. Their pages were as complicated as the computations of the revolutions of the stars to the yawning little student.

❧   ❧   ❧   ❧   ❧

The school was ablaze with patriotism. News had come that Lord Howe was in Philadelphia; General Washington withdrawing his ragged forces to Valley Forge. With fear in their hearts, men all over Virginia were enlisting in defense of their homes. Even the gentle Quakers, who as a sect are opposed to war, were joining up. Their children had caught the war spirit. It made them savage.

"Coward! Thy father's a coward!" a red-haired urchin yelled at William Temple, as after school Dolly and her brother hurried along the lane toward home.

William Temple clenched his fists. "He is not," he retorted.

"Coward! Son of a coward!"

Young Payne grabbed up a stone and turned on the boys who were following him. But he felt his sister's hand on his arm. "Don't throw at them," Dolly whispered. "Thee will be sorry."

That was the true Quaker spirit. Reluctantly, William Temple dropped the stone and walked on beside the trembling girl.

Close behind came their tormentors. "See, thee's a coward, too," shouted the red-head. "Thee's afraid to fight, like thy father—"

Shy, quiet William Temple wheeled, his face white. With one leap, he reached the red-haired boy. The big fellow struck him across the mouth. Young Payne landed a blow on his opponent's chin.

A yelling mob, the other bullies closed in on the frail, younger boy. They rolled together, over and over on the ground. Dolly was in their midst, defending her brother, shielding him from the blows that rained on his head. In spite of her corset and hampering skirt, she fought like a wildcat. Her bonnet fell off, her complexion mask. Hatless, her black curls tossed, Dolly forgot about being a girl and a non-fighting Quaker. She only knew she must help her brother.

A blow sent William Temple sprawling in the road. Seeing him go down, Dolly beat his chief tormentor with her fists. She kicked him in the shins.

"Quit that, thee Quaker cat—thee spitfire—" begged the red-haired boy.

Dolly slapped him, hard. He hit back. His fist caught her square on the forehead. With a moan, she dropped to the ground.

Afraid of what they had done, the ragamuffins swarmed about the small, gray-clad figure. "Git up, thee ain't hurt," one ordered.

William Temple rushed over to Dolly. "She is hurt. Thee boys leave her be."

His sister could still defend herself. "Get away, rats!" She lifted her face, streaked with dirt and blood. "Leave me alone or I'll hit thee again."

One horrified look, and the boys fled.

Young Payne knelt down. "Sister, are thee hurt?"

Dolly hardly knew. Painfully she struggled to her feet. Her face was grimy, her hair disheveled, her dress torn. "I want to go home," she sobbed forlornly.

It was nearly dark when the farmhouse loomed ahead. Through the window, the Payne children saw their father standing, pipe in hand, before the hearth. Mother was in the wing-chair, sewing. Softly they climbed the steps to the porch. The boy quietly opened the door. They crept in.

A floor board creaked. "Children, come in" came Father's voice.

William Temple dared not disobey. "Run!" He pushed his sister toward the stairs. Then, dirty and disheveled, he answered the command.

"Has thee been fighting, a Quaker lad?" boomed Father's deep, judgeful tones. "Get my birch rods. I'll trounce thee—"

Dolly heard no more. Frantic with fear, she stumbled up the stairs—square into Mammy Amy's safe arms.

Drawing the weeping girl quickly into her room, the devoted nurse shut the door. "Tell Mammy, lamb," she crooned, her arms about her charge.

As Dolly sobbed out her story, Amy bathed her face and applied a cold compress to her aching head.

"Now git dat dirty dress off, honey, before yer Mammy and Pappy sees ya," she cautioned.

Standing before the dresser, Dolly let her torn gown slip down about her feet. In camisole and petticoat, she looked at herself in the mirror. What she saw made her clutch her throat with dismay. In the wild scuffle with the ragamuffins, the gold chain had been wrenched from her neck.

"It's gone, Mammy," she wailed. "The chain Granny gave me."

The loss of the precious heirloom far outweighed all Dolly's previous sorrows. Never, never again would she, a Quaker child, own another piece of jewelry. She flung herself on Amy's breast in a wild spasm of grief.

"Baby, don't grieve so," her nurse comforted her. "You'll learn, before you'se as old as I is, dat nothin' in this world is worth carin' so about."

It took Dolly, who all her life was to care passionately about things, seventy years to learn that Mammy was right—there was nothing in this world worth breaking her heart over.

❦   ❦   ❦   ❦   ❦

For defending his father's honor, William Temple was whipped and given a lecture. "Quakers don't fight, even for their rights," Father said.

Dolly escaped, thanks to Mammy Amy. By suppertime, her sobs had subsided. In a clean dress, with her hair carefully combed over the lump on her forehead, her parents did not notice anything was wrong.

Later Dolly told William Temple about the loss of her gold chain. Every day they searched for it along the lane from school. Scuffling their feet through the leaves. Turning over stones. It was never found.

Gradually, the first great grief of Dolly's childhood faded. By 1778, when Lucy's place as the baby of the household was filled by the Payne family's fifth child, ten-year-old Dolly had almost forgotten the wisp of gold that had hung against her white throat.

The new baby was a girl. The boys, Dolly and chubby Lucy, peered into the hooded wooden cradle that had held them all. In the Payne family a new baby was no longer a novelty. But Dolly was fascinated by little Anna. When the other children left, the eldest daughter lingered by the cradle.

The baby had begun to cry. "Hush—hush." Dolly rocked the crib. To her delight, Anna stopped crying. Dolly touched her shell-pink fingers, so fragile and helpless. They closed over hers and clung, with a trustful grip that would not let go.

Suddenly Dolly loved Anna with her whole heart.

"Mammy Amy's going to be very busy with another baby to tend," Mother murmured from the great four poster bed. "Dolly, would thee like to help Mammy look after little Anna?"

"Oh, I'd love it!" Dolly cried.

For the older sister, it was like playing with a big doll to be Anna's "little mother." She was such a dear, flaxen-haired, blue-eyed baby, as winsome as Dolly had been at her age.

Between the sisters a great love was growing that would last all their lives.

❀   ❀   ❀   ❀   ❀

One day shortly after Anna's birth, Molly Payne called her daughter into her room.

"Dolly, thy father has sold Little Byrd Creek plantation," she said abruptly. "He has bought a plantation Cousin Patrick Henry lived on before he was governor."

"Scotchtown!" Dolly let out a most unladylike whoop.

For some time John Payne had been wanting a larger plantation for his rapidly growing family. Finally, he heard that Colonel Cary, who had bought Scotchtown from Patrick Henry, was willing to sell the place at a low figure. Father could never resist a bargain. So he had bought Scotchtown.

Patrick Henry had often talked of his former home to the Payne children. Now Dolly would actually live there! She went around the house in a dream, helping Mammy Amy close up one home and pack to move to another.

At last Mother was strong enough to make the journey. One autumn morning in 1778, the Paynes climbed into their shabby yellow coach and set out for a wild section of Hanover County.

The rays of the setting sun were burnishing the distant lavender mountains, when they finally reached Scotchtown. The children peered from the windows of the coach. Far off on a flat-topped hill, the old house loomed tall and solitary in the fading light.

It was a long, rectangular mansion which its eccentric builder, a Colonel Charles Chiswell, had erected off here in the wilderness. Its first story was of brick, the rest of the structure of unpainted wood. With its hipped roof and high brick foundation, it looked like a stranded Noah's Ark.

"It's certainly big enough," Molly Payne sighed, remembering the cosy white farmhouse they had left behind.

The coach stopped before the stone steps of a small front porch. Stiff and chilled from their journey, the Paynes climbed out. Father unlocked the door with the key Colonel Cary had sent him.

Cold, damp air burst upon them. Forming a timid line, the children trailed their parents into a dim, dusty hall, wide as a room, that ran the entire depth of the house.

Dolly and William Temple remembered a story Patrick Henry had told them. How when he owned Scotchtown, the British lieutenant, Tarleton, had raided the countryside. To spite Patrick Henry, Tarleton had led his dragoons on horseback up the front steps of Scotchtown, through this hall, and out the opposite door.

Keeping close to William Temple, Dolly walked the length of the cobwebbed hall to the back door. Unbolting it, the children stepped out onto a second small porch. Before them in the dusk, the hillside sloped in dreary fields to the North Anna River. Dolly shivered and wished herself elsewhere.

When she re-entered the house, she found Mammy Amy swaying from side to side and crying. Dolly's eyes grew big and frightened. "What's the matter, Mammy?" she asked.

"Little missie, yer done come in one door and go right out de other—dat's bad luck," the old woman moaned. "Somethin' terrible goin' ter happen to us in dis old house."

JOHN PAYNE'S DECISION TO GO TO WAR CAME OUT OF THE blue. For four years he had fought a battle between his Quaker principles and the natural yearning of a courageous man to defend his freedom. With the war off in the north, staying at home had been easy. But when Lord Cornwallis invaded Virginia, John was stirred to enlist.

One morning in 1781, Friend Payne called his family into the Green Room, the room in which Patrick Henry had composed his fiery speeches. They saw he had taken down his musket from above the mantel.

"Children, I am going to war," he said in his most impressive voice. "Boys, thee must care for thy mother and thy sisters."

Dolly stared at her father in amazement. Never had he looked so happy. The doubts that had troubled him were gone.

"Can't we go, too, Father?" chorused the boys. Walter was nineteen; William Temple, fifteen. Every lad big enough to carry a gun, they argued, had put aside his school books and shouldered his musket.

But their father said no, they must stay at home. "Who else would see to the tobacco?" he asked sternly.

That was the trouble. No one knew better than visionary John Payne that there was almost no tobacco; that the Scotchtown plantation was hopelessly infertile.

When he had tried to plant tobacco on the thousand acres

that Colonel Chiswell had carved out of the wilderness, Friend Payne found the fields encrusted with rock. Niles, his practical overseer, had left him to work for a more successful planter. With the aid of Walter, a big stolid youth who wanted to be a Quaker preacher, John struggled on. But as they planted the fields that May of 1781, Cornwallis came to Virginia. And soon Father was off to war, leaving two inexperienced boys to handle the sprawling acres.

In the dark days that followed, thirteen-year-old Dolly often had cause to remember Mammy Amy's premonition that trouble would come to them in the remote Scotchtown mansion.

Virginia was now the center of the conflict. General Nathanael Greene had moved his men south, leaving the state with only young Lafayette in charge of a small force to defend it. Several thousand strong, the British began their pursuit of "the boy," as they sneeringly referred to Lafayette. Joined by General Anthony Wayne, Lafayette retreated southward from Fredericksburg, the British after him.

Meanwhile Cornwallis had sent his dread cavalry man, Colonel Banastre Tarleton—"the fox," they called him—with dragoons to Charlottesville. Tarleton was to capture Thomas Jefferson, Patrick Henry and the fleeing Virginia legislature. Prowling over the state, Tarleton raided the countryside.

People fled Hanover County in droves. Those who stuck to their isolated plantations, like Molly Payne and her children, did not know what each day would bring them. The hills were full of Tarleton's dragoons. Cornwallis and his army were not far away. Thomas Jefferson's wife with their little daughter, Martha, so the Payne's heard, had fled their home, Monticello. Even Martha Washington felt herself unsafe at Mount Vernon.

Would Tarleton come again and devastate Scotchtown,

Dolly wondered. Because of Patrick Henry, the haughty British officer had a special hatred for the place. If Tarleton came, the Paynes would face him alone. They had no neighbors for miles.

Life in the twenty-room mansion was wretchedly uncomfortable. Built of materials imported from Scotland by Colonel Chiswell, the huge rooms were paneled in walnut from floor to ceiling. All her life Dolly was to remember the bizarre black mantels over the corner fireplaces. Some had fluted columns; others were supported by figures.

Under the high gabled roof was a garret a hundred feet long. Colonel Chiswell had used it as a ballroom. John Payne partitioned it off into small rooms for his children.

The only cheerful place was the small, detached kitchenhouse. Its walls were bare, except for Mammy Sue's gleaming pots and skillets. Hams hung from the low, smoke-stained rafters. Barrels of flour and cornmeal stood about.

The fireplace was so big that logs for it had to be dragged in by a horse on a sled. At night Molly Payne and her children gathered there before the fire to work and talk. It was warm and cosy. One wasn't as afraid out in the kitchenhouse, thought Dolly.

But even three-year-old Anna was conscious of the fear that hung over the household; the fear of what might happen to Father, now a captain in the army, and of what might befall the little family at Scotchtown if Tarleton came. The dread was constantly in Molly's mind, and in the thoughts of the children who were old enough to realize their danger. Tiny Mary—a fourth daughter, born after Father's departure—caught the suspense somehow and reflected it in her baby face.

Before the kitchen fire one night, Mother knitted and Dolly whirled her spinning wheel. Lucy carded wool, or

MRS. JAMES MADISON

Pencil drawing by T. C. Lübbers

MRS. JAMES MADISON: AGE THIRTY-SIX

By Gilbert Stuart

MONTPELLIER, VIRGINIA

As the house appeared when Dolly Madison lived there

AARON BURR: AGE FIFTY-THREE

By John Vanderlyn

helped Anna to sew on a sampler. The boys read, curled up
on a settee at the chimney corner. The faithful servants were
there too, as part of the family. Mammy Amy, turbaned head
erect, amused the children by relating Scotchtown legends,
whispered to her by the slaves.

There were tales of an Indian attack, of a duel—responsible
for the "bloodstain" on the hall floor, that all Mammy Amy's
scrubbing could not wash away. But the story over which
Dolly shuddered most deliciously was that of the wicked Mr.
Forsyth, a former owner, who had chained his wife in the
dungeon.

The "dungeon" was a tunnel under the house, where the
Paynes stored their potatoes. It had been built by Colonel
Chiswell as a means of escape in case of an Indian raid, and
was reached by a trap door in the hall, to the left of the front
entrance. A hidden spring in the woodwork, that pushed the
walnut paneling aside, fascinated the children.

One of the rumors said that the ghost of the beautiful
Mrs. Forsyth still haunted Scotchtown. On windy nights you
could hear her screams and the rattle of her chains.

"As if Scotchtown wasn't lonely enough, Amy—to have
thee talking 'haunt talk' and frightening the children!" Molly
scolded. "I don't believe that horrible story anyhow."

But the children believed it.

As the wind whistled around the kitchen-house that night,
Dolly suddenly exclaimed, "I hear a haunt now, Mammy
Amy." Her eyes had a listening look. "What's that noise?"

It was footsteps, coming nearer.

"It sounds like someone running." Walter frowned. His
brother jumped up in alarm, and started to investigate.

William Temple was halfway to the door, when it was
flung open. In burst Banjo, all out of breath. The enemy
soldiers were on the plantation, he cried, and they must flee.

"Tarleton's comin'," he panted. "You'se got ter git away from here."

The British raiders were all over Scotchtown. They had burned the barns, set fire to the slave quarters. Hidden behind a hay rack, Banjo had watched them plundering. Any minute now, the enemy troops would attack the big house.

Molly Payne sprang to her feet, Mary in her arms. Lucy ran to hide her face in her mother's skirts. Anna clung to her "little mother."

They must hide—and quickly. But where?

Dolly thought of it. "The dungeon, Mother?"

"Yes, children. Come, Amy, Sue and Timothy. And thee, Banjo."

Molly herded her household from the kitchen-house into the mansion, and through the darkened hall to the secret door. It took some time for William Temple's trembling fingers to find the hidden spring in the raised carving. He pressed it. Slowly the paneled woodwork slid back. The hole gaped before them, rank and damp.

Steep steps led down into the blackness. As the Paynes faltered, pistol shots rang out close to the house. They must go quickly. Shading a candle's flame with his hand, Walter stepped inside the hole. Molly Payne, the other children and the servants followed him down the dusty stairs. When Timothy, the last one, was in, the secret panel slid back without a sound.

At the bottom of the steps, the little group huddled together, teeth chattering with cold and fright. Mud oozed under their feet from the water dripping from the rocky ceiling overhead.

"We'll stay here," Walter said.

For hours they crouched against the wet, rocky walls. To Dolly it seemed an eternity, but it was only overnight.

Mammy Sue divided the food she had brought. The tired children tried to sleep.

But there was no sleep for Dolly. Nestling against Mammy Amy, she listened to her own heartbeats. Once during the night, she rolled over and touched something round and hard. It was an iron link, with a chain attached to the wall. Shuddering, Dolly knew Mammy's legend was true. Mr. Forsyth had chained his poor wife, perhaps in this very spot.

It was morning before the chilled, cramped Paynes dared come out of hiding. Upstairs the house was in confusion. Tarleton had again ridden his horse through the great hall of Scotchtown, in one door and out the other. His dragoons had despoiled the stately rooms, ripped the furniture open with their swords.

Worse still, they had ransacked the kitchen-house. The hams were gone from the chimney, the bread from the oven, all Mammy Sue's little stock of flour and cornmeal. Most frightening of all, they had carried off every Negro slave they could lay their hands on. Then the raiders had ridden away laughing, leaving desolation behind.

Why Tarleton had not burned down the Scotchtown house over their heads, Molly Payne and her children would never know.

❧　　❧　　❧　　❧　　❧

The gloomy old mansion was set among broken locusts, ancient oak trees and tattered box—all that remained of a once beautifully laid-out garden and grounds. In front of the house, some of the old boxwood had grown into the shape of a comfortable armchair.

Dolly sat for hours that fall of 1781 in this curious seat, where Patrick Henry, too, had liked to sit. From it, she

could look down the Negrofoot road that skirted the plantation. Along it might come a passing stranger, who would stop
in to avoid paying a tavern bill. In return for the Payne's
hospitality, he might tell the family news of the outside
world.

There were so many questions Dolly wanted to ask. Had
Tarleton captured Governor Thomas Jefferson, Patrick
Henry and the Virginia legislature? . . . Would the patriots
win the war? . . . Had the stranger heard of her father,
Captain John Payne?

One day as Dolly and Lucy scanned the road, they saw a
rider coming toward them. He was a young man, about
thirty; short and with a pale, solemn face. At the sight of the
bright-eyed girls, he paused to say good-day.

"Won't thee come in, sir?" Dolly begged.

The traveler smiled and shook his head. "I'm in a hurry
to reach Philadelphia and attend the Continental Congress,"
he replied proudly, for it was his first term as a member from
Virginia. "I come from Richmond. I've a long way to go."

Dolly regarded the young man with respect. "Will thee
see Benjamin Franklin in Philadelphia?" she asked eagerly.

"Yes, I'll see Franklin and also Alexander Hamilton."

"And surely thee will meet James Madison."

The rider stared at Dolly curiously. "Yes, I'll even see that
prig of a Jimmy Madison," he replied with a dry smile.

The girl frowned. She did not like the way the young
man spoke of Mr. Madison. Father admired James Madison
because he had helped to write in the new Virginia Constitution an amendment for religious freedom. All Quakers were
grateful to Mr. Madison for that.

The stranger gathered up his reins. "Well, I must be off—
good-bye!"

Dolly watched him trot off down the road. She liked the

surprising twinkle in his blue eyes, his shy manner. She remembered the questions she had meant to ask, and wished he had stopped in for dinner.

At noon another man trudged down the road on foot. He was a sharp-faced peddler in ragged garments. Tied on his back was a tin trunk.

His name was Chepa Rose and for forty-eight years he had tramped the countryside, selling his wares. Dolly did not like him. But trunk peddlers are notorious news-bearers, so she said sweetly: "Won't thee come in, sir? My mother would like to see what thee has to sell."

Would he! Chepa Rose fairly leaped over the gate.

Quickly the news of the peddler's arrival spread about the plantation. The Negroes gathered. Even Mother and Walter came to chat with him, as he devoured a meal in the kitchen-house.

Prompted by the Paynes' eager questions, Chepa Rose told how Tarleton had pursued the Virginia Assembly, that had fled from Richmond to Charlottesville, riding at the head of his dragoons. Their white uniforms faced with green caught many a frightened eye that peered forth from roadside houses. But warned by Captain Jouette, Patrick Henry and the legislature escaped again. This time to Staunton in the Shenandoah Valley.

And what of Thomas Jefferson? The Paynes heard how he had watched through a telescope for Tarleton's coming. When he saw Charlottesville swarming with troopers in white coats, Jefferson mounted his horse and barely managed to escape to Poplar Forest in Bedford County before the enemy reached Monticello.

The Paynes relaxed. "Where did Tarleton go then?" asked Walter.

"Back to Yorktown to join Cornwallis, Lafayette at his

heels." His meal finished, the peddler rose from the table. "Of course the French had bottled up Cornwallis by sea—"

"The French?" His listeners looked mystified.

"Didn't you country folks know 'bout the French, who came to help us before the battle of Yorktown?" The peddler began to unpack his goods. "With the army that Washington and that Frenchman, Rochambeau, brought down from the north, we beat the Redcoats—"

Chepa Rose broke off suddenly and began to display his wares. Before he gave out any more news, the Paynes knew they would have to buy from the peddler. Everything he offered, they bought. He must be kept in a good humor.

When Chepa Rose packed his trunk and hoisted it on his back, Dolly begged, "Please tell us more."

The man sneered. "You folks don't know anything— *Cornwallis surrendered in October at Yorktown; America's won the war.*"

The Revolution was over! No longer need Molly and her children listen each night for Tarleton, and Father could come home! But months passed, and John Payne did not appear. His family began to despair. Was he sick? Dead?

One night Dolly, who slept with her mother, was awakened by a sound outside. It came again, a loud knocking. Half asleep, she forgot that the war was over, and drew the covers over her head.

"Mother!" Dolly whispered. "Somebody's at the front door."

Mrs. Payne sprang from her bed and opened the window. It was moonlight. But the visitor was in a shadow.

"Who is it?" she called.

"Thy husband," answered a familiar voice.

Molly caught up her shawl, and hurried down the stairs. Dolly, the boys, and sleepy-eyed Lucy followed her. But

Mother reached the front door first. Fumbling excitedly at the bolt, she flung it open. Father stretched out his arms.

"Molly, my dear!" he said huskily.

Then Dolly, Lucy and the boys were embraced.

"John, thee forgets Anna," Mother said. And Captain Payne turned to still another daughter, a round-eyed child of three, standing on the stairs.

"That's not our baby? This great girl!" Father mounted the stairs, picked Anna up, and came down again. "Oh, God is good, I'm home again! Thee cannot know what that means, Molly."

"I didn't expect thee, John. No letter—"

"I came as soon as I could."

What rivalry there was among the children as they waited upon Father, getting him food, bringing him his pipe. Lucy climbed into his lap and patted his face. Dolly smiled at him adoringly. Mother looked sweet and young again, not worn and pale as she had been lately.

Presently Father went up to the nursery to see Mary, born after his departure. He lifted the frail child from the crib and kissed her. And she cuddled sleepily against his neck.

"John, our Mary knows thee for her father," cried Mary's mother, delighted.

❀   ❀   ❀   ❀   ❀

With Father home, everything would be all right, Dolly assured herself. The shadow over the gloomy Scotchtown mansion would vanish. She would be able to laugh at Mammy Amy's melancholy prophecies.

And everything was all right, for a time. John Payne settled down to try to grow tobacco on his rocky acres. He did not want to talk about his war experiences, which had been hard and bitter. He wanted to forget.

Not even his family was aware of the dissatisfaction with which John returned to the life of a Virginia planter. Many times Dolly found him in the tobacco fields with his sons.

"The color of these shoots is only fair, boys, the leaves mighty small," Father would point out in a dejected voice.

"It's the best we can do in this rocky soil, sir." Walter was almost in tears.

"I know it. Well, top the tobacco when it's ready and cut off the ground leaves." Father sighed and walked away.

The year after John Payne came home, there was a new baby, named John. The following year there was still another boy, Isaac, for Mammy Amy to nurse. By 1783 there were eight Payne children, with Dolly, then fifteen, a handsome girl, almost grown to womanhood. It began to look as though even Scotchtown would be too small to hold them all.

Father talked frequently of Philadelphia. After being de-mobilized, he had visited the city founded by the Society of Friends.

"I'd like to live there, Molly," Dolly heard him say. "We'd be among Quakers, our own kind."

He had never been contented in his native state. Virginia with its cock-fighting, horse-racing, and rum-drinking, was too "dissipated and ungodly" for the austere John Payne.

After the Revolution, the Church of England remained the established church to which the aristocracy belonged. They had little love for Quakers and other non-conformists, al-though the article on religious freedom which James Madison had helped to draft into the Virginia Bill of Rights was the first declaration for religious freedom in America. It distinctly said:

. . . religion, or the duty we owe to our Creator, and the

manner of discharging it, can be directed only by reason and conviction, not by force or violence, and therefore all men are equally entitled to the free exercise of religion according to the dictates of conscience.

When Father predicted that Mr. Madison's declaration of religious tolerance would be copied by other states, Dolly remembered the solemn-faced young man who had stopped on his way to Congress.

"Mr. Madison must be a fine man, Father." Dolly's face was aglow. "He wants everyone, even us Quakers, to worship as we please."

"He is more tolerant than most Virginians. But even he—" Then John Payne quoted a remark Madison was reported to have made, "A man may be a Christian in any church, but a *gentleman* belongs to the Church of England."

Dolly frowned. So even Mr. Madison looked down on Quakers, as did so many people. The horrid man! Perhaps the traveler had been right, after all.

🏵   🏵   🏵   🏵   🏵

On a spring day in 1783, John Payne gave up his hopeless struggle with the rocky soil of Scotchtown. "Children, we're moving to Philadelphia to live," he announced bluntly.

"Leaving Scotchtown? Oh, goody!" Dolly cried—anything for a change from her dull country life. She started excitedly for the door. "I'll go tell Mammy Amy. She'll have the others pack—"

Her father's grim look stopped her.

"I haven't told thee, Molly." He turned, in some embarrassment, to his wife. "Amy and the other Negroes aren't

going with us. The Lord has commanded me to give up my
slaves."

Mother gasped. "John, thee doesn't mean give them their
freedom?"

Father patted her shoulder, and tried to calm her. He meant
just that; he had been talking it over with God for a long
time. "I fought for freedom in the war," he explained. "Can
I deprive anyone of it?"

"But, John, how can we live without our Negroes?"
Mother pleaded. "Our tobacco's a failure. The only money
we have is in slaves."

Dolly listened in amazement. She had always thought of
her father as rich. And so he was. Slaves were worth from
one hundred and fifty to fifteen hundred dollars each. John
Payne, who had fifty slaves and a thousand acres of land,
rocky as it was, was worth about forty thousand dollars—
quite a fortune in those days. But he had no stocks and bonds,
no money out at interest. Like other southern planters, he
lived on the labor of his Negroes.

Yet the Quakers, as a sect, were against slavery; and Friend
Payne was ready to do the heroic thing, pay a dear price
for his convictions. Not even Molly's tears, nor the children's
pleas, could turn him from his resolve, now that he had seen
the Light.

His docile wife finally gave in—since naming her eldest
daughter, she had seldom opposed him. "But what will we
live on?" Molly asked.

Father shrugged. "We'll sell Scotchtown. We'll have the
money from that, until I find work in Philadelphia."

Convincing his family, John Payne found, was an easier
matter than breaking the news to Mammy Amy and his other
faithful slaves. When the master offered them freedom, several of the most devoted refused to accept their liberty.

"We belon' to ye, massa," cried a chorus of voices. "Don't turn us out!"

Mammy Amy clung weeping to Dolly. "Massa John, don't take my chile from me. She's mine—"

"There, there, Mammy." Dolly dried the old woman's tears. "Nobody is going to separate us. Thee will go with us. I'll ask Father."

It was not easy for Dolly to ask her stern father anything. But for Mammy's sake, she gathered her courage. So touching was his daughter's plea that John Payne finally relented. Amy could go to Philadelphia, not as a slave, but as a servant. She was to be paid for her labor in money.

"Money, what's dat?" Mammy Amy had never heard of wages. But she did not care how she went to Philadelphia, as long as she went.

So Amy was with John Payne and his family on the July day in 1783 when they boarded the packet that would take them north.

In her gray cape and poke bonnet, Dolly stood with her brothers and Lucy in the bow of the boat. As it moved down the James River toward Chesapeake Bay, Dolly gazed ahead eagerly. Even more wonderful than Williamsburg or Richmond would be Philadelphia—the largest town in America— where she was going to live.

THE NEW HOME OF THE PAYNES IN PHILADELPHIA WAS A typical Quaker brick dwelling, high and narrow, with white trim. It stood at 410 Third Street, just around the corner from William Penn's own. (Now standing in Fairmount Park.)

How small it looked after Scotchtown! When the tired travelers mounted the white steps to a tiny porch and looked down the brick row of houses, Dolly exclaimed, "Why, they're all exactly alike!"

The family crowded into the narrow hall to see if the interior was more original-looking. But like so many Philadelphia homes of the Friends, it was just as monotonous as the exterior.

The lower floor had two rooms. In one corner of the front room was a large iron stove called a "Franklin Stove," after Benjamin Franklin, who invented it. The back room with its white-washed walls and sanded floor had an open fireplace. Upstairs there were four small bedrooms. Walter and William Temple would have to double up in one. Lucy and Anna would push Dolly out of bed in the second. Mother and Father took delicate little Mary, while Mammy Amy watched over the babies—quiet John and boisterous Isaac.

There were so many Paynes! A dejected group, they gathered around the Franklin stove, too tired to unpack and lay out their belongings. Mary began to cry—

Suddenly there was a knock; the front door opened. Into the bleak little room swept a plump woman and two young girls dressed in Quaker gray.

"Molly Payne, oh, I'm glad thee has come!" Then turning to John Payne, the visitor said, "And thee, John, welcome, too."

It was Mistress Henry Drinker and her daughters, Sally and Nancy, who lived two doors away. Elizabeth Drinker and Molly Payne were old friends. Their fathers had both come from County Wexford in Ireland. A month before, Molly had written Elizabeth of their move to Philadelphia.

"Thee must be starved," cried the energetic Mrs. Drinker. "I've brought thee a hot meal." While Mammy Amy brewed tea, Elizabeth unpacked the basket piled high with warm, tempting food.

The famished Paynes sat down to eat the crisp rye bread and cheese, the savory sausage. In a brown earthen crock was a dish new to the Virginians, Philadelphia pepper pot. Dolly thought she had never tasted anything more delicious than the mixture of tripe, peppers, tomatoes, tender little dumplings and strange spices. They washed down the food with Mammy Amy's scalding tea and felt better.

"We've need of thy eloquence, John," said Mrs. Drinker, when the meal ended. "Our meeting is bare of the Spirit."

The Drinkers belonged to the Free Quaker Meeting House on the southwest corner of Fifth and Mulberry Streets. That was the congregation of Friends the Paynes would join. Already they were among their own kind.

While their elders talked, Dolly sat between the Drinker daughters, two girls about her own age. The elder, Sally, was blond and beautiful. Brunette Nancy was less pretty. But she had a gay, witty tongue.

"All thee Paynes will go to our school, of course." Sally smiled across the table at William Temple and Lucy. "It'll be nice knowing new boys and girls."

Dolly could not believe her ears. The Drinkers were Quakers, but their young people were allowed to have fun. The country maiden leaned forward eagerly as Nancy and Sally described boating parties on the Schuylkill and drives on the good roads around Philadelphia. Were they, the Paynes, to be included in these jolly parties? She looked doubtfully at her father.

"See thee tomorrow," Sally cried when she bade her new friend good night. "Scrubbing the steps," added Nancy.

Scrubbing the steps was a Philadelphia custom, they explained. The Friends were proud of their white marble steps, that led up to their tiny porches. They must be kept spotless. So on Wednesdays and Saturdays, regardless of weather, the stoops were washed, usually by the younger girls of the family.

Next morning Dolly was out early with her bucket of soapy water and her clean rags. But Nancy was there first. Down on her knees, she mopped the steps to the Drinker porch. "Hello, Neighbor," she called.

Dolly looked down the row of brick houses. Before each porch was a woman or a young girl, scrubbing the marble. As they worked, they threw gay remarks to and fro.

The tiny stoops promoted the sociability of the neighborhood in another way. On summer evenings, Philadelphia families sat out on their porches until bedtime. There were so many Paynes that they overflowed theirs. Dolly, red-haired plump Lucy, and little blond Anna curled up on the white steps so they wouldn't miss one of the fascinating sights of the busy, lamp-lit street.

Shortly after supper, Walter and William Temple were off with the other neighborhood boys, promenading up and down.

The first night, a freckle-faced youth had stopped at the

Payne house. "I'm Jacob Downing," he said. "Don't thee want to come and walk?" He spoke to Walter but he looked straight into Dolly's blue eyes.

Jacob lived three doors down the street. He, too, went to the school run by the Free Quaker Meeting. To John and Molly Payne, he was an acceptable companion for their children.

Dolly thought seventeen-year-old Jacob homely, but very old and so interesting. When he passed the house and tried to catch her eye, she blushed. But Jacob was really Nancy Drinker's beau. Dolly could hear Nancy call out a greeting, when the boys neared her front stoop. Nancy was in love with Jacob; anyone could see that.

It was September, with a hunter's moon. Dolly sat on the little porch and sighed. She was fifteen; a rosy-faced country girl, who once, long ago, had danced gaily in a blue satin dress. Would she ever dance again? Would she—and Dolly buried her face in Anna's golden curls—ever have a beau?

❧   ❧   ❧   ❧   ❧

On Chestnut Street, all the fashionable Philadelphia world promenaded in the late afternoon. Gentlemen in powdered wigs and cocked hats, ladies in hooped gowns and enormous calash bonnets or feathered hats atop monumental wigs, sauntered along or paused to look in the shop windows that lined the street.

Whenever she could slip away, Dolly walked on Chestnut Street. She, too, liked to look at the displays of the dressmakers, milliners, tailors, shoemakers, and jewelers. This was Philadelphia—this was the life, exciting and fascinating, Dolly had always wanted. She loved the crowds, the shops, the paved and lamp-lit streets, the portly watchmen who called out the hours when all was still.

Her quick eye took in all the pretty clothes. "Look, Lucy—" She pointed to the clocks on a girl's bright stockings peeping from under her petticoats. "And those earrings—oh, Lucy, I wish Quakers could wear earrings!"

Under her demure kerchief, the girl's heart yearned for all the vanities against which the Friends were warned in meeting. She had soon learned that in Philadelphia there were Quakers who wore hoops, silk bonnets, buckles and bright colors right under the disapproving frowns of the elders. They were known as "Wet Quakers." Highly condemned for the elasticity of their principles, "Wet Quakers" were only allowed to come to the Weekly Meetings, not to the Monthly or Quarterly ones.

With Father an elder, none of the Paynes could be "Wet Quakers." But John Payne could not forbid his daughter to look at the lovely clothes in the stores on her way to meeting. There was one shop where she always lingered. In its window stood one of the fashion dolls sent from Paris to display the newest styles in dress. The French doll wore a gown of shimmering white satin. On her golden hair was a cascade of white tulle fastened with orange blossoms. It was a bridal doll.

Dolly held her breath in rapture. She had never seen anything so beautiful. As she imagined herself wearing such a wedding outfit, her eyes shone.

Father's patience gave out. "Daughter, come!" he called.

Meekly she followed him down the street.

But Dolly never forgot that wedding dress. Nor the thought of herself in it, coming down a church aisle to where a handsome bridegroom waited, the sleeves of his velvet coat edged with ruffles of Mechlin lace.

❀   ❀   ❀   ❀   ❀

In Philadelphia, John Payne achieved his life's ambition. He became an elder, or lay preacher. On First Day, he exhorted in meeting.

After that he became stricter than ever. No dancing and cards, of course, for the young Paynes. No dresses other than the Quaker's quiet gray for the girls. But Dolly's black curls and bright Irish-blue eyes triumphed over her sombre garb. As she walked with the Drinker girls, or her new school friend, Eliza Collins, the boys lined up on the street to watch her pass.

"Thee should wear a mask, the men stare at thee so." Eliza gripped Dolly's arm to protect her.

At school, it was the same story. It had been no fault of Dolly's that Jacob Downing preferred her to Nancy Drinker. Before a month had passed, he was waiting one morning when she started off to school. "Let me carry thy books," he said abruptly.

Snatching the books, he stalked along beside her. Dolly pitied Nancy, ahead with her sister Sally.

"Give me back my books, Jacob," she said firmly. "What will people say—thee walking to school with me in the morning." She hurried to catch up with the other girls.

He reddened under his freckles. "I want them to think it."

"Think what?"

"That I'm thy beau."

It was Dolly's turn to blush. Her wish had come true; she could have a beau, like the other Philadelphia girls. But Jacob Downing—she stared at his sandy hair, his freckled face, his lanky body. She thought of Nancy Drinker, who loved him. She remembered the bridegroom with ruffles of Mechlin lace, the bridal gown of shimmering white. No, Jacob Downing was not the handsome bridegroom; not the man to lift the long tulle veil and fasten the orange blossoms in Dolly's heavy dark curls.

"I haven't a beau," she said airily. "I don't want any."

❧   ❧   ❧   ❧   ❧

In late October of 1783, Dolly scrubbed the Paynes' steps on Saturday morning. Down the street came a tall, sandy-haired man, holding a little girl by the hand. To Dolly's surprise, he stopped and introduced himself, "I'm Thomas Jefferson from Monticello, come to see my old friends, the Paynes."

Dolly dropped her pail in astonishment. So this was Thomas Jefferson, for whose words the Liberty Bell had tolled, "We hold these truths to be self-evident . . . that all men are created equal . . . life, liberty and the pursuit of happiness. . . ." This was Mother's old beau—Tom Jefferson, with whom on visits to her cousin, John Coles, in Albemarle County, Virginia, pretty young Molly Coles had once danced and ridden.

Now in the front room, a sobered Molly sat knitting. Her face was pale and sad. A fifth daughter had been born to her in August. They had hardly named the little mite Philadelphia, after their new home, when she died.

But at the sight of the tall visitor, the color rushed again to Mother's cheeks. "Tom Jefferson!" She jumped up, her hands outstretched.

"You haven't changed a bit, Molly," he told her later over the tea cups. "And that's a lovely daughter you have. Dolly is very much like you were when I was courting you."

Thomas Jefferson, heartsick over the death of his wife, could no longer enjoy his beloved home, Monticello. He was glad to be going to Europe, he said. Congress was sending him over to help John Adams and Benjamin Franklin arrange trade treaties.

"I'm taking Patsy with me." He directed a fond look at the forlorn little girl, seated on the sofa beside Dolly. "Patsy's only twelve, but I think we can manage. I'll put her in a convent school in Paris. I've two younger children at home— Polly, who is six, and a baby, Lucy. Their aunt is looking after them."

But it was not until the following July that Thomas Jefferson and his Martha, or Patsy as he called her, sailed from Boston. That winter, while her father was in Congress at Annapolis, Martha went to school in Philadelphia. Dolly Payne looked after Martha like a big sister. And between the two girls grew a deep and lasting affection.

🏵   🏵   🏵   🏵   🏵

One May day in 1787, Dolly Payne and her sisters, Anna and Lucy, pushed their way through the crowd that had gathered around Independence Hall. Philadelphia was the scene of great excitement. Delegates from all the states were there to write a Constitution.

Suddenly the voice of the Town Crier was heard, "The debates began today that will establish our form of government, based on a new Constitution. It has been decided that these sessions will be closed to the public."

Disappointed murmurs rose from the crowd. Everyone had hoped to throng into the brick State House and listen.

The Payne girls, craning their necks to watch the delegates enter, were disappointed, too. Pushing Lucy and Anna forward, Dolly caught her breath at the sight of the first imposing figure. It was George Washington, handsome in black, and wearing his dress sword with grace.

Walking briskly beside him was a dapper young man. "That's Alexander Hamilton . . . a clever fellow . . . delegate from New York, and Washington's aide-de-camp in the war," Dolly heard a man tell his companion.

Along came other delegates. Governor Randolph of Virginia. Elbridge Gerry. Roger Sherman. Rutledge from South Carolina. As the last man stepped inside, the great doors of the hall were closed. The crowd turned reluctantly away.

"We might as well go home," Dolly told her sisters. But their path led them around Independence Hall. And as they passed, they saw an open window. Dolly's face brightened. It was only a short distance from the ground. Just one look inside. Why not?

The three girls tiptoed over to a rain barrel, right under the open window. Forgetting the dignity of her nineteen years, Dolly boosted the younger girls onto the barrel and then climbed up after them.

Their arms linked, the three sisters glued their excited faces to the window that opened into the hall. George Washington sat in his high-backed chair. Eighty-one-year-old Benjamin Franklin nodded his white locks. Edmund Randolph, in a soft southern voice, spoke eloquently of the "Virginia Plan."

Then a little man with a small face, and the nearsighted eyes of a scholar, who had been seated near General Washington taking down copious notes of everything that was said, rose to his feet. He spoke in a quiet, thin voice, that sank almost to a whisper at the end of each sentence.

"Governor Randolph, let me add a few ideas to yours," he said earnestly. "True, the Constitution does not wholly satisfy any of us. But I think it should be adopted, and the States should ratify it. The Constitution could have a Bill of Rights added to it, that would take care of any objections—"

Dolly listened intently. It was obvious that the other delegates were impressed with the speaker's wide knowledge of his subject.

When he finished, Randolph bowed. "It's thanks to your efforts this convention has met at all, Mr. Madison. The Virginia Plan, the basis for the proposed Constitution, was worked out by *you*. I've only the honor of presenting it. If the document is ever drawn up and ratified, I predict, James Madison, that you'll go down in history as the Father of the Constitution—"

The shy little man turned crimson and sat down.

James Madison! Dolly looked hard at the short, solemn-faced man, who received Edmund Randolph's compliments with blushing confusion. She nudged her sister.

"It's the stranger we saw riding to Congress. Remember, Lucy, the day the peddler came?"

Lucy shook her head. She had been too young to remember. But Dolly did. She was fascinated by Mr. Madison's pale, serious face. She remembered how he had helped the Quakers in Virginia gain the right to worship as they pleased, and how she had once admired him. She would have liked him now, but for that later remark of his, which Father had repeated, "A man may be a Christian in any church, but a *gentleman* belongs to the Church of England."

Dolly tossed her dark head so high that she almost fell off the rain barrel. Let people call James Madison the "Father of the Constitution," and think him a great man, she looked down on him. He had dared to patronize the Quakers.

"Dolly!" Lucy's frightened voice brought her sister up with a start. "Get down! A soldier's coming."

Dolly jumped down, and helped Anna and Lucy to the ground. Then the sisters ran off, as fast as Anna's short legs would carry her. Too lazy to chase them, the soldier stood shaking his fist as the Payne girls scampered out of sight.

☙   ☙   ☙   ☙   ☙

Not until September 17th was the Constitution favorably voted on. Then the delegates scattered to their homes to plead with their states to adopt it. Alexander Hamilton returned to New York; James Madison to Virginia. Both had their minds on the Federalist papers they would write, pleading for the Constitution. Madison was already planning the ten amendments, known as the Bill of Rights, which would protect the freedom of the common citizen against oppression from the government—nine of which he would introduce in Congress.

But by September, Dolly Payne had forgotten James Madison and his "child," the Constitution. Troubles lay so heavily on her heart that she gave little thought to the May morning when she had peered into the window of Independence Hall.

That September of 1787, Grandmother Coles died down in Virginia. Before Dolly could recover from her grief, Mammy Amy took ill.

For weeks the old Negro woman lay sick in bed. The Payne children, except the two older boys, had never known life without Amy—"to wait upon us, love us, and always be there" as Anna put it. Now it was their turn to care for their aged nurse, and by their love, repay her devotion. All of them did. Dolly, most of all.

Day after day she waited at her mammy's bedside. She was there the night Amy died. Raising herself on her elbow, the dying woman whispered, "Take it . . . it's all dyar fer you," and pointed to an old shoe on the floor.

Puzzled, Dolly picked it up. A roll of money fell out.

"Count it. I didn't touch none o' yit," Amy gasped. "It's all fer you, chile."

The roll of bills uncoiled in Dolly's hand. Amazed, she counted them. They added up to *five hundred dollars.* In a flash Dolly understood—it was Mammy's wages.

Since Amy had lived in Philadelphia with the Paynes as a servant, not as a slave, Father had insisted on paying her a salary of ten dollars a month. Without a word, Mammy Amy accepted the money. But she had not spent a cent of it. She had saved it for her "chile."

Tears in her eyes, Dolly looked up. "Mammy, dear—"

For once, her old nurse did not return her smile. With a little sigh, she sank back on her pillow and passed away.

IN MAY OF 1789, PRETTY DOLLY PAYNE REACHED HER twenty-first birthday. But she was still unmarried. At an age when most of the belles of Philadelphia had become decorous matrons with a child or two, Dolly had refused to make her choice.

The dark-haired, blue-eyed girl was highly popular. In the mild social activities of her set and at meeting, she mingled with men and boys of the Friends. But Dolly, hoping, dreaming, looked ahead into more exciting spaces. Somehow she felt that her greatest triumphs—and her deepest sorrows—lay very far beyond her.

John Payne often worried because his eldest daughter was well on the way to being a spinster. He also worried because Dolly had never felt the Spirit, had never spoken in meeting. Lucy, nine years younger, had already risen and given her testimony. Plump, round-faced and serious-minded, Lucy was a pious child.

"I don't have incomes of the Spirit like thee," Dolly told her sister. "I can't think of a thing to say."

"But thee must soon have the Spirit, or it shows there's something wrong with thee," said Lucy smugly. "Father says so."

Added to the humiliation of having a daughter "bare of the Spirit," was John Payne's constant battle with poverty. The Revolutionary money, left from the sale of Scotchtown, was now of little worth. A large lump of it had gone to send

Walter, John's favorite son, to England in 1785—a long, expensive journey for a poor Quaker boy.

Walter had not returned, nor had he repaid the money. Now, four years later, the family finances were so low that even Father knew he could no longer postpone going to work.

"There's a fortune in starch," John Payne announced one night. In a determined voice, he began to explain its many uses: to size yarn, to dress cloth, to thicken colors in calico printing. "I'd like to find a nice starch business, already established, and buy it," he said.

He found one—belonging to Zebe Smith, at 89 Elm Street, a successful starch maker with ten years' experience. Too ill to continue in business, Smith would sell his starch factory for five hundred dollars.

Father was jubilant. "Fortunately, we've the money Mammy Amy left us," he reminded the family.

Dolly opened her mouth to protest. But her father's expression stopped her. He needed money so desperately. Surely there would never be a moment when she herself would know a greater need.

So Father bought the starch business with Mammy Amy's savings. Almost at once, he departed for Ohio to visit a Friends' meeting. He had it all figured out—Zebe Smith's old employees would keep on making starch for him; being in business would not interfere with his preaching at all.

While Father was in Ohio, Zebe Smith opened a competing plant right in Philadelphia. His equipment was the newest, the best to be had—Mammy Amy's money had made it possible.

Father was furious. But Zebe's original promise to give John Payne all of his business had not been put in writing. Philadelphia was deep in the depression that followed the Revolution. Customers did not pay their bills. Payne went deeper and deeper in debt.

One morning when breakfast was ready, Father did not appear. Timidly, Dolly opened the door and addressed the figure muffled in blankets. "I am not coming down," Father muttered.

The doctor called it a nervous breakdown. He said Mr. Payne must have complete rest and freedom from worry. His business troubles had been too much for him.

With Father lying in bed, life was harder than ever for his family. Dolly's back ached from carrying up trays. Father's creditors had taken over the starch business. His son, William Temple, did not dare tell him.

One August day in 1789, the Paynes received a letter from Walter, John Payne's favorite child. Perhaps a message from him would bring Father back to health. Dolly rushed upstairs to hand the letter to her ailing parent.

But when the invalid had read it, he sank back on his pillow with a moan. In gasping words, he told her the dreadful news. Walter had married out of meeting, an English girl who was not a Quaker. Because of his marriage, he had been disowned by the Devonshire House Meeting. And—oh, the most dreadful part of it—Walter added, he did not care.

Marrying out of meeting, outside the membership of the Society of Friends, was the blackest sin a Quaker could commit. Dolly could not believe it of Walter, next to Father the most devout member of the family. What would Mother say?

But when Molly Payne returned from market, Father was so ill that Dolly had frantically summoned the doctor. Walter's terrible deed became of secondary importance. Mr. Payne had had a stroke, the doctor said.

So continued the long months that John Payne lay in bed, a helpless invalid. His devoted family, particularly Dolly, catered to every whim. Meanwhile, money grew scarcer, and Molly Payne more worried and worn.

All these cares Dolly took with her to meeting one First Day morning. It was Lucy's turn to stay home with Father. In the large, bare room filled with gray-clad, silent people, Dolly sat on the women's side between Mother and Anna. During the long meditation, she turned her troubles over in her mind. There was no solution.

A sob shattered the silence. The valiant Molly had broken down completely, hiding her face in her hands. "If Mother gives up—" thought Dolly in panic. Suddenly life became more than she could bear, alone. She rose slowly to her feet.

There was a slight turning of heads, a faint stir of expectation. The girl stood silent a moment, swaying like a flower in the breeze, her lashes downcast, her hands clasped tightly before her. She began to speak, frightened at first, then gradually gaining courage.

"I feel drawings in my mind to place my troubles on Thy shoulders, O Lord. I cannot bear my afflictions alone any longer. Lord, I am too weak. Only Thee can help me—"

With her downcast eyes and folded hands, the girl was lovely. There was a heavenly light in her face. Surely she was "in the Spirit."

Seated across the room among the men and boys, the young Quaker lawyer, John Todd, watched Dolly Payne. He saw the rosy flush mount to the girl's clear skin. He listened to her sweet voice, calling on the Lord for help. What was she saying? That her life was hard. That her cross was more than she could bear without God's aid.

John Todd's kind heart went out to the suffering girl. That anyone so beautiful should be in such trouble grieved him. Couldn't he help her? Take her troubles on his own shoulders? John longed to leap across the aisle to the women's section and grasp her hands. He longed to shield and protect her.

For John Todd, serious-minded Quaker, had fallen in love at first sight. It happens like that sometimes.

Despite her downcast eyes, Dolly felt the young man staring at her. He looked at her so hard, she could not but be conscious of him. Yet his face seemed dreamlike, unreal. For suddenly the Lord was with her; she felt the Divine ease.

"Oh, thank Thee, Lord, for answering my prayer. Thee has taken my troubles and given me peace—" Dolly began to tremble. Then suddenly she could say no more. Sinking back into her seat, she knew the blessed relief of tears.

After the meeting, many of the congregation stopped to speak to Dolly Payne. Everyone was pleased that John's daughter had finally bloomed with the Divine word; that she had borne such rich testimony and spoken so well.

"Thy father would be proud of thee," an elder praised her.

Dolly saw a tall, young Quaker shouldering his way through the crowd toward her.

"May I tell thee that thy testimony tendered my heart?" he asked, looking squarely into her blue eyes. "My name is John Todd. Will thee forgive my introducing myself? I couldn't wait to find someone who knew us both, and go through the formalities. May I help thee?"

Dolly thought how nice-looking he was. Not really handsome, he was too thin and pale. But his brown eyes were kind.

She shook her head. Just now, still shaken by her testimony, still trembling from the power of the Spirit that had flowed through her, Dolly longed to be alone.

"Please, if at any time you need me—"

She put out her hand to grasp his. "Thank you," she murmured, eyes downcast.

Later she caught sight of John Todd's beaver hat, towering
above everyone's, as he hurried past the young men gathered
on the steps of the meeting house to exchange shy words
with the girls.

❀   ❀   ❀   ❀   ❀

From the day Dolly gave her testimony, Father grew
worse. He lay on his pillow, his face so white one would
think him dead. John, then Lucy, then Dolly, Anna or Isaac,
sat beside him.

One night Mother walked the floor up and down, too
upset to sit still. Their landlord would not be put off any
longer. They must pay their rent or be put out of the simple
brick house at 410 Third Street. And where would they find
the money?

Suddenly the brass knocker sounded through the house.
Faces turned pale. Who could it be? Not the doctor. He had
come and gone. It must be the landlord.

"Mother, dear—" William Temple put his arm protectingly
around her, as Dolly went to answer the door.

In the hall, she stopped a moment to gather courage. If it
were the landlord— Trembling, she opened the door. It was a
tall, thin man in a broad-brimmed beaver hat.

"John Todd!" She forgot she hardly knew him.

"None of thee Paynes came to meeting. I knew thee must
be in trouble," he told Dolly. "Then tonight I had a concern.
The Lord led me to thee—"

Dolly welcomed him, grateful tears in her eyes. She was
soon to know that the kindly John Todd often had "con-
cerns" for those in trouble. All over Philadelphia were unfortunates who could tell of good deeds he had done. But that

evening she felt his coming was a miracle. God had answered the prayer in her heart.

Even proud Molly Payne told him her troubles. In the telling, she already felt better. John's manner was so calm and quiet. He listened with such understanding.

When he heard their landlord's name, his face brightened. "Why, he's a friend of my father's!" he exclaimed. "And really a good man. I'll go see him tomorrow and explain."

John Todd, Senior, was a well-known Philadelphia school teacher. He taught at a Quaker school for boys on Fourth Street below Chestnut, known as Proud's School. At twenty-six, John himself was already a promising young attorney. The landlord was impressed; he agreed that the Paynes could remain in their house a few months longer.

That evening John appeared with the good news and a basket of food, a turkey and fresh vegetables. Anna and Mary ran to meet him at the door. Lucy ushered him over to sit in Father's wing chair. But it was at Dolly that young Todd looked.

The next time John came he asked to see Father. Molly feared that a visit from a stranger would be too much for the invalid. But John Payne took to the serious young Friend at once.

"I'm a lawyer; I can help." John Todd had already heard about his business difficulties. "Thee bought thy starch business with the understanding Zebe Smith would leave Philadelphia, Friend Payne?"

Father nodded weakly.

"Then it's a clear case of misrepresentation and fraud. Let me see Zebe Smith. I'm sure I can get a settlement."

A few days later, John Todd again lifted the Payne's knocker. The lawyer had investigated Zebe Smith's reputation. The starch maker had forged deeds; he had been in jail

three times. When Todd threatened to institute a suit against
Smith in behalf of his client, Zebe suddenly found he must
go to New York. He sent John Payne two hundred dollars.

What joy there was in the Payne household! The landlord
was paid. On the balance, the Paynes could live for a while.
John Todd became like an older brother to the family.

But it was Father who clung to John the most. He began to
take Walter's place in the invalid's heart. When he died . . .
The family had tried to keep it from John Payne. But Father
knew he was dying.

"Thee will look after my family, John?" he asked one day.
He must have known the secret in the young Friend's heart,
for he added, "Thee will look after Dolly?"

John took his frail hand. "I'll watch over them all, Mr.
Payne," he promised solemnly. "Especially Dolly."

At twilight, John Todd came into the Payne's front room.
Dolly, seated on the sofa, was suddenly very busy with her
sampler. But he took it away from her. "Dolly," he said
softly, seating himself beside her, "I love thee. Darling, won't
thee love me a little? Won't thee marry me?"

Dolly's grateful heart ached for him. He had been so good
to them all. Why must she hurt him?

"I like thee a lot, John," she said. "But I don't—love thee."

"Wouldn't liking be enough, dear?" he asked patiently.

"No, no!" Then she added quickly, to ease the pain, "John,
I shall never marry anyone."

When Father heard what Dolly had said—especially that
ridiculous remark that she never expected to marry—he flew
into one of his old rages.

"Thee must marry John Todd. Thee must obey thy
father," he poured words of wrath on his daughter's head.

"I can't marry John; I don't love him," was her reply.
Stubbornly, she held on to her dream of a life far removed

from this quiet Quaker lawyer.

Father reared up in bed, his face livid. "Then I disown thee. Ungrateful child—" Suddenly he fell back, gasping for breath.

One look, and terrified Dolly ran to fetch Mother. The doctor said he thought Mr. Payne was dying. The children were called. Silent and afraid, they stood around the bed.

"Father, don't die," Dolly cried. He was weak, helpless and terribly ill. She was the strong one, young and well. He was asking something of her. Such a little thing, so he could die happy.

What John Payne's rages had never done, pity now accomplished. Dolly fell on her knees by his bed. "I'll do as thee wishes," she promised, trying to break down the wall of coldness that had always existed between them. "I'll marry John for thy sake."

❁   ❁   ❁   ❁   ❁

John Payne did not die then. He lived, a helpless invalid, for two years after Dolly plighted her troth to John Todd.

They were married in the Friends' Meeting House on Pine Street on the seventh day of First Month, 1790. January whitened the Philadelphia streets with snow; and Dolly, her face no less white, walked like a girl in a trance.

It was the short, simple ceremony of the Quaker faith. Dolly and John sat among the elders on the high seat facing the congregation. First came the long silence. Then John rose, took Dolly's hand, and repeated a solemn marriage service:

"*I, John Todd, do take thee, Dorothea Payne, to be my wedded wife, and promise through divine assistance to be unto thee a loving husband, until separated by death—*"

Dolly's clear voice repeated the vow. There is no priest or

minister in a Quaker marriage. The bride and groom simply declare themselves willing to live together as a married couple. They marry themselves in the sight of God. Then the certificate of marriage is read.

Lively Eliza Collins, her gray gown billowing, her demure bonnet a frame for her piquant face and auburn curls, was Dolly's bridesmaid. Another young Quaker lawyer, Anthony Morris, flaxen-haired and amiable, graduate of the University of Pennsylvania, was John's best man.

There were no flowers, music, or decorations. Dolly Payne's wedding gown was her usual gray dress. Her dark hair was drawn back simply under her scooped bonnet. Her kerchief was fragile muslin, but it was plain.

It was all so different from the wedding of which the romantic girl had dreamed . . . that fashion doll in the store window on Chestnut Street, the doll's white satin dress and filmy tulle veil. Nor was John Todd the handsome bridegroom of her dreams. He wore no velvet coat with ruffles of Mechlin lace. No white peruke, no buckled shoes. Never had his face seemed more sallow, his nose more hawklike.

It was the Quaker custom for all who signed the marriage register to be entertained later at supper in the bride's home. But the Paynes could afford no such hospitality. So it was only a small family group of Paynes and Todds that gathered in the little brick house on Third Street to enjoy Molly's Virginia cooking.

At twilight, John and Dolly Todd walked the short distance to their new home at 83 Chestnut Street, next to the corner of Third. There they began married life. Dolly had always longed for glamor and excitement. Now a quiet Quaker existence, such as her mother had become resigned to, stretched before her.

7

South Fourth Street Matron

$\mathcal{M}$ISTRESS TODD, WEARING A TULLE MOB CAP, A FOUR-STRAND gold chain about her throat, and her kerchief fastened with a large brooch (for the devoted John Todd leniently stretched his principles to indulge his wife's love of finery), turned her head to hear the watchman call the hour. "Eight o'clock," his voice echoed down South Fourth Street. Dolly went on pouring John's tea, listening, also, to what her husband, seated across the breakfast table, was saying.

"Yesterday I saw a robin," John observed. "But now it seems to be snowing." It was a March morning of 1792. A late snow squall beat against the windowpane.

"A long winter is hard on the poor," he continued, "and for those unfortunates trying to escape to Canada."

Fugitive slaves from the southern plantations were beginning to pass through Philadelphia. There they were helped by the Friends to travel north and over the Canadian border to freedom.

"I feel for any poor Negroes caught in this blizzard and sent back to their masters," Dolly sighed.

"I, too," said her husband earnestly. He went on to talk of the plans being made among the Friends to establish stations for the aid of these Negroes.

Delia, a slim brown girl, came into the room with a plate of hot waffles. An escaped slave herself, she was staying with the Todds until John could find a way to get her to Canada.

Meanwhile, Delia cooked the southern dishes that Dolly

loved. She also helped care for Dolly's month-old son, asleep in his crib upstairs. He was John Payne Todd, born on February 29, for 1792 was a leap year.

The Friends had to be careful about their activities. "If we're caught," John often said, "we'll be in grave trouble." Dolly worried. Since the baby's birth, she wished John would not take such risks. But Friend Todd had a great "concern" for anyone in distress. He helped the needy whenever he could.

Breakfast over, John rose to go to his law office. Dolly followed him into the hall. "Oh, it has already stopped snowing!" she cried. The young matron was going to a tea that afternoon at Mrs. George Washington's. She wanted to wear her First Day dress.

Dolly kissed her husband good-bye. Then she stood in the doorway, watching his thin, angular figure go off down the brick walk. Looking at her white steps, she thought of the many times she had bent to wipe similar steps at home before her marriage.

So much had happened since that day, over two years ago, when she became John's wife. Her father had died late in 1791, depressed by a sense of failure, but happy in his daughter's marriage.

After Father's death, courageous Molly Payne had moved to a slightly larger house—96 North Third Street—and begun taking in boarders. Thomas Jefferson was one of them. As President Washington's Secretary of State, Jefferson was now a very important man.

These boarders were fortunate people. With true Virginia hospitality, Molly treated them like honored guests. Living "at Mrs. Payne's" was vastly different from stopping at the Indian Queen, a dirty inn noted for its discomforts.

The Indian Queen was not far from the John Todd's new

home, Number 51 South Fourth Street. The Todds had not
lingered long on Chestnut Street. Their present home was a
newer house, but still another of those sedate Quaker brick
dwellings, high and narrow, with white blinds and door, and
a white stoop.

There the young couple lived comfortably, but not luxuri-
ously, on the small means of a lawyer of twenty-nine who
could not charge large fees. But Mistress John Todd was a
good manager. Her little house shone. Her meals were hot
and prompt. Her baby was a dimpled darling in his hooded
wooden crib.

If the twenty-four-year-old wife still cherished dreams of
a more worldly life than her modest Philadelphia dwelling af-
forded, there was no indication of it in her serene composure.
Her marriage had made her father happy. It had given her
mother, her younger brothers and sisters, a male relative on
whom they could depend for sound advice. Any regrets at
her decision had long ago been stifled. After the baby's arrival, Dolly seemed completely happy.

She was about to shut her front door and go up to little
Payne when her two sisters, Anna and Mary, rushed down
the street to greet her.

Anna and Mary lived with their mother in the boarding
house on North Third Street. But not Lucy. To the family's
great surprise, Lucy was now a Washington.

A month ago, at the age of fifteen, the plump and rather
plain girl had astonished them all by marrying George Washington's nephew—George Steptoe Washington, son of the
President's brother, Samuel, by his fourth wife. With her
husband, Lucy had returned to Virginia. Her new home was
Harewood, in Jefferson County, not far from Harper's Ferry.

William Temple was also living in Virginia, at Coles Hill,
which Mother had inherited from Granny. The two younger

boys, stolid John and rowdy little Isaac, remained with their mother. They were students at Proud's School, where Dolly's father-in-law was one of the four masters.

Anna was fourteen now, growing into a blond, vivacious beauty. Her promise to vie with Dolly for good looks had been borne out. Frail little Mary, a thin, brown-haired eleven-year-old, was not so radiant a girl. But with her sweet smile and gentle, brown eyes, she was always appealing.

The two girls followed Dolly upstairs to the nursery.

"Oh, isn't Payne precious!" Anna knelt down by the baby, who lay in his cradle, kicking and crowing.

"Isn't it time for Payne's nap?" asked Mary.

Dolly laughed. "He doesn't nap any more. Payne's so full of life. He never wants to sleep."

"But shouldn't he be made to? Naps are good for babies."

"Payne isn't going to do anything he doesn't want to— ever." Dolly pressed her lips together. "John and I have decided that. His father used to flog him for nothing; and I've known, too, what it means to have a strict parent. We want Payne to know nothing but love."

Her sister spoke with such bitterness that Anna hastily changed the subject. "Dolly, I've wonderful news. Mother has a new boarder. Who does thee think it is?"

"President Washington."

"Oh, no! It's the Senator from New York—Aaron Burr. He's simply wonderful, Dolly. Not tall, but so handsome, with the most fascinating eyes. Mr. Jefferson says the Burrs have a lovely home in New York, called Richmond Hill. He's married and has a little girl, Theodosia."

Dolly smiled at Anna's chatter. Her young sister had always been a hero worshipper.

"Senator Burr asked Mother if she could take in his friend,

James Madison, too," Mary said. "Mr. Madison finds the Indian Queen very dirty. But Mother hasn't a vacant room."

Dolly listened with increasing interest. James Madison was a famous Virginian; a congressman, as well, representing his home county of Orange.

Anna rose and tied the strings of her plain gray bonnet. "I wish I could wear a flowered hat to Lady Washington's instead of this hideous scoop," she pouted. "Oh, I hate the ugly old thing!"

"Thee looks sweet in it, dear." Dolly gave her sister an affectionate hug. She knew how Anna felt. Quiet little Mary did not seem to care about worldly things. But fair, blue-eyed Anna loved gaiety and pretty clothes. Dolly wished it was in her power to give them to her.

Young Mrs. Todd tried to maintain a dignified calm. But she was as excited as Anna at the thought of going to tea at Mrs. George Washington's. Ties of relationship are strong in Virginia. Because the Paynes had become by Lucy's marriage a "kin" of the President and First Lady, Dolly and Anna—whose mother ran a boarding house—had been invited today to the Washingtons'.

To do the family honor, Dolly donned her First Day dress, a well-fitting gray, and her big scoop bonnet. With Anna, she set off late that afternoon for the President's house.

As they passed their mother's home on North Third Street, a man came out of the door. From across the street, he lifted his cocked hat and bowed to Anna and Mary. The girls bowed back.

Anna squeezed Dolly's arm. "That's Colonel Aaron Burr."

Dolly's scoop of a bonnet was like a horse's blinders. To see, she had to turn her head clear around. What she saw was a short, handsome man, walking off briskly down the street.

But one quick glimpse told her that never before had she seen such assurance in any man's carriage.

❀ ❀ ❀ ❀ ❀

The Washingtons lived in one of Robert Morris' houses on High (now Market) Street. It was a small brick house with nothing about it to indicate that it was the home of the president of the United States. But Dolly's knees grew weak from nervousness as she approached it.

The Payne sisters climbed a narrow carpeted stairs, which led to an upper hall. To the left was a room crowded with people. Mrs. Todd was conscious of the buzz of voices, and to ease her nervousness thought hard about her mythical ancestor, the Earl of Wigton. Thinking about the earl gave Dolly assurance, as head high, chin out, she entered the drawing room with Anna. To her surprise, she saw it was simply furnished.

Before the fireplace a sweet-faced little woman in plum-colored silk was pouring tea. On her white hair rested a lace cap. In the glow of a chandelier, well-dressed ladies sat chatting. Several gentlemen stood in a group by the window.

A plump lady came toward Dolly and Anna. "I'm Mrs. Knox." She smiled. "May I introduce you?"

The wife of General Knox presented the sisters to Martha Washington, who greeted them cordially. The gentlemen bowed.

Then Dolly sat down stiffly on the sofa near a slim young woman with beautiful black eyes. Her breath failed her—she was actually sitting by Mrs. Alexander Hamilton!

A sweet little girl brought Mrs. Todd a cup of tea. It was Mrs. Washington's granddaughter, Nellie Custis. Plum cake was passed. Dolly made note to write Lucy that Lady

Washington served plain plum cake.

"How does your sister Lucy like Harewood?"

Gracious Martha Washington had left the tea table to sit beside Mrs. Todd on the sofa. The younger woman longed to tell the First Lady that she was the namesake of her cousin, Mrs. Patrick Henry. But Dolly was too shy. She was more at ease, however, when the President's wife talked about household matters, a topic in which she seemed interested.

Mrs. Todd glanced at her sister. The two fourteen-year-olds, Anna and Nellie Custis, were having an animated discussion. In fact, things were going well, when suddenly—

A tall, white-haired man passed with dignity by the door on his way upstairs. *President Washington.* For a breathless moment Dolly Todd thought he was coming in. Forgetting the tea on her lap, she sprang to her feet. Over the cup went, its contents staining her own gray dress and Lady Washington's rich plum-colored silk.

Dolly's cheeks were scarlet. Oh, if the carpet would open and swallow her! "I—I'm so sorry—" she stammered.

"It's nothing, Mrs. Todd. A mere spot." Martha Washington's kindness made it all the worse. For anyone could see that her dress was ruined.

With everybody trying so hard to put her at her ease, and Anna looking reproachful, Dolly never knew how she got through her visit. Finally the sisters rose, said their thanks and good-byes.

Sure that there was no place for her in this gay world, Dolly Todd followed Anna down the stairs. She had had a taste of the life for which she had always longed. And what had she done? Behaved like a clumsy country housewife. Disgraced Lucy. She knew she would never again be invited to the George Washingtons'.

Perhaps it was just as well, Dolly reasoned, as she hurried

to the modest house on South Fourth Street, back to the world to which she belonged. She had deserved her social downfall. What right had she to mingle with these fashionable people? Her place was with the plain Quaker lawyer, John Todd, and her baby. Almost running, Dolly reached the steps of her little brick house and opened the white door.

She found John in the kitchen. With Delia, he was packing a big basket of food.

"I thought thee would never return," he greeted his wife. "Thee must come with me, Dolly. I never had surer leading, a suffering soul needs us."

"Who? Where?" asked Dolly. She was used to these errands of mercy. Often John Todd routed her out of her warm bed to go with him on such trips, when he felt a "concern" for someone in trouble.

"It's a woman, I think. Somewhere near Bush Hill."

Dolly took off her First Day clothes. When her husband drove up to the door in the chaise they kept at the livery stable, Mistress Todd, wearing her every-day dress, bonnet and shawl, was ready. Carrying the basket of food, she went out to the carriage.

"Shall we take Delia?" John asked. "She might be of help."

"Oh, John! Then who would stay with Payne?"

John was like Father sometimes, Dolly thought, always thinking of outsiders before his own family. Otherwise, the two men were very different. John Todd was almost inarticulate in meeting; he made no grand speeches like Elder Payne. But John gave most of his time and too much money to persecuted humanity.

Over the rough roads the kindly Quaker and his wife started for Bush Hill in the darkness. The chaise lurched and bumped. Each time the horse sank into a mud hole, it threatened to overturn. Dolly sat clutching the basket of food, frightened and wishing herself back home.

But they found the object of John's "concern"—a starved, hunted Negro girl who had been hiding in a barn for days. Her child lay in the straw, wrapped in rags, crying from hunger.

At first, the terrified slave girl fled from the strangers. But calmed by John's soothing words, she soon realized they were Friends who had come to help her to join her husband in New York.

When the fugitives had eaten, the Todds drove them to their home under cover of darkness. There in the South Fourth Street attic, they hid them until John arranged for Delia, the girl and her child, to go by boat to New York. The owner of the boat was a Quaker.

There were grateful tears in her eyes as the young mother took Dolly Todd's hands in hers.

"Everybody in de South dey's sayin', git to Philadelphia and a Friend will help you," she murmured. "Dey's de finest folk in de world."

❀   ❀   ❀   ❀   ❀

In May of 1793 a second son was born to John and Dolly Todd. He was named William Payne for Dolly's favorite brother, William Temple, now a contented Virginia planter at Coles Hill. He was a good baby with a solemn face and John Todd's dark eyes.

Payne, the adored older boy, had become a plump, vigorous youngster of fifteen months. He grew so fast that no clothes fitted him for long. He was so active that his mother dared not leave him alone a minute.

Dolly was slow in recovering her strength after William's birth. When John Todd came home, he often found his wife lying on the sofa. For months she failed to go to meeting. Those of the congregation who liked to hear Mistress Todd recite the Psalms in her sweet voice went home disappointed.

One hot mid-August morning, Dolly appeared again at First Day meeting. "The Lord has blessed me," she rose to say. "He has given me another son. Dear God, I thank Thee." Then she sat down.

After the meeting, gray-garbed men and women gathered about Mrs. Todd to welcome her back. But they also talked of another thing. "Peter Aston has died of a strange illness," Dolly heard them say.

"Peter Aston has died," she told John on the way home. They knew him slightly.

Soon all Philadelphia was full of excitement over Peter Aston's death. For Peter Aston had died of yellow fever.

With what dread men whispered the words—*yellow fever!* When Peter Aston's death was followed by others, panic assailed even the bravest. In the bank, the market, or the church, nothing was talked of but the disease, its symptoms and its remedies.

No one dared shake hands for fear of infection. People huddled in terror in their homes. Anyone forced to venture out held a handkerchief soaked with camphor to his nose. Some carried pieces of tarred rope in their pockets. Others chewed garlic or put it in their shoes to keep off the fever.

But nothing could stop the spread of the epidemic or the fear that gripped Philadelphia. Rich and poor had but one thought—to escape the plague. Every road out of the city was crowded with frightened people in any sort of vehicle.

Among this panic-driven throng was the Todd chaise in which Dolly rode with her husband and two small children. She had not wanted to leave the city, by her going add to the confusion. But John had insisted. For the sake of the children, she was being driven to the inn at Gray's Ferry, where many people were taking refuge.

When the carriage finally crossed the Schuylkill and reached the secluded country resort, Dolly was glad her little family was safe among the trees and pure air. Soon they were united with Molly Payne, who had driven out with her children.

Reassured as to the safety of his wife and babies, conscientious Friend Todd decided to return to Philadelphia. He must look after his father and mother.

Dolly burst into tears, and pleaded with her husband not to leave. He was adamant. "I must," he said. "God tells me to go."

There was nothing she could do, for every good Quaker follows his Inner Light, no matter where it may lead. Sobbing bitterly, she clung to her husband's arm with a burst of affection almost unknown to her.

"I'll come back as soon as I can," he promised, "and then I'll never leave thee again."

In the city, John found both his parents dying of yellow fever. On all sides, friends and clients were ill. Desperate, they appealed to this kindly lawyer for help.

John Todd stayed on. He cared for his mother and father, until both died of the plague. Then, exhausted from the strain, already ill himself, he returned to his wife and children.

When Molly Payne met John at the door of the inn, she cried out in fright at the sight of his haggard face.

"Where's Dolly?" the sick man gasped. "The fever's in my veins . . . I must see her before I die."

At the sound of her husband's voice, Dolly rushed into the room. She, too, paled at the sight of him. With no thought of danger, she threw herself in John's arms.

"I'm dying, Dolly." He held her close. "My love. . . ."

The two women half-carried him to a bed. There John Todd lay for days, desperately ill, tossing and muttering with fever.

"Dolly," he called hoarsely. "Dolly—"

When, frightened and wild-eyed, she came to his side, he did not recognize her.

"Oh, Mother, is he going . . . to die?" Dolly whispered.

Frantically she wrung out cold towels to cool John's hot face. When in his delirium he tried to leave the bed, she held him down with her strong young arms.

"Dolly's sick . . . she's dying of the fever," he cried. "I must go to her."

"Lie back, John, please—Dolly's all right," she assured him. Even then she was shaking with fever. So was their five-months-old baby, William. By noon he was a very sick little boy.

Only vaguely aware of the passing time, Dolly kept going. She was coming down with yellow fever. But her only fear was that her family should know. John's room was so cold. Kneeling on the hearth, Dolly tried to make more fire. But no flames could warm her. Suddenly the log fell from her shaking hands. She crumpled up in a heap upon the hearth.

For three terrible weeks Dolly Todd lay at the point of death. Her body ached cruelly; she shook with cold. John was dying and the baby. But there was nothing she could do. She was slipping, slipping. . . .

"Mummy!" Across the void came her son Payne's demanding voice.

Had the boy actually called to her? Or had her heart spoken? Suddenly Dolly knew that she must not die and leave Payne. She must live and care for him all her life.

So Dolly Todd began the long fight back.

After three weeks the ache and shivering suddenly left her.

She woke one morning, as from a long slumber. Her mother stood beside her bed.

"Mother," Dolly whispered. "How are John . . . and the baby?"

Molly's sweet face was very sad. She had to call on all her strength to speak. "The Lord has gathered them *both* to Him, dear," she answered with Quaker truthfulness, taking her daughter in her arms.

Wrenching herself free, Dolly buried her face in the pillow. "Oh, Mother, I can't bear it!" she sobbed.

John had broken his promise never to leave her again. Always he had obeyed God's voice with implicit trust. When the Lord commanded John to come, no earthly love could hold him. Taking tiny William in his arms, he had set out dutifully on the longest journey of all.

8

The Widow at Payne's

Seated listlessly at her window in south fourth
Street Mistress Dolly Todd stared with blurred eyes at the
familiar landscape. It was frosty December now, and the
pestilence had ended. Quarantine was relaxed. The same carriages that had been driven with frantic haste along the roads
leading out of Philadelphia, had trundled slowly back. The
streets ceased to look like those of a dead city.

But everywhere there were sorrowing hearts. Out of a
population of fifty-five thousand, over nine thousand Phila-
delphians had died of the plague in less than three months.

Buried in the Quaker cemetery lay Friend John Todd and
his infant son, William Payne. The double loss, following her
own serious illness, had left the usually healthy and cheerful
Dolly weak and stunned. She went about in a daze, clinging
to Payne, her surviving child, with a desperate fear. Only
when caring for the robust youngster did her face lighten a
little.

This intense preoccupation was bad for both Dolly and her
boy, and practical Molly Payne knew it. One day she urged,
"Sell thy house, dear. Come live with me. I need thy help
with the boarders."

It was the sensible thing to do. The Widow Todd could no
longer afford to keep the comfortable little brick house on
South Fourth Street. She was executrix of John's will in
which he called her "the dear wife of my bosom and first and
only woman upon whom my all and only affections are

placed." He had left his son, Payne, his silver watch—but to his wife, very little money.

So Dolly and her boy went to live with her mother in the now famous Payne boarding house on North Third Street. It was only a small brick house, but Molly made every inch of it pay. She knew how to pack people in and still make them comfortable. The three small bedrooms were rented to eight congressmen and Senator Aaron Burr—three men to a room. The fourth room, the Secretary of State, Mr. Jefferson, had all to himself.

Molly's own family slept over the kitchen. It was crowded, Anna complained, but Mother was fiercely determined to make money.

To the Senator from New York, Colonel Burr, southern cooking was a novelty. At Oeller's Tavern and the Coffee House, at the Indian Queen and in the halls of Congress, he told envious colleagues about Mrs. Payne's candied yams, her crab croquettes, her oyster pie and Sally Lunn.

Besides the food at Mrs. Payne's, Colonel Burr described another attraction for which his boarding house was to achieve renown. Everywhere, he told people about "the widow at Payne's."

She was dark-haired and fresh-faced, he said. She had the bluest eyes in the world, and the most charming smile. She was industrious, too. All day, she helped her mother with the dishwashing, bedmaking and marketing. She also took entire care of her spirited, handsome little son.

These things and more, Burr told his Princeton College friend, James Madison, who roomed with James Monroe at the uncomfortable Indian Queen. Mr. Madison envied his friend Mrs. Payne's delicious southern cooking. But of Burr's new acquaintance, the pretty Widow Todd, James, a sedate bachelor of forty-three, was not envious.

Congressman Madison was a busy man. Also, he had good reasons for disliking the fair sex. Ten years ago, the scholarly young James had fallen in love for the first time with Catherine Floyd, daughter of General William Floyd of Long Island. The pretty, sixteen-year-old Catherine accepted Madison's proposal; but later, when she fell in love with a young clergyman who bent over her at the harpsichord, she sent James a letter of dismissal sealed with a bit of rye dough. Catherine's behavior wounded James so deeply that thereafter he avoided girls.

But if the solemn Congressman from Virginia closed his ears to Burr's description of the winsome widow, plenty of Philadelphia gentlemen wanted to hear.

Gradually Dolly's healthy, happy nature reasserted itself. She was only twenty-five that winter of 1793-4, prettier than in her girlhood, and with the added independence of a married woman.

"One can't cry forever," she told herself an April morning as she fastened on her mob cap.

Flushing deeply, she remembered her first meeting with Aaron Burr. He had been in New York when Dolly came to live with her mother. On the afternoon of his return, she came into the dining room, carrying a bowl of fragrant punch.

Jumping to his feet, Burr gallantly took the dish from her hands. "It's I who should be serving you," he said softly.

His hazel eyes, the most striking thing about him, were on a level with her own blue ones. The Senator was short—five feet, six inches—although very erect and dignified. His smile was captivating. She found it hard to look away.

"Come, talk to me. I want to know you." He caught her hand and made her sit down beside him.

It was the rush hour; the dining room was crowded. In the

kitchen, Molly Payne, with Mary sick again, and only Anna to help her, was trying to get a dozen dinners at once. "I should go . . ." Dolly murmured. But she lingered on. Burr's eyes were so compelling she could not move.

The Senator's dark face with its high forehead and unexpected light hazel eyes, his mocking humor, his European ease of manner; all these fascinated the inexperienced young Quaker widow. She had never known a man like him.

Before she left him to return to the kitchen, Aaron Burr had asked John Todd's widow to accompany him on a walk the next afternoon.

"Mrs. Todd, I'm very lonely here in Philadelphia," he confided, as he bade her good night. "Would you mind if, because of my loneliness, I saw you rather often?"

"Oh, no!" Dolly blushed. "I'd be glad for thee to see me—frequently."

❀   ❀   ❀   ❀   ❀

Evenings, that spring of 1794, pretty Dolly Todd sat with Senator Burr before the keeping-room fire in her mother's parlor "to prevent him from being lonely." Aaron did most of the talking. Dolly listened, fascinated, to stories of a world she had never known.

Burr often spoke of his wife, Theodosia Prevost, a Tory widow, whom he had married after the Revolution. She had been ten years older than Aaron, neither a wealthy nor a pretty woman, but extremely intelligent. Theirs had been a happy marriage.

A year ago, Mrs. Burr had died. Now Aaron's love centered on their daughter, Theodosia, whom he had left at Richmond Hill, his beautiful estate in Greenwich Village, outside New York. The stately mansion had been built by

Sir Abraham Mortier. It was Washington's headquarters during the Revolution, when Burr worked as his aide. Aaron had bought the place—although he couldn't afford to, he laughingly told Mrs. Todd—and had spent a great deal of money to make it a suitable background for the extravagant hospitality he liked to dispense with so careless a hand.

When Senator Burr entertained, at the head of his table, as hostess, sat the eleven-year-old Theodosia. "Conducting herself with a dignity and *savoir faire* that charms my guests," declared her proud father.

Aaron Burr adored his "Miss Prissy," as he called her. No matter how busy he was at the Senate, he put aside a time each day to write to her; to scold his daughter if she misspelled a word, or if her writing was not neat. Theo must learn to ride, sing, dance, and skate. She must play the harp and the pianoforte. She must study history, geography, and the languages.

Colonel Burr was passionately interested in learning, even for women.

"Theo's not like other little girls," her father explained. "She speaks German and French, and is the most intelligent child. I've had her educated like a boy. She translates Latin better than her stepbrothers."

Dolly, who had had little schooling, heard with amazement of a child of eleven, who read Horace and Virgil, who was studying Greek grammar, and could discuss philosophy and political economy. A pitiful little bookworm, she thought. She grew indignant when Aaron added, "Isn't it time you sent your boy to school? He'll grow up a dunce."

A dunce! Dolly stroked the brown curls of the handsome child seated on her lap. "Why, Payne's only two," she murmured fondly. She had made up her mind her son should never go to school. Payne's grandfather had flogged his students. She would teach him herself.

Tactfully Dolly changed the subject and encouraged Senator Burr to tell her about his experiences during the Revolution. He had accompanied Benedict Arnold to Quebec. Later, for a while, he had been General Washington's aide. But the cocky Burr had not gotten along well with his commander in chief. They had parted "rather unpleasantly," Aaron admitted, and he had joined General Putnam's staff.

Aaron Burr had never had a more flattering audience. So evenings he joined his landlady's daughter in the little parlor, when he could have been going to the theater, to fashionable routs and balls. Mrs. Payne's boarders were not unaware of the romance unfolding in their midst. Thomas Jefferson scowled over his newspaper, the *Advertiser*. But most of them watched it with approval.

"Senator Burr says he likes it here," said Mother one day, as she shelled peas for the hearty three o'clock dinner.

"Yes," answered Dolly, lowering her eyes. "I think he does."

How cautious her answer! She could have repeated glowing statements as to how much the Senator "liked it."

Afternoons Dolly and Aaron joined the promenade on Chestnut Street. Colonel Burr loved fine clothes. He wore rich velvet suits, silk stockings, and silver buckles. Although his income from his New York law practice was large, he was always in debt. Money slipped through his fingers.

One day they saw President and Mrs. Washington drive past in their cream-colored coach drawn by four white horses. And Aaron complained bitterly because Washington had denied him the use of the official documents he needed to complete a history of the Revolutionary War.

"Washington has never liked me," he told Dolly. "Alexander Hamilton has influenced him—*he* is my real enemy."

Another day, they met him—the great Alexander Hamilton.
They were on Chestnut Street when the short, dapper Secretary of the Treasury passed. He wore a blue coat and a cocked
hat on his sandy hair. People turned to admire his handsome,
erect figure.

Hamilton and Burr bowed coldly.

"My friend, Hamilton, how he hates me!" Aaron laughed.
"He has never forgiven me for defeating his rich father-in-
law, General Schuyler, for the Senate."

In New York, Alexander Hamilton and Aaron Burr were
competing lawyers. In politics they belonged to rival parties.
Hamilton was leader of the Federalists, the conservative party
thoroughly entrenched in power. Burr was a Republican.

Dolly was glad that Aaron had cast his lot with the Republicans and so was friendly with her dear Thomas Jefferson,
whom she loved like a father. If the Republicans could only
get into power, Aaron Burr would go far, she thought.
Hadn't he graduated from Princeton at sixteen? Wasn't he a
United States senator at only thirty-eight? Dolly wished
more people appreciated Aaron, and that he had fewer
enemies.

She was seeing the Senator from New York daily now.
"Dolly" fell easily from his lips, instead of the more formal
"Mrs. Todd." He accompanied her to market, carrying her
basket, to the shocked surprise of other pedestrians. He
scandalized Mrs. Payne by going with Dolly to a Quaker
meeting. The whole town buzzed. Senator Burr's romance
with his landlady's daughter was the favorite gossip from
mansion to tavern.

"Are thee going to marry him?" Dolly's best friend, Eliza
Collins, wanted to know.

Was she? Blushing, the Widow Todd wished she knew.
She was sure Aaron liked her. Wherever she went, there he

was. Each night he waited until she came from the kitchen to join him by the keeping-room fire. But did he love her? He had never said so. Inexperienced Dolly felt a pang. There might be heartbreak ahead, but she shut her mind to it. She loved the present as a child loves it.

❦   ❦   ❦   ❦   ❦

Colonel Burr's social life took him into a far gayer world than the sedate circle of Martha Washington. He played cards with lovely Mrs. John Jay, who had once been mistaken by a Paris audience for Marie Antoinette. He attended Mrs. William Bingham's balls in her magnificent home with its white marble staircase in the most exclusive section of Third Street. The supper tables were decorated with real orange trees. Punch was served with the first dance.

"Anne Bingham has lived in both Paris and London," Burr explained to Mrs. Todd, "and knows how to entertain fashionably."

Dolly listened, enraptured. Each word Aaron said fed her hunger for this gay, glittering life. Was he the handsome lover who had come to take her out of her drab existence into the glamorous world for which she had always longed? Dolly began to wonder, and to hope.

But Aaron Burr was not a Quaker, she reminded herself sternly. If she married him, she would be disowned by the Friends' meeting, as her brother Walter had been. Dolly thought of the sorrow it would bring to her mother. And she tried to stem the swift tide that was carrying her along.

One day Senator Burr returned from Congress greatly elated. The Minister to France, Gouverneur Morris, unpopular with the French, was being recalled. And because of his Francophile sympathies, the Republicans had selected

Colonel Burr as their candidate to succeed Morris.

"I've always loved everything French. I'll make them a good minister." Aaron smiled happily, as he told Mrs. Todd of the great honor that had come to him.

Burr's friends, James Madison and James Monroe, were to go to President Washington and inform him of their party's preference for the appointment.

On the morning of their visit Aaron Burr left his boarding house and went off confidently to attend Congress. "I'll let you know as soon as I hear officially," he told Dolly.

The morning passed slowly. The young widow tidied up the lodgers' rooms; she helped Anna prepare dinner. Over and over she wondered excitedly, would Aaron ask her to marry him before he left for France? Would he marry her and take her with him?

Dolly was the first to hear Senator Burr's step on his return. Running to greet him, she asked, "What happened?"

His face was a white mask. "Washington refused to have me," he muttered.

"Oh, Aaron, I feel for thee!" Dolly sighed, reaching for his hand.

Burr's head was high. "Rather feel sorry for France, and for America, that have lost my services," he replied, with an attempt at bravado. "I was especially fitted for this appointment from which Washington—with Mr. Hamilton at his elbow—has blocked me."

Aaron Burr had striven hard for this high honor. But having failed, he was not one to brood. "Come, we'll talk of something pleasant. I'm taking the afternoon stage to New York. I want to get away from Congress for a while. Everything here is run by Hamilton."

They sat close together by the fire. And at the sight of

Dolly's pretty, sympathetic face, the bitterness faded from Aaron's eyes.

"It's good to be with you, dear." He patted her hand. "You understand."

In the simple firelit room there was peace. The hours passed. Gradually the candles began to cast long, wavering shadows against the wall.

"Aaron, it's time for thy stage," whispered Dolly.

"What would you say, if I told you I'm not going?"

Wild joy stole into her heart. "I dreaded thy departure," she confessed.

A mad evening followed. At suppertime, when she must leave him, Senator Burr followed Dolly into the busy kitchen. The Senator's lack of dignity shocked his landlady. But he ignored her displeasure, and insisted on helping Dolly at every turn.

Wrapped in a huge apron to cover her frock, Mistress Todd was perched on a stool beside the kitchen table, plucking a turkey. On a stool beside her was the Senator from New York, tearing the feathers from the bird's drum sticks.

Molly Payne watched them, her hands on her hips. "Dinner's ready, Senator Burr," she said tartly.

He had to go back to the dining room to eat, and leave his charming companion. And for a while Dolly was busy, with Anna and Mary, waiting on the table at dinner and then washing the dishes.

"Has anyone taken up Senator Burr's warming pan?" Mary asked.

Dolly grabbed the metal pan filled with hot coals, which, thrust into a bed, kept it warm. Anything for an excuse to go to the front of the house, where she might see her sweetheart. She ran up the stairs. In the darkness of the upper hall, she met him coming down.

He took the warming pan from her hands. Then suddenly
she was in his arms, close, close. Aaron Burr was saying all
those things Dolly had dreamed of his saying—only far more.
He was demanding that she love him—she who had loved him
from the very first.

Both arms about Burr's neck, Dolly clung to him with a
terrible earnestness. Her response surprised and delighted the
sophisticated New Yorker. A Quaker maid, she was as ardent
a girl as he had ever known.

"Isn't it strange," Dolly thought, as, deliriously happy, she
went to bed later that evening, "that one's heart can sing like
this and nobody hear it?"

❧   ❧   ❧   ❧   ❧

The Widow Todd slept well that night. She woke radiant,
dressed and hurried downstairs. Aaron would be there, waiting to smile at her over the tea and waffles.

There was no one about but Anna, clearing the table.

"Aaron—Senator Burr—has he had breakfast?" faltered
Dolly.

"Yes," Anna replied with embarrassment. "He took the
early stage to New York."

Dolly felt a cold chill. Aaron had gone without saying
good-bye. And after last night— "Did he say how long he'd
be gone?" she asked. "Did he leave a message for me?"

Pretty Anna shook her blond head. She shared her sister's
disappointment. Both she and Mary understood how much
Aaron Burr meant to Dolly.

Busy with her boarders, Molly Payne had been unaware of
the romance. But the night when Senator Burr burst into the
kitchen after Dolly, the truth came home to her.

Watching her daughter's unhappy face this morning, Molly

decided to speak. "Dolly," she demanded sternly, "how long is thee going to accept the attentions of Senator Burr? Aren't there enough good men at Friends' meeting to please thee? Colonel Burr is not a Quaker. And I would not want him to marry thee, if he were. I do not like the man . . . If thee does not avoid him, I'll have to ask him to leave my house."

Not see Aaron again! Dolly's heart turned over. She was so deeply in love, she could not find words to reply.

Her mother was firm. When Dolly remained silent, she repeated her threat, "Daughter, thee must not go out pleasuring with Senator Burr again or see him alone." Then after a long pause, "I'm waiting for thy promise."

"I can't promise," Dolly answered. And later, with a stamp of her foot, "I won't promise."

"Has he asked thee to marry him?" asked Molly coldly.

Dolly went crimson at the burning memory of Aaron's kisses. Could she admit that, although he paid her pretty compliments, Senator Burr had been very careful not to commit himself?

"I thought so." Mother's lips set in a hard line.

❦   ❦   ❦   ❦   ❦

As the days passed, Dolly Todd's common sense told her the truth. The impulsive Aaron Burr was only playing with her affections. Even now he probably regretted the reckless things he had said and done. A widower for only a year, he might dread losing his liberty. Or perhaps he did not consider Mrs. Todd intelligent enough to become the stepmother of the prodigy Theodosia. Or perhaps the grandson of Jonathan Edwards was too much of a snob to marry—his landlady's daughter.

Dolly flung herself weeping into Anna's arms. "I want him so," she sobbed. "I'll do something awful if I can't have him."

After two weeks Aaron Burr came back. James Monroe had been named Minister to France. And Burr, bitter at Alexander Hamilton who had blocked his appointment, wished he never had to see Philadelphia again. But there were his duties in Congress. And there was the Widow Todd.

The night of his return they met in the parlor of his boarding house. Dolly was carrying an account book in her arms. The distress in her eyes touched Aaron.

"What are you doing with that big book?" he asked.

"Trying to balance Mother's accounts," she replied stiffly. "I never was any good at cyphers."

"Let me help you."

He sat down beside her on the sofa. But he made sure of the distance between them, and held the book at arm's length. He added up all the figures and wrote them down.

"There, that balances now," Burr finally declared. Handing her back the account book, he left to dress and go out for dinner. The formality in his manner was almost an insult. As he disappeared up the stairs, Dolly's eyes stung with tears.

A few days later Senator Burr took Mrs. Todd for a walk along Chestnut Street. But evenings he was always out now with his fashionable friends. Dolly sat alone by the fireside, trying not to cry. Then Aaron asked her to go walking again. After which he avoided her for a week. Oh, dreadful regularity! It was plain that Colonel Burr was being only moderately attentive. It would not be fair to keep serious suitors away from the charming Widow Todd.

Where did Aaron go those days she did not see him? Was he with the fascinating Anne Bingham? The beautiful Misses Allen and the Misses Chew? In that gay, glamorous world where his landlady's daughter could not follow him.

Dolly tortured herself by wondering. For the first time in her life, she cared more for a man than he did for her.

O<small>N A MAY MORNING IN</small> 1794, <small>DOLLY TODD HURRIED DOWN</small> North Third Street toward the market sheds that stretched along the Delaware River. In one hand she held her basket; in the other, the chubby fingers of her two-year-old son.

Payne had been naughtier than usual that morning. He had refused to take his nap. He had spilled his porridge on the rug. He had fretted and cried continuously.

"Little mischief, I declare I'll have to punish thee," his mother had sighed. But Payne was not frightened of her gentle scoldings. In all his spoiled life, Dolly had never really punished her child.

"Mummy . . ." Payne lifted his plump arms and grinned, showing his new tooth. That was too much for his doting parent. Catching him in her arms, she covered his round baby face with kisses. Then tying a cap over his dark curls, she had taken him with her to market.

Soon Dolly was down among the market stalls, bright with mounds of yellow carrots, ruby beets and fat cabbages. As she paid the grocer for her purchases, she turned her back on Payne.

Suddenly the child was missing. Unnoticed by his mother, he had toddled off down the aisle toward the flower stand.

"Payne! Baby!" Dolly hurried after him.

She caught up with her son, as a short, dignified gentleman turned the corner of the cheese stall. A package under his arm, he stopped to admire a tempting array of fresh pot cheese. Just then Payne toddled between the gentleman's legs, almost knocking him over. His package fell to the ground.

"Watch out where you're going, youngster," he snapped. Dignity gone, his tricorne hat and wig awry, the man bent to retrieve his parcel from the mud.

"Oh, I'm sorry, sir!" Dolly's cheeks were scarlet with embarrassment. She almost added "Mr. Madison . . .", for to her horror, she saw that it was "the Great Little Madison." "Forgive my baby, please. He has just learned to walk."

James Madison found himself staring intently at a brunette young beauty, whose distress made her all the more appealing. He was annoyed at having the duck, just selected for his dinner, rolled into the dirt. But the child's mother was so lovely that he replied gently, "Madam, it's nothing."

Mrs. Todd smiled then. Mr. Madison thought it the most enchanting smile he had ever seen. Then, picking up her heavy son and the basket of vegetables, she hastened home.

On the way she paused to rest, and chanced to look back. There, to her amazement, was Congressman Madison, a short distance behind. Could he be following her?

It appeared so when Madison passed the Indian Queen, where he lived, and trailed Mrs. Todd right to her door. Watching him from behind a curtain, Dolly saw him stare intently at the house, then turn away.

A few nights later, Aaron Burr stopped after dinner to speak to Dolly. She had hardly seen him all week.

"Are you free tomorrow night?" he asked.

Her eyes glowed. "Yes, of course."

"Then wear your prettiest dress, my dear. I'm bringing a colleague of mine in Congress, James Madison, to call on you. He has been pestering me for days to introduce him."

Dolly said the proper things. But as Aaron left her to go

out for a gay evening, her lips quivered. James Madison, that dull old bachelor!

With a heavy heart, Mistress Todd arranged her dark curls on the following evening. She did not want to share an hour of Aaron's society with the "Father of the Constitution."

An idea came to her. She would invite Eliza Collins in for the evening. Eliza could entertain Mr. Madison, so she could have Aaron to herself. Dolly sat down and wrote Eliza a little note:

Dear Friend: Thee must come to me. Aaron Burr says that the Great Little Madison has asked to be brought to see me this evening. . . .

At nightfall, in the candlelit parlor of the boarding house, Dolly waited with her friend Eliza. Gowned in her First Day dress of soft gray, Mrs. Todd had never looked prettier. The tulle cap on her dark hair, the dainty kerchief about her shoulders, set off her exquisite skin, the young widow's chief beauty.

The two men entered. Nervously Dolly fingered the brooch that fastened her kerchief. As Senator Burr introduced the staid Madison to the captivating widow, there was a pleased smile on his lips—he was ridding himself of an obligation.

Swiftly Dolly compared her callers. Aaron Burr was graceful, vivacious and charming. James Madison was a little man, dressed all in dignified black, except for his ruffled shirt and pewter shoe-buckles. He was solemn of speech, precise in manner, with an air of fatigue about him. Furthermore, he was forty-three; Mrs. Todd, twenty-six. Her smile as he bent over her hand was polite, but scarcely enthusiastic.

Dolly had planned to pass Congressman Madison on to

Eliza, so that Senator Burr could sit beside her. But somehow
—Mrs. Todd never knew how it happened—it was Aaron who
went over to Eliza, and Mr. Madison who seated himself
stiffly by her on the sofa.

Dolly was so annoyed that for once her talkative tongue
was stilled. Smiling slyly, Burr picked up the conversation.
He and James Madison talked of their undergraduate days
together, for they had both gone to Princeton. Madison had
been in the class ahead of Burr. But they had often debated
together in the "paper wars" between the two Princeton
literary societies. James had led one college debating society,
the American Whigs. Aaron belonged to the rival Clio-
sophics.

"Remember your graduation, Jim, when you won the right
to give the first oration as the most outstanding graduate of
your class?" Burr reminded his friend.

"Yes, and by sleeping only three hours out of the twenty-
four, so I could do two years in one, made myself too ill to
speak."

"You've plenty of brains behind that white face of yours,
but you never had the fun at college that I had." Aaron
laughed. "President Witherspoon used to tell us, 'Madison
never did an indiscreet thing all the time he was at Princeton.'"

Dolly smiled. She knew Aaron Burr had done plenty of
"indiscreet" things, at Princeton and elsewhere.

Now, for instance. Turning to the flattered Eliza, he was
whispering to her and laughing into her eyes. Trying to ig-
nore Aaron's behavior, Mrs. Todd turned to her other caller.

"Tell me about thy work on the Constitution, Mr. Madison," she said sweetly. "I've heard so much about thee."

How ridiculously pleased he was at her interest, this shy,

plain little man! "What does a pretty girl like you know about politics?" he ventured.

"Not very much." She fluttered her long lashes. "But thy friend, Mr. Jefferson, told me of thy service to our country. He said it was thy profound familiarity with English constitutional law which helped write our Constitution; thy sound logic that defended it when it stood in grave danger."

It was a long speech, but prettily said. James Madison leaned forward eagerly. The Widow Todd was even more charming than he had thought. Could it be that she was intelligent, as well?

"I know, too, how thee defended the Constitution in Virginia, and won its adoption against the opposition of my very own cousin, Patrick Henry."

They had found another mutual friend. They talked of Patrick Henry and of their native state. Madison was pleased to learn that Mrs. Todd was a fellow Virginian.

This studious, middle-aged man in black was not at all the sort of person who should have attracted gay Dolly Todd, or, for that matter, have been attracted to her. But retiring and small as James Madison was, he could be entertaining in a quiet way. Dolly began to like him.

Later that evening, as the candles burned low, she confessed, "Mr. Madison, I've long borne a grudge against thee. Does thee remember saying, 'A man may be a Christian in any church, but a *gentleman* belongs to the Church of England.'"

Madison laughed. There was a twinkle in his mild eyes.

"Perhaps I did say that, politicians say many foolish things at times," he admitted. "But, don't forget, I fought for religious freedom for people like you Quakers."

🌫   🌫   🌫   🌫   🌫

Soon it was Dolly and James Madison who sat evenings
before the fire in Mrs. Payne's little parlor. Senator Burr was
seldom present. More important social engagements took him
away directly after dinner.

What could Dolly do? Aaron had tired of her, if he had
ever cared at all. So it was a comfort to have the unexciting
little Mr. Madison's company. When James sat on the sofa
beside her, Dolly stared into the fire and thought of Aaron.
Dreamily she half-listened as her new admirer talked of
Montpellier, his parents' plantation in Orange County, Virginia, and of his career in politics.

Madison was the eldest of eight children. Graduated from
Princeton—a solitary youth, in bad health, and a trifle morbid
—he had returned home to Montpellier to study for the min-
istry, and to act as tutor for his younger brothers and sisters.

Later James had gone into politics. First, as a member of
the Virginia Convention, the first Assembly, and the Council
of State. Then as a delegate to the Continental Congress.
He was now in the House of Representatives thanks to Mr.
Patrick Henry, who had caused Madison to be defeated for
the Senate because of his stand on the Constitution.

Congressman Madison could not be said to have lost his
youth. He had never had any. All his life he had studied hard;
there had been no time for fun. Now, for the first time, he
relaxed. He idled long evenings in the company of the pretty
widow, who teased him about his reputation for being so
solemn.

One night Congressman Madison handed Mrs. Todd a
copy of the Bill of Rights; the ten amendments to the
Constitution, nine of which he had drafted. He had a strange
request. Would she please write him her opinion as to what
they did for humanity?

Poor Dolly! When James had gone, she read over the

long, serious document. Little of it made sense to her.

Aaron Burr, just in from a game of loo at Mrs. Bingham's, found her frowning over the pages. "What's the matter?" he asked.

Eagerly, Dolly repeated Madison's odd request. "What shall I do, Aaron?" she wailed.

Senator Burr was amused. "Give it to me, I'll write an opinion for you," he replied.

Next morning, at breakfast, he handed her a paper.

"Copy this in your best handwriting," he said, "and give it to James. He'll be impressed."

When Burr had left for Congress, Dolly copied what he had written. So careful was she that there was not even one misspelled word.

The Bill of Rights has made us free men. It has given us the right to worship as we please, say what we please, and read what we please. The Bill of Rights has given us the security of our home against unlawful search and seizure. By means of the Bill of Rights the basic rights of a Democracy are made the law of our land, so that we and those after us can live in happiness and peace.

That evening as he read these words, Madison's face glowed with pleasure. "Why, this is excellently put, Mrs. Todd," he exclaimed in surprise. "I congratulate you. You've expressed what my amendments to the Constitution do, exactly."

Dolly flushed. Quaker honesty compelled her to try to explain the deception. But James, regarding her in rapture, interrupted her halting words. He had doubted the pretty widow's mental qualifications to become his wife. But now he thought he had proof that Mrs. Todd's intellect equalled her beauty. He had found the first woman he wanted to marry since Catherine Floyd.

"Will you be my wife, Dolly?" he begged, catching her hand in his. "Will you try to think of me as a lover . . . as a husband?"

The Widow Todd pulled her hand away. "Oh, I couldn't marry thee. I don't love thee."

"I know. But I hoped you liked me well enough. Oh, Dolly, I want to take you out of this drab life into the world for which your beauty suits you! I'd—" His voice stumbled. "I'd be so proud to introduce you as my wife."

How he tempted her! Dolly hid her face in her hands lest James see the eager look in her eyes.

"Besides, I'm a Quaker. I couldn't marry out of meeting," she told him.

"I don't believe you're so inflexible, my dear," he said flatly. "Isn't there some other reason why you won't marry me?"

With downcast eyes, she nodded her capped head. "I'll not lie to thee, James. There's another man I love, very much."

"Then why don't you marry him?"

"He doesn't love me."

To Madison it seemed incredible that any man should not love this enchanting creature. "Then won't you think it over . . . about marrying me?" He caught her hand again. "I'll never ask who the man is you love, Dolly. Only be my wife."

"Thee would want me, James, knowing I love another?"

"Any way you wish, only say, yes."

Her answer was a whisper. "Yes, then, if Mother is willing."

"Bless your heart—" He was suddenly the lover. As suddenly Dolly knew she did not want him as such. When he opened his arms, she shrank away. "Oh, thee mustn't!" she cried. "Someone might see us."

James Madison bent to kiss his loved one's hand. He dared not kiss her lips.

❦   ❦   ❦   ❦   ❦

In the kitchen, next morning, Dolly revealed her secret. Her mother was making bread, her hands in the dough.

"Mother, I want to marry out of meeting—" Dolly began.

"It's not that Senator Burr, is it?" Molly asked sharply.

Sadly, her daughter shook her head. "No, it's James Madison who has asked me to be his wife. But he's an Episcopalian."

Mrs. Payne took her hands out of the dough and wiped them carefully. "I've no fault to find in Mr. Madison," she said. "He's a good, serious man, although rather old for thee. I don't object to him as I did to Aaron Burr. It's only that James Madison is not a Quaker. First, Walter married out of meeting . . . then Lucy . . . and now, thee. . . ."

Dolly saw the sorrow in her mother's eyes and flushed.

"I'll not forbid this, as thy father would have done," Molly Payne continued, sadly. "But to marry out of meeting is a grave step, dear. I ask thee to wait and let me think it over."

Dolly knew she had caused her mother pain. She was ashamed. But an exciting future seemed to open before her. Married to James Madison, she would live among the world's people, wear bright colors, go to the theater and to balls.

"I want to live," Dolly thought stubbornly. "I want—oh, I want everything there is in life!" Eagerness, an urge to begin living, surged up within her.

❦   ❦   ❦   ❦   ❦

The report that the Widow Todd had captured the heart of Congressman Madison, always thought to be an irreclaimable old bachelor, spread over Philadelphia. The fact that the recluse scholar, Madison, was calling on any lady would inevitably excite comment.

Finally the news reached the President's mansion. The First Lady, who liked Lucy Washington's sister, sent for Mrs. Todd and asked her if the rumor was true.

"Don't be ashamed to admit it, my dear, rather be proud," said Martha Washington. "James Madison will make you a good husband, all the better for being older. President Washington and I admire him, although we regret he left the Federalist party to become a Republican." And she added, looking hard at her young kinswoman by marriage, "Yes, President Washington and I approve of your marrying *Mr. Madison.*"

Dolly understood, and flushed. Well she knew that the Washingtons did not approve of Aaron Burr!

Martha Washington saw that her guest had caught the point. To soften her reprimand, she escorted Mrs. Todd to the door, her arm around her.

"I know you and James will be happy, dear," she said in her motherly manner. Then she added sternly, "And I wouldn't see any more of Senator Burr, if I were you."

Cheeks flaming, Dolly Todd nodded.

The First Lady's praise of Mr. Madison helped. But on the morning when a committee of elders arrived at her house, Molly Payne had not given her consent to her daughter's marriage.

Two stern men and three stony-faced women filed into Mrs. Payne's keeping-room. The men frowned under their broad hats. The women's arms were folded in their shawls.

"Friend Todd," Elder Jones, the spokesman, addressed

Dolly. "We have come to plead with thee. Thy engagement is rumored to Congressman Madison, an eminent statesman, but one of the world's people."

Dolly faced them proudly. Last summer this committee had smashed her mother's best chinaware, because the pattern on it was in blue, a sinful color. Surely their punishment of her would be severe.

"If thee marries out of meeting, thee will be disowned," Elder Jones warned the young widow. "Thy family will be disgraced."

As he spoke, the women of the committee stared disapprovingly at Molly Payne's pink window curtains. The lush colors of the roses in the flowered carpet scorched the soles of their shoes.

"I'm astonished at thee, Friend Molly." One of the women turned indignantly on Mrs. Payne. "Thee must get this vain and worldly floor covering out of the house and burn it before the next Monthly Meeting."

Molly turned white. "I'll do no such thing, Friend Truely. My mother gave me this carpet. It belonged in my childhood home, Coles Hill, and was one of the few things I brought from Virginia. It means a great deal to me."

"Thee did not have it down while thy good husband lived."

"No, it was stored in the attic."

The committee had scored a point. They exchanged glances.

"I did not know that worldly things had such a hold on thee, Friend Payne; and thy husband, an elder, too," scolded Elder Jones. "Thy carpet is red, a wicked color, forbidden Quakers. Therefore thee must burn it."

"It would break my heart!"

"Very well, Friend Payne, then thee shall be reported to the meeting." Elder Jones stood up, a signal for the others to rise. Then, suddenly remembering why they had come, he added, "Both thee and thy erring daughter."

Dolly held the door open for the Friends to file out. Then she returned to the keeping-room, where Molly continued to stare at the flowered carpet.

"Mother, I'm sorry I brought this trouble on thee."

"Perhaps it's just as well they came and acted as they did," Molly answered bitterly. "It has opened my eyes to their narrowness. I'm not going to burn my flowered carpet, Dolly. And if thee wants to marry out of meeting, and live among the world's people, I'm going to let thee."

"Oh, Mother!" Dolly threw her arms around her. "But won't the disgrace ruin thy boarding house?"

"I'm going to close it, dear. I decided, while the committee was berating me, to do as Lucy has often begged me to do, go and live with her at Harewood. Our meeting here is too strict."

The next day Dolly Todd told the delighted James Madison that she would marry him. But when James urged her to name the wedding day, she could not bring herself to do it. If only she would hear from Aaron Burr, who was in New York! Secretly, Dolly had hoped—oh, vain hope!—that the report of her engagement to another man would bring Aaron rushing to her. Even now, if he wrote her just a line . . . But nothing came.

In July Mrs. Payne closed her famous boarding house. Her disappointed lodgers moved elsewhere. Dolly wrote to one of them in New York a little note—oh, so calm in spite of her ardent love! She told him that he would have to find new quarters in Philadelphia; that she was engaged to his friend Madison; and that she was going to Harewood, the home of her sister Lucy Washington, in Virginia. After the condemnation of the elders, Dolly did not dare to marry James Madison in Philadelphia.

At Harewood, a sturdy gray stone house, three miles out of Charleston, West Virginia, Dolly continued to contemplate a placid union with her middle-aged suitor. From Montpellier, James wrote frequently; formal, stilted letters that urged Mrs. Todd to name the wedding day.

"Can I marry without love a second time?" she asked herself. And was she throwing herself away on "the Great Little Madison"? James had had his day of glory writing the Constitution, people said. Now he was only a minor congressman, although Jefferson was fond of him. The future looked very different for the brilliant Aaron Burr.

So Dolly waited. What if Aaron should follow her to Virginia? But as the days flowed into weeks, hope died within her. Burr was not coming. He had not even answered her letter. He did not care that she was marrying his friend Madison.

What was the use of saying "no" any longer? Why not make James Madison happy? After weeping most of the night, Dolly wrote him an encouraging note and mentioned a possible wedding day.

James replied immediately to her "precious favor" with its endearing "stile."

Orange, Aug. 18, 1794: I received some days ago yr precious favor. I cannot exprefs, but hope you will conceive the joy it gave me. The delay in hearing had filled me with extreme inquietude, and the consummation of that welcome event was endearing to me by the *stile* in which it was conveyed. I hope you will never have another deliberation on that subject. If the sentiments of my heart can guarantee those of yours, they assure me there can never be a cause for it. . . ."

When her staid suitor reached Harewood, Dolly was in the garden, gathering flowers. At the sight of James, so safe and dependable, she stretched out her arms like a frightened child.

"James . . . " she half-sobbed. Madison caught her close, kissing her forehead, her lips, her rosy cheeks.

"You'll be my wife," he said. It was not really a question. But he could not believe it until he heard her say it.

"Yes, I'll be thy wife," she whispered. "But oh, marry me quickly . . . quickly!"

They were married at Harewood on September 15, 1794— a day that to his death, James Madison would speak of as the luckiest day of his life.

In the handsome paneled drawing room of Harewood, Dolly and James were united by the Reverend Dr. Balmaine of Winchester, Virginia, a relative of the groom, in a Church of England ceremony. The bride wore her plain First Day dress of gray. But at her throat gleamed a blue mosaic necklace, James' wedding gift. The groom's coat was green velvet, with ruffles of Mechlin lace.

After the ceremony, fiddles and banjos played for the formal minuet, as well as for the sprightly Virginia reel. Everyone danced, but the bride and her Quaker family.

From their cabins, the Negro slaves flocked to the edge of the gathering to gaze at the beautiful bride. There was a huge wedding cake out under the trees, tables heaped with rich food.

In typical Virginia fashion, the relatives, neighbors and friends who had gathered for the wedding stayed on for days of prolonged merry-making. So her second wedding was as gay an event as the pleasure-loving Dolly could have wished.

Then one morning Congressman and Mrs. Madison left on their honeymoon; two weeks at Belle Grove, the home of

Mrs. Isaac Hite, James' sister Nelly, in King George County, Virginia.

Dolly descended the carved staircase, her flowing gray cape about her shoulders, her high scoop bonnet rising above the clustered curls on her forehead. At the bottom of the stairs James stood in his green velvet coat and shining buckles, waiting to hand his wife out to the carriage.

Tears in her eyes, Anna rushed forward. "Dolly, don't leave me," she wailed, throwing her arms around her. The devoted sisters had never been separated.

They could not be now, not even on her honeymoon, Dolly quickly decided. "James, can't we take Anna with us?" she begged. "And Harriot, too." For there beside Anna stood Harriot Washington, the young sister of Lucy's husband, George.

"Anything you want, dear." Madison was to say that often during a lifetime of indulgently granting his wife her slightest wish.

So Anna and Harriot went with them on that strange honeymoon. And, of course, Payne. Not for a moment could Dolly be without her child.

Mrs. Madison leaned back in the crowded coach. She looked at James in his green velvet coat, sitting stiffly beside her. The Mechlin lace on his coat sleeves, as well as his shirt ruffles, was in shreds. It had so fascinated the girls at the wedding, they had rivaled each other in tearing off pieces as souvenirs.

The dignified Madison had behaved in a sprightly fashion. With all the dash of a young man, he had insisted that each lady present cut herself a piece of the exquisite lace.

"It's a shame what thee girls did to James' ruffles." Dolly shook her head at Anna and Harriot.

Then she smiled wanly. Out of the past came the memory

of the fashion doll in the show window on Chestnut Street. Dolly had always wanted a bridegroom in a velvet coat and ruffles of Mechlin lace. She looked at James Madison . . . well, she had one. Now, she told herself, she should be very happy.

FROM A WOODED KNOLL IN THE BLUE RIDGE COUNTRY, FIFTY
miles northwest of Richmond, Virginia, the square, pillared
house faced the mountains. It owed its classic beauty to the
four widely-spaced Doric columns on its portico that rose
directly from the ground. In the rear stretched the tobacco
fields of the Madison plantation.

"Oh, James," cried Dolly, when she first saw it, "thee
didn't tell me . . . Montpellier's beautiful!"

James Madison gazed adoringly at his bride of two weeks.
There was an odd pulse in his voice, a glow in his eyes, that
contrasted oddly with his usually chilly reserve. "My dear,
you can't describe Montpellier," he said. "It's within a squir-
rel's jump of heaven."

And it was. Dolly's heart warmed as their carriage approached her husband's beloved home, which he always
spelled with two "l's." Dropping one, he said, was a "Yankee
notion."

On the porch before the house, James' parents awaited
their son's bride. James Madison, Senior, a tall, thin man in
his seventies, embraced Dolly with courtly dignity. Nelly
Conway Madison, a smiling gray-haired woman, kissed her
new daughter-in-law's pink cheek. When she saw Payne, she
exclaimed, "What a handsome child!" and kissed him, too.

"Welcome home, son," rang out Father Madison's voice.
"Let Mother take your wife to her room. I've a thousand

things to ask you. I never know just what to do when you're away."

On the arm of her father-in-law, Dolly entered a narrow hall. On either side were two rooms paneled in simple white woodwork. Montpellier, she saw, was not as large as the impressive portico led one to believe.

The Madisons were not of the Tidewater aristocracy, James had told her, but comfortably well-to-do planters, descendants of an English ship carpenter who had put his money in land. His father was not a rich man; but rich enough to have sent him to Princeton.

Here, in 1760, Madison, Senior, had built the first brick house in Orange County. It stood on land his own father had wrested from the Indians. His son, James, had added the portico only the year before, at the suggestion of Thomas Jefferson.

Up a graceful staircase to the second floor, Dolly and her child followed James' mother.

"These will be your rooms." The elder woman opened the door into a sunny sitting room, furnished in polished mahogany and with dainty curtains. Through an archway Dolly saw a second room with a canopied bed.

"My dear, come look at the Blue Ridge," her mother-in-law said from the window.

Dolly came to her side. Across the green sloping lawn, she could see the purple mountains that extended in a great arc for ninety miles. Comfortable as the house was, the chief charm of Montpellier lay in its superb view of the Blue Ridge.

Mother Madison introduced Nany, a smiling Negro woman, who would serve as Dolly's personal maid and Payne's nurse. "Now I'll leave you until dinner time," she said. "Do try to rest."

"She's sweet!" thought Dolly, as the door closed behind
James' mother. The warm glow embraced his father, too.
"I'm going to like them," she decided. "We're all going to
live together happily at Montpellier," she told her little boy,
who, tired from his journey, had already crawled up on the
big white bed.

She would show them by her tact and sweetness that,
contrary to general belief, a house could be large enough for
two families. And she did. As long as Madison's parents lived,
Montpellier was their home as well as their son's. Dolly was
all that a daughter could have been to the lovable elderly
couple.

After breakfast the next morning, James went into the
library to write a letter.

"I'm asking Chisholm, the architect, to come and help me
fix up the house," he told his wife. "I want to make it a
fitting background for your beauty, my darling. It isn't nearly
large enough. Some day you'll be the mistress of Montpellier."

Thus Madison began the remodeling he would carry on for
years. He was in his element—busy, happy, full of plans. At
his honeymoon's end, James would have liked to remain at
Montpellier the rest of his life. Helping to write the Constitution had given him his fill of glory. He was tired of public
life.

But Dolly was younger, and for her there had been little
glory. Montpellier, lovely as it was, was not what she wanted.
As in her girlhood, she grew bored and restless in the country.
Fired with tremendous energy and ambition, she was eager
to begin to live—

❀   ❀   ❀   ❀   ❀

So within a month the James Madisons were back in Philadelphia. Their new home was at 115 Spruce Street; a house that James Monroe, now in Paris as American Minister, had occupied the previous winter. And Madison was busy in Congress—the first congressman to rise and say "Mr. Speaker!"

115 Spruce Street was not a big house. Virginia allowed her congressmen their family expenses, three servants and four horses, house rent and fuel, two dollars a mile for travel, and twenty dollars a day while in Philadelphia. Madison's only private income came from Montpellier. He was financially dependent on his father until he was fifty.

But Dolly's new home had maple furniture, chairs with horsehair seats, English carpets and silver on the sideboard. Mrs. Congressman Madison no longer had to rise at dawn, make the lodgers' beds, and wait on the table. She could lie in her bed until nine, then breakfast elegantly on ham, salt fish, hot breads, jam and tea.

This was a new Philadelphia for Dolly, the Philadelphia for which she had always yearned. As pretty Mrs. Madison of Montpellier, she plunged into the fashionable world with all the stored-up zest of her restrained girlhood.

It was at one of Martha Washington's Friday Evenings that Dolly Madison first wore bright colors.

She had arranged her dark unpowdered hair as usual, parted and braided around her head. But as she slipped into the new pink gown, the change she saw in her mirror was startling.

The sleeves on the dress were puffed and short. The neck cut astonishingly low. Dolly blushed. Against Nany's protests, she ordered her maid to fill in the neck with tulle. Then throwing a scarf about her shoulders, Mrs. Madison hurried downstairs.

James was in the library, writing to Virginia his quarterly

accounts of their household expenses. Dolly took off her scarf, and stood revealed in the pink gown. "How does thee— I mean, you—like it?" She was trying to remember to use the world's speech.

"It's beautiful," James murmured. He could not take his eyes off her loveliness.

With sudden shyness Dolly caught up the scarf and wrapped it around her. She had not foreseen the effect her first gay dress would have on her husband. As he rose and stepped toward her, she shrank back.

"No—oh, no," she whispered.

He stopped instantly.

"Sometimes you're cruel," he said.

"I don't mean to be. Oh, I'm sorry—" She put out her hand and he caught it, trembling.

"My dearest, I do want you to love me," he told her in low, moved tones.

And she wanted to, also. James was so kind to her. He was trying so hard to be an understanding father to Payne. Dolly despised herself for shrinking from her husband whenever he touched her.

To make amends, Dolly slipped her hand in his, as they drove down High Street toward the brick house of the Washingtons, with its two lamps glimmering owl-like before the door.

It was six o'clock. Official society had donned its best to climb the stairs to the reception rooms on the second floor and pay its respects to the President and First Lady.

That night Dolly Madison's beauty shone with an almost unearthly quality. She was like a tree with pink buds suddenly burst into bloom. But it was not the pink dress alone; it was happiness that entranced her. She was beginning to live.

President Washington, dignified in black with powdered

hair, came up to meet Mr. Madison's charming new bride.

A moment later, gracious little Martha Washington—calling Mrs. Madison, "Cousin Dolly"—joined them. Martha remembered that Dolly was the namesake of Dorothea Dandridge Henry. Perhaps the First Lady's memory also went back to the time when she herself had not been so exalted socially, and Dorothea's mother had introduced her, a shy debutante, to Williamsburg society.

As pink-clad Dolly moved through the crowded rooms, constantly watched over by gallant cavaliers, who filled her plate from the buffet table, or brought her a glass of punch, the evening seemed like a dream. Here she was the center of attraction. No longer a poor relative of the Washingtons, but the popular young wife of "the Great Little Madison."

She met Alexander Hamilton, suave, handsome, and so like Aaron Burr that her heart jumped painfully beneath her pink bodice. She chatted with his slender, vivacious wife, wondering if Mrs. Hamilton remembered the gauche episode of the dropped cup at Mrs. Washington's tea. "Elizabeth Hamilton has everything—youth, position, money," she thought enviously. "Most of all a fascinating husband—like Aaron would have been," her heart added.

When would she see Aaron? Dolly wondered. All evening she waited for him to stride into the room.

But Aaron Burr, one of the "filthy democrats" whom Lady Washington accused of leaving dirty finger marks on her wall paper, was not invited to the President's home. The Republican Madisons were different. James Madison had been a Federalist until, partly due to his friendship for Jefferson, partly because of his disgust with Hamilton's "administering" of the Constitution into the form he desired, Madison had broken with the conservatives and gone over to the liberal party of Thomas Jefferson.

Besides, George and Martha Washington did not approve of the private life of the Senator from New York.

❀   ❀   ❀   ❀   ❀

Dolly's first winter as Mrs. Madison slipped by quickly. Scented and powdered, gowned now in bright colors and the latest fashion, the charming wife of Congressman Madison lunched with the McKeans, the Butlers, Boudinots and Mifflins. She drank tea with the Chews, Conynghams and Hamiltons at their country seats.

Everywhere, clever Dolly Madison quietly studied how society carried itself. She learned about black beauty-patches, lace handkerchiefs, ivory fans and snuff boxes. When she had had enough tea to turn her cup upside down in the accepted manner. And not to blush at a favorite topic of gossip —Aaron Burr.

In spite of his fine law practice, Senator Burr, said the Federalists, was heavily in debt and likely to lose Richmond Hill unless he stopped his extravagance. He was always giving money to the poor, educating young protégés, or investing in crazy inventions such as heating a whole house without stoves.

Yet you couldn't help liking him, exclaimed the ladies, the Senator from New York had such charming manners. And Burr was so clever and unscrupulous, added the men, that no doubt he would some day become president.

"Aaron Burr, president . . . what a calamity!" cried the rich and conservative, who were led by Alexander Hamilton, for the grandson of Jonathan Edwards was a traitor to his own class, a dangerous radical. And they lowered their voices, as they said this, lest the Republican Madisons, who also belonged to the party of Thomas Jefferson, the party of the common people, should be offended.

Listening, Dolly knew that this criticism would only amuse Aaron. He cared very little what people thought of him. She heard of Burr going his debonair way, busy in Congress, dancing at gay parties; happy enough, no doubt, not to be invited to President Washington's stiff functions.

Of course, Senator Burr attended the fashionable Dancing Assemblies. And, one Thursday night in April, 1795, so did the James Madisons.

Dolly, radiant in yellow satin, her hair elaborately dressed now—powdered by the fashionable hairdresser Lacave and festooned with ostrich feathers—sat on a sofa beside her solemn husband in the ballroom of Oeller's Tavern on Chestnut Street. Before her, handsomely gowned ladies and gentlemen swayed to the languorous music of the violins, cellos and flutes. But Dolly did not dance. She, who had once tripped through the minuet with Patrick Henry, remained sedately beside her black-clad mate. At this time when men dressed as gay as peacocks, James Madison always wore sombre black. A white wig covered his bald head.

The chairman of the dance came up. Louis Philippe, later to be Louis XVIII, one of the many exiles of the French Revolution living in Philadelphia that winter.

"Madame Madison, will you lead the next set?" he asked.

Dolly shook her head. "I cannot dance, Your Highness. My Quaker parents thought it wicked."

"Come, let me teach you." The affable Frenchman held out his hand.

"No, Your Highness, I prefer to stay with my husband," Mrs. Madison replied firmly. What held her back? She had taken eagerly to the theater, to card-playing and other pleasures denied to strict Quakers. But the more Louis Philippe urged Dolly to dance, the more she knew she could not. Was it due to her stern upbringing? Or that the Prince was not the one for whom, unconsciously, she waited?

Then across the polished floor, erect and military, came the answer—a graceful figure in a wine-red velvet suit. There were snowy lace frills at his wrists, silver buckles on his shoes. Dolly clutched her fan with icy fingers.

"So it's Mrs. Madison now!" As he kissed her hand, Aaron Burr's sparkling hazel eyes told Dolly how lovely he found her. "My two old friends, your marriage makes me very happy, for I consider I made the match."

A cold chill crept over Dolly. If only Aaron had looked sad! But here he was, so distressingly handsome in spite of his short figure and big mouth, obviously pleased over what he hoped was her married happiness.

As the music struck up, the dancers gathered for the next set. Dolly's lips parted with expectation. When Aaron Burr asked her to dance, she would extend her hand and say "yes." Together they would glide and sway over the polished floor—

Aaron adjusted his lace frills. "I must go and draw my partner for this set," he said lightly. "Too bad, my Quaker Dolly, you don't dance."

"But I do dance," her heart called after him, as he moved gracefully away toward a group of ladies.

Dolly's head with its nodding plumes was held high. But her eyes were blurred; her hands trembled.

"It was nice seeing Aaron again," said James.

His wife nodded, her throat too tight for speech. The next set started. Its leader was Senator Burr. His partner was Anne Bingham, a beautiful young woman in blue satin, her powdered hair wreathed with roses.

Dolly could stand no more. Pleading a headache, Mrs.

Madison, who enjoyed perfect health, begged James to take her home.

❦   ❦   ❦   ❦   ❦

The smart frivolity of official Philadelphia life entertained twenty-eight-year-old Dolly Madison far more than it did her husband, who was over forty. But the cause went deeper than youth and middle-age. James, looking beneath this pleasant exterior, grew daily more disgusted with the envy, hatred and malice that underlay political life. Increasingly he longed for his beloved Montpellier, for his solitude and his books.

"I think I'll resign from Congress," he threatened frequently, "and content myself with being a Virginia country squire."

Nothing made Dolly more unhappy than such a prospect. She did not want to bury herself at Montpellier. In her lonely Scotchtown girlhood, she had had her share of plantation life.

It was Thomas Jefferson who saved her from this fate, for a time, at least. He, too, was anxious to keep his devoted lieutenant in public life; "little Madison" was too valuable a man in the Republican party. From Monticello, Jefferson used every argument likely to influence Jim Madison to stay in Philadelphia. As extra persuasion, he added at the end of one of his letters, "Present me respectfully to Mrs. Madison and pray her to keep you where you are, for her own satisfaction and the public good."

No doubt for the public good, and certainly for her own satisfaction, Dolly begged her husband to stay in Congress until the end of Washington's second term. And she continued to make friends for him, even among his political enemies.

That staunch Federalist, John Adams, regarded Madison as a traitor who had deserted Alexander Hamilton to follow Jefferson. But he admired Dolly. She charmed everyone who met her. How did she do it? Perhaps the explanation lies in a remark made some years later by one of her nieces, "I always thought better of *myself* when I had been with Aunt Dolly."

To his Abigail, pompous John Adams wrote of dining with the Madisons and of chatting with his hostess, "a fine woman, and her two sisters are equally so."

For Lucy Washington and Anna Payne had come to Philadelphia on what was to have been a happy family reunion; Walter Payne, back from England with his wife, was a guest of the Madisons. But Lucy and Anna brought sad news, too terrible to write. In a tavern brawl, Isaac, Dolly's wild younger brother, had offended a man, who shot him dead. And her darling William Temple had been thrown from his horse at Coles Hill and killed.

Dolly, whose warm heart vibrated to every family joy and sorrow, took the twin blows hard. When it came time for Lucy Washington to return to Harewood, Dolly refused to let Anna leave her.

So Walter Payne went to Coles Hill to take William Temple's place on the old family plantation. And Anna, as Dolly's "sister-child," became part of the Madison household.

By the time Dolly had recovered from her grief, it was March 1797. George Washington's administration was over. So was James Madison's term as congressman.

Now the Washingtons were free to return to Mount Vernon, and the Madisons to Montpellier. As for Aaron Burr, his six years in the Senate were over, and he, too, was a private citizen. But before the general exodus from Philadelphia, all men prominent in the government met in March at the inaugural of President John Adams.

Gowned in her handsomest red velvet cloak and bonnet, Dolly Madison joined her husband after the ceremony to tell Aaron Burr good-bye. He was returning to New York to run for the Assembly.

"We've got to beat this fellow Hamilton somehow, Jim," he said. "The place to do it is at home, in the great state of New York. If we build up the Republican Party, if we break the grip that the Schuylers have through Hamilton on the Federalists, the presidency is ours."

Dolly smiled gently. As always, Burr's great incentive was to defeat Hamilton. The two men were born to be enemies. In politics there was never room for both.

James wished his old friend luck. Aaron kissed Mrs. Madison's hand. As he turned to go out of her life, Dolly closed her eyes to hide her tears. With Senator Burr in New York, fighting to become a power in the Republican Party, and the Madisons in Virginia, it was not likely that their paths would cross again.

❦ ❦ ❦ ❦ ❦

Back in his library at Montpellier, James Madison, scholar and country gentleman, was a contented man. After three years in Congress, he was tired. He needed all the rest his beloved home could give.

The architect, Chisholm, had redecorated the homestead, but there were plenty of touches that only the master and mistress could add. From James Monroe, their neighbor, they bought handsome linen, brought from France, and later offered for sale. There was new French furniture, too; small, dainty gilt pieces, unlike the heavy carved furniture in the rest of the house.

Dolly tried hard to become a contented rural wife. If she missed the gaiety of city life, she did not complain. No woman ever understood better than Dolly Madison how to mask her feelings with a smile.

Her sister Anna's bright companionship helped to pass the time. Dolly read to her sick father-in-law, or chatted with James' brothers and sisters, who often came to Montpellier. She played with Payne, now a handsome, willful child of five, and tried to teach him to read. She helped Mother Madison with the housekeeping.

There were visits to be paid. The Monroes were at Ash Lawn, within driving distance. So was Monticello, Thomas Jefferson's "Little Mountain" home; the noblest mansion in Virginia.

This trip of thirty miles, which could be made in one day's drive, was sure to end in a warm welcome for Dolly and James. A guest room at Monticello, known as the "Madison Chamber," was always kept ready for them, for Dolly's girlhood friend, Martha Jefferson Randolph, looked forward to her coming. As for Jefferson, his affection for Dolly was heightened by his long friendship with her husband and his youthful love for Molly Payne.

At Monticello, James spent many hours showing his stepson Jefferson's inventions that filled the big red-brick house. He whirled Payne in Jefferson's revolving chair. He carried a pocket of corn for the boy to feed the tame deer on the estate. Unused to children, and shy with them, Madison was making a sincere effort to gain the confidence of the dark-eyed, spoiled child.

Dolly was more expert with kisses and affectionate reprimands than with the kind of discipline needed by so willful a little boy. Sensing this, James devoted himself to the five-year-old, encouraging him to talk, and spurring on Payne's interest in outdoor things.

In 1798, when James Madison was elected to the Virginia legislature, the placid life at Montpellier was broken. He was off to Richmond the following autumn to help Jefferson fight the Federalists' Alien and Sedition Laws.

It looked, too, as though there might be war with France. Again George Washington agreed to become commander in chief of the army. But, this time, Alexander Hamilton was the real head.

At isolated Montpellier, the Madisons heard how Aaron Burr had asked President Adams for an appointment in the new army. The President promised it to him. But Alexander Hamilton would grant Colonel Burr no favors. He was a dangerous man, he explained; it was his patriotic duty to thwart his ambitions. So General Washington refused Burr's services.

Hamilton again snubbed Aaron Burr—all in the line of patriotic duty, of course—just as he had blocked his hopes of the ministership to France, and of being governor of New York, back in 1792, before Dolly knew him.

But war with France was averted. And in December 1799 came the sad news that George Washington had died at Mount Vernon.

Dolly Madison, like many in the nation, wore the same deep mourning at Washington's death as for the loss of a relative. Along with Thomas Jefferson, the Madisons went to Mount Vernon to offer what consolation they could to the grief-stricken Martha.

The same year, on June 6th, Patrick Henry died at Red Hill, Virginia. The next year the Madisons went to visit Dorothea Dandridge Henry, who had remarried another cousin of Dolly's, Isaac Winston. They also attended the marriage of Mary, Dolly's sister, to John G. Jackson of Virginia.

Otherwise, life at Montpellier moved slowly. Payne Todd, despite James' efforts, remained a spoiled and pampered child. Dolly seemed resigned to country life. And Madison claimed that he was fulfilling his public duty by going to Richmond and taking part in the state legislature.

There was nothing Dolly could do about it. Nationally her "little Madison" was forgotten; his political career was over. It looked as though ambitious, thirty-two-year-old Mrs. Madison would spend the rest of her life quietly at Montpellier.

Then the presidential campaign of 1800 got under way. The Federalist candidates were Adams and Pinckney; the Republican, Thomas Jefferson and Aaron Burr. When the electoral votes were cast, the result was a tie between the two Republicans; the House of Representatives must now vote to decide which would be president. Everywhere, people said that Burr would be chosen.

So Aaron would be the next president! At Montpellier, Dolly Madison shut herself in her room and gazed into the mirror. "President Aaron Burr . . ." she had always known this would happen. She had not seen him for nearly four years, yet how often he had been in her thoughts.

But Burr was not chosen. One morning Mrs. Madison sat at her sewing. She was worrying about Payne's indifference to his studies, his fondness for teasing the farm animals. Suddenly her husband burst into the room.

"Jefferson's won," he cried—for Alexander Hamilton, who considered Jefferson the lesser of two evils, had used his influence to block Aaron Burr again; this time, just as the presidency was within his grasp. "But Aaron is vice president," Madison continued. "We couldn't have two better men."

There was no envy in James. But Dolly's heart contracted with jealousy as she thought of Burr's rapid rise in politics. He might be in line to succeed Jefferson. While her little Madison—tears blurred her eyes—remained forgotten at Montpellier.

It was more than Dolly could bear. But then, she told herself bitterly, she had known how it would be when she married James.

However, Madison's chance was on its way. One morning as James and his wife sat at breakfast, a letter came from Thomas Jefferson asking his faithful lieutenant to be his secretary of state.

Dolly jumped up from the table, almost knocking over the teapot in her excitement. Mob cap awry, she snatched Jefferson's letter and read it. "Oh, James, how wonderful!" she cried. "We'll go to the Federal City to live."

After ten years in Philadelphia, the national capital had once more been moved—this time, permanently. The new site was one laid out by George Washington along the Potomac River, on a ten-mile-square tract given by the State of Virginia. Only three months ago, the government had moved to its new location.

Madison smiled at his wife's girlish delight. How he loved to see Dolly happy! Of late, she had been so silent and moody.

Still James hesitated. "Father's desperately ill," he reminded her. "Perhaps it's my duty to stay home and run Montpellier."

His wife's heart sank. "My little Madison," she pleaded, "you'll be in Jefferson's Cabinet . . . you'll be almost as important as Vice President Burr."

In the end, James Madison gave in. "All right, I'll accept," he said, although still with reluctance. His reward came when he saw Dolly's glad smile.

A fever of excitement ran through her. James' political career was not over. They were not forgotten and cast aside. They were going to the wonderful new Federal City to live, back into public life.

She followed James into his study, when he went to answer Jefferson's letter. He stood for a moment at the window, looking out, saying good-bye to all that he loved. His eyes on the Blue Ridge, he ached already with homesickness for their peace and beauty.

Dolly could not understand his mood. Here they were important again, once more in national politics—and James looked mournful! People, not places, meant the most to Dolly Madison. Montpellier was beautiful, but she had not been really happy there.

Coming close to her husband's side, Dolly put her arm through his. "Mr. Secretary of State Madison," she whispered proudly.

Oh, how wonderful it sounded!

*I*T WAS APRIL, 1801, A MONTH AFTER THOMAS JEFFERSON took the oath as third president of the United States, before Secretary of State Madison and his lady drove into the new capital on the Potomac. James' father had died on the 27th of February. To Jefferson's disappointment, his dear friends from Montpellier could not be present at his inaugural.

As the Madison coach splashed along a muddy, unpaved road called Pennsylvania Avenue, Dolly shaded her eyes for a view of the Federal City. The place that had seemed so majestic on the plans drawn by Major L'Enfant was nothing more than a straggling line of government buildings, brick kilns and laborers' huts. Much remained still to be done before Washington, as many called the new town, acquired the dignity of a national capital.

Nor was the President's Palace, as the Federalists, still under English influence, called it, really fit for occupancy. The first public building in Washington, it was built of buff sandstone painted white. Its Irish architect, James Hoban, had modeled it on the Duke of Leinster's town house in Dublin. George Washington had laid its cornerstone nine years before.

That spring day it did not look much like a Palace to Dolly. It was a gaunt, naked-looking building, with no porticoes, standing on an unfenced stretch of ground, barren of trees and shrubs.

From the door of this sorry residence, the new chief executive, Thomas Jefferson, strode forward to greet his old friends. He was informally dressed in a homespun coat, red waistcoat, worn corduroy breeches, insecure woolen hose and slippers. His red hair was touseled.

Since the main stairs were not built, Jefferson took his guests up a back way to an upstairs oval sitting room, handsomely furnished in red damask. Of the six rooms then finished, it was the only pleasant spot in the bleak barn of a house.

Jefferson had brought from Monticello eleven servants, including a French cook and butler. He had scattered his personal belongings about the bare rooms, even in the still unplastered audience chamber to the east where Mrs. John Adams had hung her washing to dry. About him were his fossils waiting to be classified, his experiments in horticulture, his musical instruments, and his books. But it was obvious that the new President was not a happy man. Something was missing—

"I've a request to make of you, Dolly," Jefferson said, when his guests had been fed and rested. "Will you be my First Lady?"

"Your first what?" stammered the astonished Mrs. Madison.

The President explained. With no wife, with his daughters, Martha and Polly, able to visit him only occasionally, he needed a hostess. Aaron Burr was also a widower. So the next in line to preside when the President entertained, and ladies were present, was the wife of his Secretary of State.

"Besides, you're like a daughter to me, Dolly," Jefferson added.

Of course, Mrs. Madison accepted without demur. What woman wouldn't? Then and there, she began her duties as the President's official hostess.

These would not be heavy, she learned. Jefferson cared

little for formal social affairs. He had already decided to omit the weekly levees established by George Washington, as well as the President's Birthday Ball. A reception on New Year's Day and one on the Fourth of July were enough, he said.

This news threw social Washington into consternation. Not to be cheated of the privilege of calling on the President, a group of ladies appeared uninvited at Jefferson's door and pretended they did not know the weekly reception had been cancelled. The busy President had to spend an hour chatting with them.

"You'll have to take these females off my hands," he told Mrs. Madison. "I can't be bothered with them."

So while the new President busied himself with putting the ship of state on her "republican tack," Dolly received all officialdom in the half-finished parlors of the executive mansion.

Whatever their estimation of the President, everyone was charmed with the new First Lady. Only a handful of congressmen, who had been in Philadelphia and remembered "Mrs. Payne's" boarding house, thought her daughter had traveled rather far from her humble Quaker upbringing. Everyone else accepted her as Mrs. James Madison, bedecked with jewels, her dark curls topped with the towering turbans which were to become distinctive of Jefferson's First Lady.

On New Year's Day of 1802 the President greeted a hundred people gathered at noon in the Palace. At his first reception, Jefferson shocked his guests by not wearing a wig, the badge of all statesmen. Instead of bowing, as had the Federalist presidents, he shook hands.

To the strains of the Marine Band playing in the hall, Secretary of State and Mrs. Madison mingled with the incongruous elements that made up official Washington society. It ranged from the Tunisan Minister, Meley-Meley, in rich silk robes with real jewels for buttons, to a group of half-naked Osage chiefs in blankets and moccasins, and their squaws.

Dolly Madison, who had been asked to dress the chiefs' wives for the occasion, looked at them with speculative interest. Some of her friends had suggested that the Indian women wear silk and satin; some, cotton. Anna thought they would look best in their native costumes. But Dolly had decided on large flower-patterned chintz dresses over stiff petticoats, and no beads or bracelets.

Now watching the squaws stoically enduring their ordeal, Dolly murmured to James, "Oh, dear, they do look uncomfortable!"

The chiefs, however, seemed to be enjoying the party. Especially the ice in the wine coolers, which aroused their childlike curiosity. One slyly lifted out a piece. Then surprised at its burning his fingers, he quickly passed it to a friend. Then how the Indians chattered together!

In one room, Jefferson had on display a gift; a mammoth cheese weighing 1,600 pounds, made in Cheshire, Massachusetts, and hauled to Washington on a sleigh drawn by six horses.

"I hope that no Federalist cows contributed to it," said a mocking voice. Dolly turned quickly.

It was Aaron Burr. The moment, which she had both anticipated and dreaded, had come. For the first time in five years, she looked into his bright hazel eyes. Vice President Burr had just arrived from New York to assume his gavel in the north wing of the Capitol.

"I hear Jefferson paid his admirers two hundred dollars for it," Burr remarked cynically. "A pretty good price for any cheese—"

His mockery made the President sound ridiculous. Mrs.

Madison, who had been admiring the cheese, found herself laughing at it, and at Mr. Jefferson. She hated herself for laughing.

Aaron's mood changed. "Dolly, remember my telling you about my daughter?" He smiled proudly as a tall, dark-haired girl came toward them. "This is Theo."

Theodosia Burr had married a wealthy young planter. She was now Mrs. Joseph Alston of Charleston, South Carolina. Dolly could hardly believe that this handsome young woman, with her mother's fine mind and exquisite manners, was the precocious child of whom Aaron had boasted. How the years flew!

"We were sorry you missed the inaugural, Mrs. Madison," Theo said prettily. "Oh, I'll never forget the ceremony! Papa was wonderful."

Aaron's daughter gazed at him adoringly. Her beloved father, not President Jefferson, had been the hero of the occasion to Theodosia. Dolly's heart went out to the beautiful, loyal girl. Aaron would have just such a splendid daughter, she thought.

Mrs. Alston was visiting Colonel Burr; and because she was Aaron's child, as well as for her charming self, Mrs. Madison sponsored Theodosia at dinners, teas and receptions. Delighted by his daughter's social success, the Vice President teased her about being the most popular young woman in Washington.

But that distinction belonged to Dolly Madison. With Jefferson often away at Monticello, the real center of Washington life was not in the executive mansion. It was at 2113 Pennsylvania Avenue, where the Madisons moved soon after their arrival in Washington. There rival senators, Cabinet members and foreign diplomats met every day in the most informal manner. All party differences seemed forgotten in

Dolly Madison's presence.

Being First Lady by proxy did not turn Dolly's brightly-turbaned head. Her hearty laugh rang out above the chatter of voices in her parlor. The offer of her snuff box (and she was growing increasingly fond of snuff) saved many an awkward political moment. She loved people. She longed to please, and was easily pleased. No wonder Mrs. Madison was popular. Tactful and kindly, she hurt no one's feelings, and made friends everywhere. Her amazing memory helped her never to forget a name or a face.

All this was a great help to the President, as well as to the solemn Madison, who unbent with difficulty.

"You know, Jim," exclaimed Jefferson, after Dolly had reigned for a few months, "we must both thank our First Lady for any popularity we enjoy."

Every day at the Madisons' there was company to dine, usually a dozen or more. They sat at the table from four o'clock in the afternoon until late in the evening, eating heavily, drinking toasts with the Secretary of State's fine madeira, and laughing at his droll stories.

"Mrs. Madison's dinners are more like harvest home suppers than the banquets of a secretary of state," Mrs. Anthony Merry, wife of the British Minister, remarked acidly.

"The profusion at my table reflects the prosperity of America," was Dolly's quick retort. She was proud that her invitations were the most sought-for in Washington. And she knew why Mrs. Merry disliked her. Jefferson insisted that Dolly Madison grace the head of his table at state dinners. And that had started a diplomatic feud.

Dining one night at the Palace, Mrs. Anthony Merry was the ranking lady. According to precedent, the President should give her his arm into dinner. But, true to form, Jefferson had established the rule of equality among his guests.

Besides, he was fond of Dolly Madison. So when dinner was announced, he offered his arm to Mrs. Secretary of State.

Seeing the tall, horse-faced Mrs. Merry's fierce expression, Dolly whispered, "No, take her."

Jefferson grinned wickedly. Tucking Mrs. Madison's hand under his arm, he escorted her into the dining room. The wife of the British Minister was left to crowd her way through the door as best she could on the arm of her own husband.

Immediately after dinner, the Merrys left in a huff.

Afterwards, they refused all invitations of the President and Secretary of State. But little did Dolly Madison guess that this snub, rankling in Mr. Merry's mind, would cause him later on to listen, eagerly, to some curious proposals whispered in his ear by another guest that evening—Aaron Burr.

It had been months since she had seen him. Dolly, who had feared meeting Aaron too often in Washington, found, to her surprise, that she seldom saw him. For Jefferson no longer liked Mr. Burr. He regarded him as a potential rival and enemy, who had plotted in the recent presidential election to defeat him with Federalist help and seize the presidency for himself.

Then there was the way Aaron Burr presided over the Senate. No loyal Republican could forgive him his independence. If questions came to a tie, the Vice President must cast a deciding vote. "I vote as I think best," Burr said. Often he voted with the Federalists, and angered his own party.

So now Vice President Burr was excluded from Republican party counsels, and only tolerated at their social affairs. He had attended a Federalist banquet. And it was rumored that Burr was plotting to form a third party, composed of Federalists and disgruntled Republicans. Under his leadership, they would work to defeat Mr. Jefferson and Mr. Madison.

Seated at her dinner table that summer of 1802, Dolly

listened with dismay as her Republican guests, strict party men, drank hostile toasts to the Vice President, "Burr, may he stick to Republicanism!"

As she saw Aaron lined up against Jefferson and Madison, their enemy, instead of their friend, Dolly's loyal heart grew sick.

"Jim, I no longer trust Aaron Burr," she heard Jefferson say. It might have been George Washington speaking.

Whatever Jefferson thought, Madison echoed. "I wouldn't ask Burr to the house for a while," he said to his wife. (He no longer called his old college friend "Aaron.")

"But Theo's returning to South Carolina next week," Dolly protested, "I want to give a good-bye dinner for her."

Her husband frowned. "I prefer that you didn't."

❧   ❧   ❧   ❧   ❧

When Theodosia Alston returned to South Carolina, the kind Mrs. Madison took two other young women under her wing. In November 1802, the President's daughters, Martha Randolph and pretty Polly Eppes, came for their first visit to Washington. Into their two months' stay, their old friend, Dolly Madison, crowded a round of teas, calls and dinners.

Mrs. Randolph and Mrs. Madison were often taken for each other. Once as a joke, Martha Randolph, wearing a pelisse and bonnet of Dolly's, made a series of calls on comparative strangers announcing herself as "Mrs. Madison." Those on whom she called believed that she was.

Before their visit, Jefferson's daughters had written to Dolly Madison, asking her what gowns to bring. They enclosed samples of their hair, and commissioned her to buy them the most fashionable wigs. These little tasks amused Dolly, who loved shopping. It was she who bought all the earrings, shawls and sashes, that Jefferson took home to his daughters.

This winter of 1802-3 was a happy time in Dolly's life. Popular Anna Payne attracted to the house a group of gay young people. Among them was Richard D. Cutts, the thirty-year-old Congressman from Maine. A Harvard graduate, as well, Cutts was a great beau with the girls.

Anna flirted with him so outrageously that Dolly had to speak severely to her sister. "You're overeager, dear," Mrs. Madison remarked, after a game of loo. "Congressman Cutts is a spoiled young man. You mustn't frighten him away by being too anxious."

On the Fourth of July, 1803, the Madisons joined the jubilant crowd that filled the President's house to celebrate the Louisiana Purchase. The mansion was gay with banners. The Marine Band played. There were speeches and cheers in honor of Jefferson, Madison, and the new territory bought from France that would more than double the size of the country.

No one was more stirred than Dolly Madison. This was a proud moment in her husband's life. Across the room, she saw a crowd of people around the Secretary of State, to congratulate him. Another enthusiastic group surrounded Thomas Jefferson. He had never been more popular.

Where was Aaron Burr on this occasion of Republican triumph? Dolly wondered. During the discussions held before sending James Monroe to France to buy the vast Louisiana Territory, the Vice President had not been consulted by Jefferson and Madison. Nor was he present now.

After the purchase, the attention of the country turned to the unexplored west. Jefferson selected two Virginians, his secretary, Meriwether Lewis, and Captain William Clark to explore the new territory that the nation had bought. Before their departure, Dolly Madison and the other Cabinet ladies outdid each other in giving parties for the courageous pair.

One afternoon Mrs. Madison was at the home of Mrs. Secretary of War Dearborn, drinking tea with Mr. Lewis and Mr. Clark, when Aaron Burr sauntered in.

To Dolly's surprise, he was in high spirits. Seating himself among the ladies, Mr. Burr proceeded to steal the limelight from Mr. Lewis and Mr. Clark as he amused the company with bits of New York scandal. Dolly watched Aaron's face, dark and handsome in the firelight. How could a man so gay, so charming, be the scoundrel people called him?

"Have you heard that I'm a grandfather, Dolly?" he asked proudly. "Theo has a boy, Aaron Burr Alston. But I've nicknamed him Gampy because his first word, an attempt to say Grandpa, sounded like 'Gampy.'"

He took a paper from his pocket. "Look, Gampy wrote this." He pointed to a scrawl. "Isn't that splendid for a child of nineteen months? He's going to be a genius. I wrote Theo that she must begin teaching him to read and write and some French."

Dolly smiled. Aaron's mania for education had not changed. Only now it was Theodosia's child.

"Joseph writes that Theo's not well. He's sending her north to Saratoga Springs." Mr. Burr leaned forward earnestly. "Dolly, will you let Theo stay with you on her way to Saratoga? She loves you so. Being with you would do her good."

Readily Mrs. Madison promised. Then, a little frightened, she went home to break the news to her husband.

James was seated before the fire, reading the newspaper.

"It would be embarrassing politically for me to have Burr's daughter staying in my house," he said, when Dolly finished her story. "Jefferson won't like it. In New York State, the Republican leaders, the Clintons and Livingstons, have also turned against Burr."

"Is that any reason we should, James?" Dolly's voice trembled. "You went to college with Aaron. I've known him for years. If his old friends don't stand by him now, who will?"

It was the Madisons' first serious quarrel. Anna, siding with her sister, only made it worse.

"All right, let Mrs. Alston come," James finally said. "I suppose I'm strong enough politically to stand it. But it won't help me."

So Theo came, looking listless and depressed. Mr. Madison was polite to her; but he managed to be out of the house most of the time, especially when Colonel Burr called.

"Dolly, I'm worried about Papa," Theo confessed one day. "Those dreadful lies Alexander Hamilton has spread about him—that Papa has been discredited by the Republicans, as well as by the Federalists; that he is plotting to overthrow Jefferson and form a third party. Papa only laughs when I ask him if such attacks can hurt him. He says of course not, that nobody believes them—you know how he always glosses over unpleasant things—"

"If only Mr. Jefferson would come out and defend Papa," Theo continued, as Dolly remained silent. "I don't understand why Jefferson doesn't. Both he and Papa are Republicans."

Dolly bowed her head to hide her embarrassment. James Madison, also a Republican, had not rushed to the Vice President's defense.

In a few days Theodosia Alston, still pale and languid, went on to Saratoga Springs. Worried sick about her beloved father, not even Dolly's loving attentions could restore Theo's health and high spirits.

🏵　　　🏵　　　🏵　　　🏵　　　🏵

With January 1804 came the time for another presidential election. Thomas Jefferson was assured a second term, but no one wanted Aaron Burr as vice president. The Republicans distrusted him for conniving with the Federalists. Alexander Hamilton had never ceased to discredit Burr in Federalist circles by whispers and innuendos. Jefferson refused to have him on the ticket.

Dolly could hardly believe it. Aaron Burr, whose political future had once looked so bright!

National politics might be closed to him, but that did not mean that Colonel Burr was through politically. There was a fight coming for the governorship of New York. One day Anna brought home the news that the Vice President would try to retrieve his political fortune by running for the governorship of his home state.

"As an independent, of course," Madison emphasized. Aaron Burr, whom many had expected would succeed Jefferson as president, had been repudiated by his own party.

But Dolly's heart glowed. Ah, Aaron was a brave man! How could she help him? She remembered Theodosia's words, "If only Mr. Jefferson would come out and defend Papa." Mrs. Madison knew how the President felt about Colonel Burr. But now that he was rid of him as vice president, surely, she thought, Jefferson would not object to giving Burr some mark of esteem with which to face the world.

Saying nothing to her husband, Dolly hurried to the executive mansion. She found the President at the desk in his study, among his maps and books and flowers.

"Will you do something for me?" Seating herself beside him, she took his hand. "See Aaron Burr, please, and have a talk with him."

Jefferson frowned. "Why should I? We've nothing to talk about. Burr's going back to New York."

"I know." She smiled sweetly. "But give him something to show at home—a letter with a few kind words in it. Coming from you, the leader of the Republican Party, it would mean everything to Aaron."

The man who was like a father to Dolly looked at her hard. "Why are you doing this for Burr?" he asked.

Mrs. Madison's face was scarlet. "Because he's an old friend, and I'm sorry for him." She had the grace to lower her lashes. "Please see him, for my sake."

"I'd prefer not to," Jefferson replied coldly. Then at the sadness in Dolly's blue eyes, his own softened. "But I will, because you ask it." He patted her hand. "You know, dear, you're so much like your mother at times."

Triumphant, Mrs. Madison raced home and sat down at her desk. Her pen fairly flew over the paper as she wrote Aaron Burr. He must go to Jefferson at once; the President wanted to see him.

All Washington was startled to hear that on January 26, 1804, President Jefferson conferred with the retiring Vice President. Dolly Madison waited impatiently to hear what happened. The weeks passed. At last it became apparent that Jefferson had done nothing for Burr beyond bidding him good-bye.

On February 25th, a Republican caucus renominated Mr. Jefferson for president and chose George Clinton as vice president. The name of Aaron Burr was not even mentioned.

As the Madisons sat for their portraits by Gilbert Stuart

that spring of 1804, disappointment and strain showed on Dolly's round face. Stuart's painting of the Secretary of State was the artist's usual flattering picture. He put a gleam in Madison's sombre eyes, a ruddy tone to his pale skin. But somehow the gifted painter could not pin Mrs. Madison's vivacious spirit down on canvas. His portrait of her, seated before a curtain, a set smile on her rosy face, was not the charming thirty-six-year-old matron that her friends loved and admired.

The lively Anna Payne also sat for the young English artist. "Why don't you paint yourself?" she teased him.

So Stuart drew a caricature of himself as part of the drapery background of Anna's portrait.

Anna Payne had captured the dashing Congressman, Richard Cutts, and the pleased Madisons were preparing for a lavish April wedding. But as the vows were exchanged before Parson McCormick, pastor of the chapel at the Navy Yard, Dolly's eyes filled with tears. Her dear "sister-child" would now live in Maine. To Dolly this seemed further away from Washington than Alaska does today.

After the bustle of the Cutts' departure by stagecoach, the Madison home seemed strangely lonely. Losing Anna helped Dolly to understand the sadness that came to Thomas Jefferson that April. He wrote from Monticello that his younger daughter, Polly Eppes, had died, leaving two children.

Dolly hugged her own boy, twelve-year-old Payne, and to his delight bought him a fine saddle horse.

Meanwhile, in New York State, a bitter fight for the governorship was under way. On April 25, 1804, Aaron Burr lost to Judge Morgan Lewis, a Livingston son-in-law. "Burr's finished politically," Madison chuckled. His wife was too shocked to reply.

The Stuart portraits were finished in June, and Anna's

packed off to Maine. Dolly was studying her own likeness one afternoon when James burst into the parlor, the *Washington Federalist* in his hand.

"Burr has shot Hamilton in a duel!" he cried.

Dolly turned deathly pale. She caught a chair back to keep from falling. "It can't be true," she gasped.

Madison handed her the paper.

The duel had grown out of the recent election in New York State. Outwardly, Hamilton had gone to few political meetings, taken little part in the campaign. But privately, in his library, he had written countless letters begging the Federalists not to vote for Aaron Burr—"a dangerous man, and one who ought not to be trusted with the reins of government."

Burr, hearing of these letters, was fighting mad. If he wished to continue in politics, Hamilton must cease his attacks. He wrote to him, demanding an explanation or an apology. Hamilton was evasive. So there was only one way to settle the matter. The long feud between the two men had at last reached a climax. Burr challenged; Hamilton accepted the challenge.

Hamilton and Burr met on July 11th, at seven in the morning, on the Jersey side of the Hudson, near Weehawken—a favorite dueling ground for New Yorkers. On the same spot where his eldest son, a boy of twenty, had been killed in a similar political duel, Hamilton dropped—mortally wounded by Burr. He died the following day.

Alexander Hamilton had been silenced. But it had taken a pistol shot to do it.

Horrified, Dolly read every word of the newspaper account. "Oh, it's terrible!" she said in a stunned voice. Then with a queer, choking cry, she threw herself weeping on the couch.

"Dearest . . ." James bent over her anxiously. "I didn't think you would take it so hard. Why, you hardly knew Hamilton!"

Now that Alexander Hamilton was dead, even his enemies praised him. Everything that led up to the duel was forgotten. No condemnation of his "murderer" was too severe. People said that at the duel, Burr had laughed and apologized because his bullet had not lodged in Mr. Hamilton's heart. A "devilish good shot," Burr had fired first. He had killed Hamilton in cold blood.

Where was Aaron Burr? No one knew. Persuaded by his friends that if he stayed in New York, he would be arrested for murder, he had disappeared.

Sick with fear, Dolly could not confide in James. And he, shocked at her haggard face, thought of only one remedy.

"The heat of Washington is too much for you, my dear," he said. "We'll go to Montpellier for a vacation."

Dolly closed her eyes and groaned.

In Washington, shops were closed; flags at half mast. Everyone wore badges of mourning for Alexander Hamilton. All that hot July week, while Mrs. Madison packed for the journey, she wrote frequently to Anna, the only person to whom she confided, and then sparingly.

Her letters were models of reticence. "There is so much I could tell you . . . but I am learning to hold my tongue well," Dolly wrote. Then in a letter dated July 16th, two days after the Hamilton funeral: "We go to Montpellier this week. Payne continues sick and my prospects rise and fall as this precious child recovers or declines."

Exactly one sentence was given to an event then shaking the country with wild excitement and of which Dolly thought day and night. At the close of her letter, she added, "You have heard, no doubt, of the terrible duel and death of

poor Hamilton. I sent the President word of your offer to get
the glass . . ."

Aaron Burr kills the great Federalist leader, Alexander
Hamilton, and Dolly writes about glassware—not another
word of that awful July morning when Hamilton was shot
by Aaron Burr under the rocky heights of Weehawken.

*F*OUR SEASONS SPENT IN THE FATIGUING DUTIES AND PLEA-sures of Washington official life had told on Mrs. Madison's health. That was the story that James gave the neighbors at Montpellier when Dolly, pale and suffering, came home in the family coach.

And, in truth, the capital was not a healthy place. In those days Tiber Creek flowed up to the lawn of the President's house; the Tidal Basin was a swamp. Certainly the marshes around Washington were partly responsible for the inflammatory rheumatism which attacked Dolly that summer of 1804 and was to trouble her all her life.

She had never known such pain. For weeks she lay in the white canopied bed at Montpellier, too sore to move. Mother Madison nursed her; the local doctor bled her. And James protected her from an endless stream of guests, rolling up uninvited, but always welcome in the cordial Virginia fashion.

Loving care and the dry mountain air of the Blue Ridge region finally restored Dolly's health. In the fall of 1804, when she returned to her Washington home, now at 244 F Street, she was more like her handsome, vivacious self again.

Still in process of building, Washington was a squalid, ugly little town, sprawling on the banks of the Potomac. With slops in the street, pigs in the puddles, cows and goats grazing along the imaginary "avenues," it was as uncomfortable as any frontier settlement.

But there was good hunting; quail was shot within a hundred yards of the Capitol. Washingtonians went to the races, lost a great deal of money at brag and loo, and paid morning calls. They listened to pretty girls play the harp and sing "Just like Love is Yonder Rose." They went to receptions and balls, attended by far more men than girls, so that Washington was "the most marrying place in the country." And for something to talk about, there was always Aaron Burr.

As the opening of Congress drew near, people declared, "Burr will never have the audacity to take his seat in the Senate. If he does, he'll be impeached. The Senate won't sit under a man indicted for murder."

Then Washington ate its words. On November 5th, when Congress reconvened, Vice President Burr quietly entered the Senate chamber and mounted the rostrum. Picking up the gavel, he rapped for order.

Seated beside Anna Cutts in the visitors' section, Dolly Madison could hardly believe her eyes. Some of Alexander Hamilton's friends glared at Aaron. But when the business of the day was over, many Republicans crowded around to shake his hand.

Fascinated, Dolly watched Burr accept their welcome with smiling ease. Surely no man had ever shown such courage. Once more, loyal, warm-hearted Dolly longed to help him. To get a new start, Aaron needed her as never before.

Throwing caution to the winds, she determined to plant the weight of her popularity and influence firmly behind him. In spite of the duel, Aaron Burr would again be accepted in Washington society.

First, Dolly appealed to her husband. "Dueling is terrible," she admitted, "but it's the customary way to settle disputes between gentlemen. To say that Burr murdered Hamilton isn't true. They both took the same risk."

"It's not that—" Madison began.

It seemed that Alexander Hamilton had written a letter, before he went to his death, in which he said he did not believe in dueling; that he had been forced into this fight to keep from being called a coward. The rumor was that Hamilton had reserved his first shot, hoping his enemy would apologize. Burr's friends insisted that Hamilton shot and missed.

"Aaron Burr deliberately killed Alexander Hamilton, people are saying," Madison explained, "that it was more an assassination than a duel—"

"Oh, how can you believe such lies!" Dolly's eyes flashed. She pictured Aaron as the innocent victim of the Federalists, who hated him; the Republicans, too. With the whole world against him, she, Dolly Madison, would not turn her back upon him.

"James," she gathered her courage, "I want to ask Aaron to dinner. Right away. In that way we may be able to help him—"

Madison frowned. "I couldn't have Burr in my house again. It would hurt me politically."

An abyss yawned. Standing on the brink of it, Dolly chose to jump. "Politics," she said scornfully. "Must you always think of your career, James? Can't you, for once, do something for an old friend in trouble?"

Just as Jefferson had done, Madison gave his wife a long, searching look. Then he rose stiffly.

"Since you demand it," he said in a hurt tone, "I'll ask Tom what he thinks our attitude should be regarding Burr. I'll be guided by what he says."

In a strange mood for him, the usually-amiable James left the house, slamming the door. Suddenly very tired, Dolly climbed the stairs to her own room.

To her surprise, Madison came back from the President's

THEODOSIA BURR: AGE TWENTY-SIX

By John Vanderlyn

JAMES MADISON

A copy by Asher B. Durand of the Gilbert Stuart original at Bowdoin College

MRS. JAMES MADISON

By Rembrandt Peale

THE PRESIDENT'S HOUSE IN 1814

Before the burning of Washington

THE WHITE HOUSE IN 1831

Rebuilt after the fire

looking happier. Jefferson, he said, had agreed that it would be wise to grant Colonel Burr the social recognition due the Vice President for the short time that he would remain in office. In fact, Jefferson, himself, intended to ask Burr to dine at the Palace.

One thing James did not tell his wife—Jefferson had reminded him of a service Aaron Burr had done them. The Weehawken duel had eliminated Alexander Hamilton, the great Federal leader, and their long-time rival. While Jefferson and Madison did not approve the method, they owed Colonel Burr a certain gratitude.

Then there was the coming trial of the Federalist judge, Samuel Chase, before the Senate. Jefferson wanted Judge Chase impeached. He reminded Madison that Burr, who presided over the Senate, would have influence in the decision.

The next day the Vice President was surprised to receive an invitation to dine at the Secretary of State's home. After his daughter Theo arrived for a visit, he was even more amazed to be asked to the Palace.

On the surface, all was pleasant. But there were many raised eyebrows.

"People are talking," Anna Cutts warned her sister. "You're risking your popularity by having Aaron Burr at the house so much. Oh, Dolly, I wish you wouldn't!"

Mrs. Madison tossed her gold-turbaned head. Let people talk! She was Jefferson's First Lady, the leader of Washington society. She could do as she pleased.

Yet, secretly, Dolly had been shocked at Aaron's attitude. She had expected to find him chastened. But not at all. Colonel Burr's manner was coldly defiant. Not once did he express regret at what he had done.

At parties people tactfully avoided any embarrassing reference to Alexander Hamilton in Burr's presence. But he astonished them all by deliberately bringing up the subject of the duel.

"My friend Hamilton," he said calmly one evening at the Madisons', "whom I shot . . ."

Dolly stifled a gasp of dismay. But she remained loyal to him. Her faith seemed justified when Vice President Burr presided with his usual finesse over the trial of Judge Samuel Chase before the Senate.

Mrs. Madison was a frequent visitor in the Senate chamber from January 1805, when the trial began, until it ended in March with Judge Chase's acquittal. Colonel Burr had again demonstrated his "impartiality." In spite of the courtesies shown him, that troublesome free-lance had done absolutely nothing to help Mr. Jefferson.

The day after the trial, Vice President Burr took leave of the Senate. Inauguration Day, two days hence, would deprive him of all official occupation.

Outside the Senate chamber, Dolly Madison waited to bid him good-bye. Burr came out, head high, but walking slowly, as if he hated to go. The tragedy of this brilliant man's wasted talents swept over Dolly. Tears in her eyes, she stretched out her hands to him.

John Randolph of Roanoke, who had left the chamber behind Mr. Burr, stood in the doorway—a witness to this touching scene.

Dolly saw the eccentric Mr. Randolph, long an enemy of her husband's, staring at her. But she gave him no thought. "What will you do, Aaron?" she asked anxiously. "Where will you go?"

"I don't know. Theo wants me to live with her. But Joseph's in politics. I don't want to hurt his chance of being elected governor. I can't go north. Two indictments have been filed against me . . . in New York for the challenge; in New Jersey for—murder. And imagine it, Dolly, my greedy creditors want to put me in jail for debt, as well." He shrugged, and added cheerfully, "Oh, well, I'll get along!"

Still that Burr bravado that refused to admit any misfortune. Even the fact that his beloved Richmond Hill had been sold by his creditors to John Jacob Astor for twenty-five thousand dollars to cover a portion of his debts, seemed not to worry Aaron.

Dolly listened in shocked dismay. Didn't he realize he was ruined politically, an outcast? His law practice was gone; no clients would trust themselves to be defended by an indicted murderer. His friends, all but a faithful few, had deserted him. His fortune—

But no. Others might think Aaron Burr finished, disgraced. Not Mr. Burr himself. He might be poor, homeless, and without occupation, but already his restless ambition was busy with plans for the future. He was popular in the West, where few had liked Alexander Hamilton. There he would find political rehabilitation.

"I think I'll go out and have a look at this Louisiana Territory the nation has acquired." His hazel eyes flashed. "Perhaps I can make some money out there—"

To pay off his creditors? Burr had already forgotten them. He needed money for a daring scheme, he said, an expedition into Mexico. He had talked with close friends about leading an invasion into that rich Spanish possession, if America went to war with Spain, as now seemed likely.

He kissed's Dolly's hand. "Well, good-bye, my dear. I'll give Theo your love when I see her."

Without a word of thanks for the help she had given him, Aaron Burr went out of Dolly Madison's life again. And she remained to face the consequences of her loyalty to him in a

Washington seething with gossip.

John Randolph of Roanoke, tall and cadaverous, and already half insane—a Virginian, but not one to bother with southern chivalry—saw his chance to hurt James Madison through his wife. Now, as Jefferson's second term began that March of 1805, Randolph turned his caustic oratory on Mrs. Dolly Madison.

She had been friendly with "murderer Burr" and his daughter—far too friendly—Mr. Randolph declared. She had compelled Jefferson and Madison to accept Burr again, after his disgrace. Mrs. Madison's dinner parties became "scandalous orgies" at which she meddled in politics.

"Dolly Madison is a female politician," Randolph charged.

A female politician. When this trust was repeated to her, Dolly wept. In those days the term was a disgrace. A woman might exert her influence in politics indirectly through her husband. But a woman of "polite breeding" would resent any hint that she meddled in public affairs, or even took an intelligent interest in them.

"A female politician," said *The Female Friend*, a little book of etiquette published in 1809, "is only less disgusting than a female infidel—"

Then there was Mrs. Madison's intimacy with Mrs. Jerome Bonaparte, the American sister-in-law of Napoleon, who was terrifying the world by conquering one country after another. Madame Bonaparte had been Betsey Patterson, a Baltimore beauty, who was, so Colonel Burr wrote to Theo, "by some thought too free."

But Mr. Burr did not mind that. He said he could put all Madame Bonaparte's clothes in his pocket. In spite of which Dolly Madison had sponsored her everywhere that Christmas of 1803, when Jerome Bonaparte brought his lovely bride to Washington on their honeymoon—as John Randolph reminded those who might have forgotten.

Aaron Burr was a friend of the nineteen-year-old Jerome and his Betsey, a tiny, pert girl with laughing hazel eyes. It had been Burr, according to John Randolph, who had asked Dolly Madison to persuade the Secretary of State to write to Napoleon and plead for the young couple. Dolly had also arranged through her husband to have the American Minister, Robert Livingston, see Napoleon in their behalf.

The Emperor was furious at the marriage his brother had contracted in a foreign country, without asking his advice. When Madame Bonaparte went to France, sure that her beauty would modify Napoleon, he refused to allow her to set foot in the country. Jerome left his bride, and dutifully married his brother's choice. Betsey Bonaparte returned to Baltimore with her son Jerome, whom she called "Bo." But Washington had not forgotten her history, or Dolly Madison's "meddling in state affairs." Madison's plea to Napoleon in Madame Bonaparte's behalf had not helped America's strained relations with France.

"Our female politician will have us in war yet," John Randolph went around saying.

This criticism hurt Dolly. She liked everyone; she wanted everyone to like her. But, as she remained loyal to Aaron Burr, so, too, she continued to be friendly with Madame Bonaparte and tried to help her.

Further gossip about "the female politician" reached Dolly's ears and added to her depression. At the same time, a long-neglected injury to her knee threatened to develop into permanent lameness. She spent the Fourth of July of 1805 at President Jefferson's Palace, "sitting quite still, and amusing myself with the mob." When no Washington doctors seemed to help her, James insisted that she go to Philadelphia, and consult the famous Doctor Physick.

Escorting his wife to Philadelphia, James turned her over to Philip Syng Physick, on Fourth Street near Spruce. Dr. Physick put Mrs. Madison's knee in splints. He thought he could cure her, but it would take time and patience. Dolly bore her troubles bravely. And James, often ill himself, sat beside her bed—"my most willing nurse."

At thirty-seven, the sophisticated Mrs. Madison was a far different person from the demure young Quakeress who had lived in Philadelphia twenty years before. Yet the same surroundings brought back old associations: ". . . the time when our Society used to control me entirely, and bar me from many pleasures. Even now, I feel my ancient terror revive . . . ," she wrote to James, who had returned to Washington. Among the Quakers, she slipped into the use of *thee* and *thy* in her letters to him.

The knee is mending. The doctor on his visits talks of thee. He regards thee more than any man he knows [she wrote in October]. I am getting well as fast as I can, for I have the reward in view of then seeing my beloved. I am so shut up that I can say nothing to amuse; when I begin to drive out, I hope to become a more interesting correspondent . . . Did thee see the Bishop, or engage a place at school for Payne? Farewell, until tomorrow, my best friend; think of thy wife, who thinks and dreams of thee. . . .

Payne was thirteen; and his mother, unable to make him study, had come to the reluctant conclusion that he must be sent away to school. Madame Bonaparte had told her of a good Roman Catholic academy, run by John Carroll, Bishop of Baltimore. She had promised to look after the boy.

Often Dolly worried about Payne, a handsome lad, with much of his mother's charm, but spoiled, weak and willful. Dolly was puzzled. Had she been too lenient with Payne, as

people hinted? Too occupied with society? Certainly James
Madison treated his stepson with all the kindly forbearance of
a father. He would have used more sternness had Payne been
his own son or had his wife allowed it.

By autumn, Dr. Physick pronounced Mrs. Madison's knee
well enough for her to return to Washington. Anna and her
husband Richard arrived in Philadelphia to take Dolly home.

It was pleasant to be back in her comfortable house, to
talk intimately with James, and to get an occasional hint of
"what is going forward in the Cabinet." Would there be war
with Spain? Dolly wondered. Aaron had said, if there was,
he would lead an expedition to conquer Mexico. From
Philadelphia she had written her husband to find out the true
state of national affairs. But remembering Mr. Randolph's
slander that Mrs. Madison was a "female politician," she
wrote James with caution,

I wish thee would indulge me with some information re-
specting the war with Spain, which is so generally expected.
Thee knows I am not much of a politician, but I am extremely
anxious to hear (as far as thee thinks proper) what is going
forward in the Cabinet. On this subject, I believe thee would
not desire thy wife to be the active partisan that our neighbor
is, Mrs. L., nor will there be the slightest danger, while she
is conscious of her want of talents, and the diffidence in ex-
pressing those opinions, always imperfectly understood by
her sex.

It was pleasant, too, to have Martha Randolph, her son and
six daughters staying with President Jefferson, as Martha had
done each winter since Polly's death. Now another son named
James Madison was added to the Randolph family. And the
first White House baby was very dear to Mr. Madison's wife.

Occasionally she heard of Aaron Burr. He had purchased

the Bastrop Grant, a million acre tract on the Washita River in Louisiana, intending, so he claimed, to colonize it. But the rumor was that, in case of war with Spain, Burr would lead his colonists into Mexico to win that country for the United States, or for himself. No one was sure.

There were other, uglier rumors—that Burr had plotted with the British Minister, Anthony Merry, to separate the western states and break up the Union. Embittered by Jefferson's snubs, the British Minister listened eagerly to Burr's schemes. The latter had told Merry that Kentucky, Tennessee and the Louisiana Territory intended to secede from the United States. If they did, all that immense territory might fall to England, if they would send a squadron to the mouth of the Mississippi to frighten the Spaniards, and loan his, Burr's, expedition to Mexico half a million dollars.

"It's the blackest treason," people said. Colonel Burr's army of colonists was raised, not to liberate Mexico, but to win the border states of Kentucky, Tennessee and Louisiana from the Union. Burr wished to set up an independent nation, with himself as emperor.

In March, to everyone's amazement, Aaron Burr reappeared in Washington. Apparently England had turned him down, for, abandoning all his mad schemes, he had come to Jefferson to ask for an appointment to some government post.

When Dolly heard of Aaron's visit, she asked Madison if he would be given anything. James shook his head. Perhaps it was just as well that Dolly should know—Mr. Burr had stooped to a little blackmail.

Reminding Jefferson of his services to the Republican Party, he had demanded a job. "I'm in the position to do you a great deal of harm, if I want to," Burr threatened. "But of course I don't want to and won't, if you have anything to give me."

"The public no longer has confidence in you, Colonel Burr," President Jefferson replied coldly, "so I can do nothing for you. As to any personal harm, I fear no injury which man can do me."

Dolly hung her head for shame of Aaron Burr. When he left Washington, without coming to see her, she was relieved. He had gone west again, people said, trying to raise men, supplies and money for his colonization project . . . for his expedition to Mexico . . . for an uprising in Louisiana. Nobody knew exactly.

Often during the next year Dolly thought of Aaron. He was not a man one could forget. Then, in March 1807, something happened that rocked the country. *Aaron Burr was arrested for treason.*

He was swinging down the Mississippi Valley with a band of his colonists leading them—where? The men thought they were bound for the Bastrop Grant, after a skirmish with the Spaniards. Burr said he was going to the border and, the moment war was declared, be ready to march into Mexico.

But General James Wilkinson, commander of the American forces in the Southwest, warned Jefferson that Colonel Burr's private army was raised to separate the border states from the Union and set up a rival nation. Jefferson had Burr arrested for treason.

"A traitor! It can't be true!" cried Dolly, when the news came. She had said the same when Aaron Burr killed Alexander Hamilton, and they called Burr a murderer. Then she had wept for her old friend. Now, with a worse charge against him, her eyes were dry.

On March 27, 1807, Dolly wrote to Anna, engrossed with her young babies. After mentioning that "the President has a sick headache every day, and is obliged to retire to a dark room every morning by nine o'clock," she added one of her guarded sentences, "I suppose you have heard that Burr is retaken, and on his way to Richmond for trial. We are quiet, and have few parties. . . ."

The country went into hysterics. Colonel Burr had tried to seize New Orleans, people said. He had wanted to revolutionize the West. What could you expect of a man who had served under Benedict Arnold? Aaron Burr was already tried and condemned by Jefferson's message to Congress that said,

"Burr's guilt is beyond question. He plotted not merely an expedition against Spain, but an effort to disrupt the Union."

James Madison agreed with the President, who wanted to have Burr convicted. And Dolly could do nothing but listen, as her husband and Jefferson flayed their old friend as a traitor.

From Washington, that hot August of 1807, Mrs. Madison followed the trial of Aaron Burr at Richmond, Virginia. The town swarmed with visitors, gathered to see Jefferson's triumph over the arch-traitor jailed there. The Alstons had come up from Charleston, bringing "Gampy." Loyal, serene Theodosia mingled with the Richmond gentry, accomplishing more for her father in her own aristocratic way than all his attorneys combined.

Said the defense: Colonel Burr wanted to acquire the Mexican territory for the United States. He thought he was helping his country by conquering Mexico privately, thus sparing America the necessity of going to war for it. Burr never plotted a civil war with the government over the border states. How could he? His private army consisted of only some fifty men with a dozen rifles. Did the United States fear an uprising of fifty men?

By the end of August, the most famous criminal trial in American history drew to a close. The jury gave out the decision for which the world—and Dolly Madison—held their breath: *"Not Guilty."*

Dolly wept with relief, but secretly. If James Madison was angry, Thomas Jefferson was furious. He had publicly declared Burr to be guilty. The jury's failure to commit him for treason was a blow to the President's prestige.

Where will Aaron go now? Dolly again wondered. What will he do? But by October of 1807, she had other things to worry about. That month her mother, who had been living with Mary, suffered a stroke and died. Dolly bore her grief stoically. But the shock was too much for Mary Payne Jackson, who had long been failing in health. By winter, she, too, passed away in her husband's arms.

In April 1808, Dolly once more had news of Aaron Burr. There were still indictments pending in New York and New Jersey against him. But a "G. H. Edwards" had slipped secretly into New York, the rumor said, and was hiding in the home of an old friend of Colonel Burr. There, too, appeared a Mary Ann Edwards. In Charleston, they called her Theodosia Burr Alston.

By June, Dolly was not surprised to hear that, to avoid any further prosecution from the government, "Mr. Edwards" had fled in the *Clarissa Ann* to England. But she was not prepared for the disgrace of his exit. Burr had boarded the packet after dark and slipped away like a thief in the night.

"He wouldn't have been given a passport," Madison said dryly. Although a court had declared Aaron Burr "not guilty" of treason, public opinion would not believe him so.

❀　　❀　　❀　　❀　　❀

At the close of Jefferson's second term, the President refused to run again. Everyone asked, "Who will be the next Republican candidate?"—for that party was sure to win. The men most frequently mentioned were Madison, Monroe, and that genial old widower, George Clinton. However Jefferson frankly said that he wanted James Madison, who had worked closely with him as Secretary of State, to succeed him as president.

To hear her "little Madison" mentioned for this high honor brought great happiness to Dolly. "James would make a splendid president," she thought. "At least with me to stir him to activity."

Dolly was the more decisive, the more ruthless one. James, so quiet, so retiring, had always clung to some stronger character. First he had been Alexander Hamilton's devoted follower. Then Jefferson's. And if Madison became president, his wife thought, she would have to lead him on.

But the fight would be a bitter one. There was a powerful faction against Madison. John Randolph, bitter and eccentric, was determined to prevent the election of Madison, whom he hated. In a letter to Monroe, Randolph did not hesitate to renew his attacks on Dolly Madison.

They (the old Republicans) are determined not to have as President one who has mixed in the intrigues of the last four years at Washington. There is another consideration, which I know not how to touch. You, my dear sir, cannot be ignorant, although of all mankind you have the least cause to know it, how deeply the respectability of any character may be impaired by an unfortunate matrimonial connection. I can pursue this subject no further. It is at once too delicate and too mortifying . . .

"*An unfortunate matrimonial connection* . . ." When this letter was made public, Dolly's face flushed with shame. She knew people were linking her name with Aaron Burr's. She had been friendly with him—far too friendly. Now she must share his disgrace.

As Madison's enemies closed in on him, using his wife's friendship with Burr as an argument against his succeeding to the presidency, Dolly realized what she had done to her husband's career. She had thought only of helping Aaron. She had ignored the harm it would do James.

To have the presidency so near their grasp and then to lose it! Red-eyed and trembling, Dolly rushed into Madison's study.

"Oh, my darling, what have I done to you?" she sobbed, throwing her arms around him.

"Why, Dolly, you've always been the greatest help in the world!" He gazed into her anxious eyes, smiling a little. "Whatever is worrying you?"

"That letter of John Randolph's."

"Oh, that . . ." he laughed. "Forget it." But she saw him flush, and she knew that the attack on her had wounded him deeply.

"Oh, James—" She dropped on her knees beside him, and felt his arms close lovingly about her. "Do you think I've ruined your career?"

"I think you're the best wife a man ever had," he said quickly. Then he added with his dry smile, "But I do think you're a ninny, who lets her heart run away with her head. Now run along to bed." He pushed her gently away. "I must write an answer to Randolph's letter."

The attacks on the Secretary of State continued. One day, when it looked as though George Clinton would be chosen, Dolly threw herself on her knees.

"Dear God, please make James win," she prayed. "If You do, I promise to think only of what is good for my Madison and make him the best wife I can. I promise to spend the rest of my life making up to James for what I've done to him."

Dolly rose from her knees, her mouth set, her blue eyes

darkened in thought. A new strength rose within her. And her intensity fired James Madison to increased activities against his opponents.

Dolly, too, redoubled her efforts to promote his popularity. Lovely, gracious, and apparently confident of success, she was seen everywhere. She never failed to smile at the right people, especially Mr. Smith of Maryland and Mr. Clay of Pennsylvania, the ring-leaders of the opposition against Madison. Night after night the Secretary of State and his lady entertained at dinner, with plenty of good food and wines. Dolly wore her handsomest gowns, her most towering turbans.

Soon people were sorry for gouty old George Clinton, who lived alone in a boarding house. "Clinton has no wife to help him," they said.

Powerful political alliances for James Madison grew out of these dinner parties at "Dolly's house," as people called 244 F Street. In spite of John Randolph's attacks, in spite of the strenuous efforts of the Federalists and the desertion of many Republicans, when the electoral votes were counted in the presence of Congress one February morning in 1809, James Madison was declared president-elect. The seventy-year-old George Clinton would be vice president.

Who had put over Madison? That was no secret. Although Jefferson's outspoken preference for him had helped, Washingtonians were already calling Dolly "Lady President."

In her moment of triumph, Dolly's mind, as always, fastened on Aaron Burr. She had thought she was throwing herself away by marrying Madison; that Burr would be president. How strange life was! The race had not been won by the hare—the brilliant, versatile, unscrupulous Aaron Burr. It was the tortoise, the slow and steadfast James Madison, who was to be the fourth president of the United States.

*I*NAUGURAL DAY, MARCH 4, 1809, FOUND WASHINGTON ASTIR
with excitement. On horseback, in rigs, in coaches, men,
women and children had come from all directions to see
James Madison made president of the United States.

The Jeffersonians were happy because their leader's best
friend was to succeed him. The Federalists were glad because
Jefferson was retiring from office. The nation, as a whole, was
relieved because Madison had promised to lift Jefferson's
hated embargo against foreign shipping, which was paralyz-
ing commerce, ruining merchants and sailors alike.

At dawn, cannon at the Navy Yard awakened James and
Dolly Madison with the presidential salute. By eleven o'clock,
ten thousand people lined the streets. They cheered as Madison, escorted by a troop of cavalry, rode along Pennsylvania
Avenue from his F Street home to the Capitol.

At twelve o'clock the pale, nervous little man took the
oath of office before Chief Justice Marshall. Then Madison
turned to face the crowded chamber, and as fourth president
of the United States began his inaugural address.

From her seat of honor, Dolly surveyed her husband's
small, black-clad figure, patriotically dressed in a new suit of
100% American merino wool. He was trembling violently;
his voice was low and uncertain. From under her turban, a
magnificent affair of purple velvet topped with white ostrich
plumes, Dolly's eyes flashed assurance. James caught her
spirit and lifted his thin shoulders. His voice grew more

audible. But throughout the speech, Dolly watched her husband closely, ready to come to his rescue with the rich warmth of her own courage.

So far as the public knew, James Madison had always been a sad-eyed old man. He had made no campaign speeches. His published addresses were able compositions, but lacking in catch phrases to attract the average American.

Dolly Madison, on the other hand, had all the lure of popular appeal. Everyone agreed that Her Majesty presented a beautiful figure at her first inaugural reception. Her short-waisted Empire gown was simple cambric with a train. Yet even the foreign diplomats declared that Mrs. Madison's regal dignity would grace any court in Europe.

"You're lovely, my darling," little Madison told his wife, when after the review of troops and the drive back to 244 F Street, he was ready to escort her downstairs to greet their guests. Dolly beamed. Her mirror told her the same story. Over forty, her curls were still black, her face under the high-piled turban, unlined and fair.

Smiling benignly, Thomas Jefferson paid Mrs. Madison a similar compliment, as he mingled with the throng who crowded into 244 F Street for the reception. The retiring President had declined his successor's invitation to ride in the carriage with him to the Capitol. Instead, Jefferson mounted his horse, and accompanied only by his grandson, Thomas Jefferson Randolph, he had joined the procession that followed Madison to the Capitol.

The inaugural ball was held at Long's Hotel, where the Library of Congress now stands. The new President and First Lady drove there in the presidential coach, drawn by four horses, a Negro coachman and footman on the box. Arriving at seven o'clock, they found the ballroom filled with four hundred people. Small, frail Jim Madison, only five feet six

THE OCTAGON

Occupied by the Madisons after the burning of the President's House; and still standing at the corner of New York Avenue and 18th Street, Washington, D. C.

SEVEN BUILDINGS, PENNSYLVANIA AVENUE AND 19TH STREET

Dolly Madison's home on leaving the Octagon. In the corner house, she gave her party for Andrew Jackson

Original owned by Washington and Lee University, Lexington, Virginia

JAMES MADISON

By Chester Harding

JOHN PAYNE TODD

Miniature by Kurtz

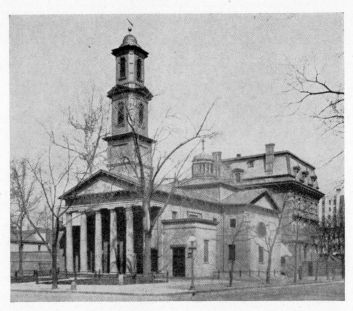

ST. JOHN'S CHURCH, WASHINGTON, D. C.

DOLLY MADISON HOUSE, WASHINGTON, D. C.

inches, and weighing but 125 pounds, was soon lost in the crowd. But his wife's plumed turban towered above everyone.

Of all the women who promenaded through Long's Hotel that evening, no one was lovelier than Queen Dolly. Every account of the affair, be it diary, letter or newspaper, described her costume. Mrs. Madison's clinging low-cut gown of buff-colored velvet with short puffed sleeves, decidedly figure-revealing, caused some feminine whispers. But all eyes were fixed on her velvet turban topped with two birds-of-paradise plumes, for it had run the British blockade from Paris straight to her charming head.

As Aaron Burr was forgotten, the criticism of Dolly Madison faded. Still, anyone so pretty should act with extra decorum, thought Mrs. Robert Smith, who was jealous of Mrs. Madison and the pre-eminence given her sister, Mrs. Cutts. The Washington ladies were pleased when they saw Her Majesty refuse to dance, even at her own inaugural ball, when Captain Tingey came to hand her a dancing card.

"What am I to do with it?" Dolly asked. "I don't dance."

"Give it to Mrs. Cutts," replied the Captain.

Gay, frivolous Anna took the card gladly. Unlike her sister, she had no prejudice against dancing. On the arm of her good-looking Richard, Anna went to join the dancers swaying to the strains of the fiddlers imported all the way from New York, a seven-day journey by stagecoach.

"Why can't I bring myself to dance?" Dolly often wondered. Only once since that childhood minuet with Patrick Henry had she been tempted. To dance with Aaron Burr— Now everything in her strict Quaker training told her that she never would dance; yet she loved to see others enjoying themselves.

With gracious dignity, Her Majesty sat and watched the

sets. When Payne, seventeen now, dark and handsome, danced by, his mother nodded proudly. Nearing manhood, the boy absorbed her interest. Payne was a son to adore, to show off to friends. Later he would marry one of the pretty girls with whom he danced tonight. Looking with happy anticipation into the future, Dolly's mind wandered over the list of belles.

The ballroom grew so crowded that one could scarcely elbow his way across. People stood on chairs to overlook the sea of heads. The windows stuck; the panes were broken to let in air. As the throng pressed around the First Lady to catch a word, a gracious look, she was almost crushed. Yet her famous smile never faded for a moment.

Mrs. Samuel Harrison Smith, wife of the founder of a Washington newspaper, the *National Intelligencer*, standing beside the President, pitied his pallid exhaustion. "I wish I had a seat to offer you," she said.

He sighed wearily. "I wish so, too."

That night the gentle, fifty-eight-year-old Madison realized fully what a burden he had assumed. It seemed to him that the ball would never end. And he was not to escape until he had sat through a long banquet.

"I'd rather be home in bed," he whispered to Mrs. Smith.

When supper was announced, Queen Dolly led the way with General Turreau de Garambonville, the French Minister, to the center of the huge, crescent-shaped table. The British Minister, the Honorable David Montague Erskine, who had taken in Anna Cutts, was seated on Mrs. Madison's left. After which, according to Mrs. Smith, the President's wife was "equally gracious to both French and English"— a most auspicious beginning for the new regime.

From the head of the banquet table, Dolly looked across the flowers at Madison. How could he look so pale, so ex-

hausted? After this long, full day, Dolly still blazed with
energy. She had presided at state dinners before for Jefferson.
But this was different. . . .

Queen Dolly was on her own at last.

❀   ❀   ❀   ❀   ❀

Thomas Jefferson was now free to return to his beloved
Monticello. And on March 11, 1809, the James Madisons
moved into the Castle, as that era called the President's home.

Jefferson had planted a lawn and encircled the mansion
with a fence. But the house was still a barren-looking place,
standing stiffly erect, without shrubs or trees about it. The
rooms were unfinished and poorly furnished. However, it
did not take energetic Dolly Madison long to give them a
touch of home.

Congress had voted the modest sum of five thousand dollars
for the Castle's refurnishing in a more elegant style. This
appropriation, Dolly had the pleasure of spending. She wisely
called in to help her Benjamin H. Latrobe, the architect of
the Capitol.

Soon there were handsome mirrors on the walls of the
Oval Parlor, as the Blue Room was called. There were new
furnishings, yellow satin upholstery on the sofas and chairs,
that matched the valanced damask curtains. Mrs. Madison
bought pier tables and card tables; a gold and crystal center-
piece for the state dining table. She spent three thousand
dollars on the great East Room, and further enlivened the
mansion with a piano for four hundred and fifty-eight dollars, a guitar for twenty-eight dollars (the latter, for Payne).
But of course the house had no running water, no sewerage
system. Such luxuries were unheard of in 1809.

In all, Dolly spent eleven thousand dollars—there was a

terrible outcry at her extravagance. And the Castle was still bare. In spite of the yellow satin upholstery and the great mirrors, its wide halls echoed to every passing footstep.

But Queen Dolly, who had never been in sympathy with "Jeffersonian simplicity," introduced a graceful, if expensive, pomp into the President's surroundings. When the First Lady took the air it was in a chariot, drawn by four matched horses, and built by Fielding of Philadelphia at a cost of one thousand five hundred dollars. The custom of elaborate receptions on New Year's Day and the Fourth of July was revived.

For the Madisons' first levee, in May 1809, a thousand candles lighted the Castle. Remembering Martha Washington's stiff functions, Dolly made her own gay and informal. The Marine Band in their scarlet uniforms played sprightly music. The ladies no longer sat and waited for the gentlemen to come to them. They strolled about—possibly because Queen Dolly's receptions were so popular there was no place to sit down.

Mrs. Madison saw that everyone in official society got to the Castle at least once a season for a sumptuous dinner. Today's cost of one of these meals would be fantastic. But in those days a turkey sold for seventy-five cents; a pig was three dollars; potatoes, forty cents a bushel. And extra waiters could always be hired; thirty-five cents for an evening's work was considered generous pay.

At a state dinner Dolly Madison surprised her guests with a new dessert, ice cream. Her recipe:

One quart of milk, eight eggs. Beat the white and yolk separately. Prepare four cups of sugar; three pints of rich, sweet cream; one teaspoonful of vanilla. Heat the milk almost to boiling. Beat the yolks and add the sugar, stir well. Pour hot milk in gradually. Beat the whites of the eggs and add them. Boil in a pail set within one of hot water.

Stir the mixture until it is thick as custard. Pour into a bowl and set aside to cool. Beat in the cream and flavoring. Have ready a quantity of ice no larger than a pigeon's egg. Pack the ice around the freezer, first a layer of ice, then one of salt, until the freezer is filled. Beat the custard and pour into the freezer. Replace the lid and pack ice and salt on it. Cover it all with a blanket, and leave for an hour. Then beat the custard again until it is a smooth, half congealed paste.

Cover, and leave to freeze for another three hours or longer. Take container out of freezer. Wrap a towel, wrung out of boiling water, around the container and turn out a solid column of ice cream, firm, close-grained and as smooth as velvet to the tongue.

In contrast to her husband, who slept badly, going to bed late and getting up frequently during the night to read and write, Dolly was a sound sleeper and an early riser. Before the day began for most people, she had planned her menus. Invaluable to her was the Negro butler she had inherited from Jefferson, Jean Pierre Sioussat, whom she called French John. Helpful, too, were her two sisters, Lucy and Anna, both of whom lived in Washington—Mrs. Cutts, during the sessions of Congress; and Lucy Washington, now a widow, who had come with her three sons to live with the Madisons.

Washington Irving, writing to his friend Brevoort in 1809, gives a picture of the famous sisters at one of Queen Dolly's functions, "Mrs. Madison is a fine, buxom dame, who has a smile and a pleasant word for everybody. Her sisters, Mrs. Cutts and Mrs. Washington, are like the two Merry Wives of Windsor. But as to Jemmy Madison—ah, poor Jemmy! He is a withered little applejohn."

At Dolly's gay gatherings, her pale, wizened husband was hardly noticed. Visitors wrote long descriptions of the First Lady, and only a perfunctory sentence about the President.

A modest man, who liked to see his wife the center of interest, Madison was content to remain quietly in the background.

With serious-minded callers who asked him questions about political history, he talked well. But casual acquaintances, who expected words of wisdom from the Father of the Constitution, were disappointed. President Madison worked incessantly. He only relaxed at dinner with close friends, when he liked to reminisce about the days of the Revolution, and set his guests laughing over his broad stories and whimsical ways of telling them.

In these dark times little Jim Madison was not in a joking mood. With a weak Cabinet (for political reasons he had been forced to make an enemy, Robert Smith, his Secretary of State), this gentle, peace-loving scholar found himself the leader of the American nation with France and England at war. Never was a man less fitted than Madison to hold the helm in troubled times.

One of our great law givers, James Madison was a student of the principles of government; but he had no gift for carrying them out. For the first time he was in an office that required executive force. And he had no knack for making decisions.

Fortunately for James, he had his blooming Dolly. When he was tired from matters of state, a visit to his wife's sitting room, where he was sure of an amusing story and hearty laugh, was as refreshing as a walk in the sunshine.

She had made a promise that if her Madison were elected president, she would do all in her power to make his administration a success. As secretary and as president, Dolly was a tremendous help to him. She was not intellectually brilliant, not a wit; but wit often hurts. And she had tact, charity, and common sense. She was frank and hearty, and always accessible. People liked her, she was good fun.

A born hostess, Dolly was never bored. Martha Washington who never cared for her duties as the President's wife, Abigail Adams who bravely endured her position, were very different from Dolly Madison who enjoyed to the utmost being First Lady.

She knew how to talk; she could listen, too. No one could heckle her into a quarrel. If there was an argument, she left the room for a few minutes, then returned and pleasantly resumed the conversation. "I would rather fight with my hands than with my tongue," she once said.

A tall, poised lady in rose satin trimmed with ermine, ostrich-feathered turban, and amethyst earrings, it seemed as though Mrs. Madison had always lived in this fashionable world. Her meager education was balanced by her remarkable adaptability, tolerance and sympathy. Her enthusiasm was that of a girl of twenty, rather than a woman over forty.

No one at the Madisons' crowded levees required a second introduction. Dolly's memory for names, her knack of getting along with people (a trait James never learned), her Irish sense of humor and robust health, made light the strenuous duties of First Lady. During all Dolly Madison's years of public life, she never lost that warmhearted simplicity that was her greatest charm.

When the young House leader from Kentucky, Henry Clay, first called on President Madison, he was so taken with the cheery smile of the maid who opened the door that he kissed her and gave her a tip.

James appeared in the hall. The "maid," who was Dolly, showed him the coin.

Clay laughed. "Had I known you were Mrs. Madison, the coin would have been larger."

Friends turned with a smile when they felt the familiar tap of Dolly's snuff box on their shoulders, as she passed among them at her crowded parties. Not always sure of herself, she was eager to please and put everyone at their ease—even the awkward youngster who in his excitement at meeting the First Lady did not know what to do with his teacup and crammed it into his pocket. She was as gracious to two country women on a Washington sight-seeing trip, who burst in on her unannounced one morning at breakfast and asked to kiss her "just to tell the home folk about," as to a foreign minister.

President Madison, being the Great White Father, must entertain delegations of Indians at the Castle. One night after a banquet for some Osage chiefs, Dolly sat at her dressing table, unclasping her pearls. Suddenly, to her dismay, she saw in a mirror the reflection of an Indian, who had hidden behind a screen. Apparently unconcerned, she walked quietly over and pulled a bell cord to summon a servant. Fortunately he came at once and persuaded the intruder to leave.

Dolly was forty-four in 1812, but she looked younger. Her rosy cheeks were the talk of Washington. Did she rouge? the ladies wondered. It was considered shocking in those days.

Mrs. Madison had played loo and other card games for money, but gave it up on becoming the First Lady, fearing that her example might be harmful. She had little leisure or inclination to read and educate herself. But she liked to enter her parlor with a copy of *Don Quixote* in her hand "to supply a bit of talk."

Her fingers were always stained, for she took snuff constantly from platina boxes, making no bones about pushing it up her nose in public. She used large cotton handkerchiefs. "This is for rough work," she told Henry Clay, after a hearty blow. Her little lace one was merely her "polisher."

Payne Todd was Dolly's one real worry. The twenty-year-old boy had inherited all his mother's zest for living, but he was unable to balance it with her more sensible qualities. For some time Payne had been at school in Baltimore, under the care of Madame Jerome Bonaparte; a strange guardian for a weak, impressionable boy.

Payne is in the Baltimore set, and as much admired as you could wish [his mother proudly wrote Anna Cutts on May 12, 1812]. He writes that he is invited out all the time. We intend to send him in a few months to Princeton. . . .

Dolly's head was full of schemes for her son's future. Ardently she longed to have him go to Princeton, where James Madison had made such a brilliant record. But Payne had no wish for a college education. He was good at languages, especially French, but otherwise he was not a student. In Washington he spent his time riding horseback with friends and playing the genial host. The money his stepfather gave him slipped through his fingers.

To keep her son amused, Dolly filled the Castle with young people. It was Dolly and Payne who began that unique ceremony connected with the White House, the egg-rolling held on the Monday after Easter.

Payne told his mother that the children in ancient Egypt used to roll hard-boiled eggs painted in bright colors against the base of the Pyramids. With her own hands Dolly dyed some hundred eggs, and invited the children of Washington to come and play with them. They came in droves. They have been coming ever since.

As the famous Queen Dolly, Mrs. Madison never forgot her old friends. She saw a great deal of Eliza Collins, now Mrs. Richard Bland Lee, married to the judge of the Orphans' Court, and living in Washington on the corner of 6th and M Streets. John Todd's groomsman, the widowed Anthony Morris, with his daughters Phoebe and Rebecca, often came from Philadelphia to be guests of the Madisons. And Phoebe wrote home about occupying a "dear little room with an alcove bed which adjoins Mrs. Washington's."

Many were the appointments Dolly Madison engineered. Washington Irving, seeking the position of secretary to Joel Barlow, Minister to France, thought that Dolly's friendship was all he needed. He wrote to his brother that he had hopes of getting the post "as Mrs. Madison is a sworn friend of mine, and indeed all the ladies of the household and myself are great cronies."

All who wished favors from President Madison felt safe if his wife would intercede for them. So it was not surprising that Dolly received a humble appeal from Theodosia Burr Alston,

. . . you may be surprised at receiving a letter from one with whom you have had so little intercourse in the past years. But your surprise will cease when you recall that my father, once your friend, is now in exile. . . .

Theodosia told how Aaron Burr was living in Paris, without money, moving from one wretched lodging to another, still poorer. She begged Mrs. Madison to get a passport from the President for her father, and a guarantee that he could come back to America without fear of arrest. "You've only to speak to your husband," the letter pleaded, "so my father can return to me. . . ."

Tears rushed to Dolly's eyes. Her kind heart ached with pity for Aaron, but it was pity merely. Love had died long ago. She remembered the criticism she had endured over her loyalty to him in the past. Then she put the thought aside as selfish. No one in trouble ever appealed to Dolly Madison in vain.

Hurrying into the President's study, she handed him

Theo's letter. He read it, his face stern.

"I won't give that traitor a passport," he said angrily. "The only passport he'll get is one demanding his arrest on reaching the United States."

"But, James, if you—"

He seemed stunned. "What do you wish me to do, Dolly? Ask that Burr be pardoned? Risk my own reputation for a scoundrel like that. Am I not unpopular enough as it is?"

Dolly hung her head. She knew that if she insisted, James would give Aaron Burr a passport, regardless of what it did to him politically. But did she really want him to? Which of the men in her life did she want to help? Which to harm? Madison or Burr?

James had turned away and was busy again with the mound of work on his desk. He looked worried, old and sick.

Impulsively, Dolly put her arms around him. "I'm sorry I bothered you, my darling, when you're so busy," she said, and kissed him lightly on the top of his wig.

He patted her hand. "Promise me you won't answer that letter of Mrs. Alston's, Dolly. It would hurt me."

She hesitated only an instant. "I promise, James," she said. Her poor Madison needed her more than Aaron Burr, who was beyond her help now.

Slowly she turned and dropped Theodosia's letter into the wastepaper basket beside the desk.

❀　　❀　　❀　　❀　　❀

The naming of Joel Barlow, the poet, as envoy to Napoleon, was one of the appointments that Dolly Madison sponsored. The Barlows were close friends of hers. During their residence abroad, Joel and his wife kept up a brisk correspondence with Mrs. Madison.

In those days when Napoleon's conquests were shaking Europe, and England and America were on the verge of war, their letters were chiefly about "cloaths." Mrs. Madison wrote to Mrs. Barlow in Paris asking her to send over by "some safe vessel" several headdresses, some flowers, feathers, gloves and silk stockings, both black and white, and "anything else pretty, suitable for an economist."

Thin, heelless slippers of soft kid or satin, laced on with crossed ribbons, were among Dolly's extravagances. She also liked long, wrinkled gloves of sheer silk and huge Oriental turbans. Sometimes these turbans matched her gowns. Sometimes they were of spangled muslin; sometimes of velour. Trimmed with pearls or ostrich feathers, they were bulky affairs that hid Mrs. Madison's hair and forehead. Only a cluster of dark curls showed at each side of her face. Perhaps they did cost a thousand dollars a year, as people said. But they took the place of the crown that many of Queen Dolly's court felt she had the right to wear.

When Mrs. Madison wrote to Mrs. Barlow in the spring of 1812, she mentioned that "Vice President Clinton cannot live until morning," and there were rumors that Napoleon had seized the *Hornet.* Then she got down to the real subject of her letter—the flowers, trimmings, and ornaments that ran the English blockade had arrived safely. She thanked Mr. Lee, American Consul in Bordeaux, for the trouble he took in sending her such "enchanting" things,

. . . the bill was immediately paid, but you will be astonished at the amount of duty—two thousand dollars. I fear I shall never have money enough to send again. The heads (turbans) I could not get on, being a little tight, so I shall lay them aside until next winter, when I can have them enlarged to fit. . . .

Part of this Parisian finery was for the wedding trousseau of Lucy Washington, who was married in March 1812 to Supreme Court Justice Thomas Todd of Kentucky, a widower with five children. He was much older than Lucy, whom a host of younger men were courting. And she turned down Judge Todd's first proposal. Then, changing her mind, Lucy sent a letter by horseback messenger after her elderly suitor, returning dejectedly to Kentucky. It overtook him at Lancaster, Pennsylvania. He lost no time in getting back to Washington.

There were gay doings at Lucy's wedding, the first held in the White House. Phoebe Morris was one of the bridesmaids. Payne Todd and Dolly's cousin Edward Coles, Madison's secretary, were the Judge's groomsmen. Dolly was glad that Lucy, who must live in Kentucky, would at least be in Washington for two months each year while her husband sat with the Supreme Court.

But through the light-hearted chatter at Lucy's wedding rang an ominous note. For over a year, the dread of another war with England had haunted every day. Now as Great Britain and France, at war with one another, continued to seize and search our ships, and impress our sailors into their service, to prevent neutral America from trading with the enemy, war seemed a certainty.

The Twelfth Congress, filled with fiery "war hawks," and speakered by Henry Clay, clamored for a fight—because of the old enmity with England rather than with France, although both nations were seizing our ships to halt American trade with the other. And some hot-heads, such as Clay, wanted war with both countries.

Instead President Madison, unable to keep his campaign promise to have no more embargoes, retaliated with another in April, 1812, which he thought preferable to war. No goods could be exported from any American port; no ships could sail to any foreign country. Again our boats lay idle, the tar barrels on their mastheads to protect the wood from rotting derisively called Madison's Nightcaps. For these unpopular embargoes were harder on the Americans than upon the English and French. Hundreds of our sailors were thrown out of work.

For years Madison had struggled to carry on Jefferson's peace policy and avoid war with England, because he knew that America was not prepared to go to war with the greatest naval power in the world. But the "war hawks" in Congress had decided to fight England. To do so successfully, they needed a more aggressive warrior as president. The timid Madison's term was nearly over. The nominee of the Democrats, as the old Republican party was now called, was sure to win. Aspirants for the Democratic nomination were James Monroe and DeWitt Clinton, Mayor of New York, both eager for war.

"The world seems to be running mad, what with one thing and another," Dolly wrote Anna in a moment of panic. If James Madison was not given another term, they would have to go back to Montpellier. At forty-four, she would again be relegated to plantation life.

Seated in the Oval Parlor, the scene of so many brilliant parties, tears filled her eyes. She couldn't leave her yellow brocade furniture, her handsome mirrors. She wouldn't. Madison must have another term. His wife set to work to see that he did.

Every night now the Castle was ablaze for dinners and receptions. The President's fine port and madeira flowed. His table was piled high with pheasants, Virginia ham, ice cream and rich desserts. After dinner, in the Oval Parlor, guests drank tea (not coffee) and listened to music from the piano, which caused such a sensation when it was listed as one of Dolly's extravagances.

When Madison dined his Cabinet, Dolly entertained the men's wives at "dove parties." These affairs were a great help to James Madison, but Dolly indignantly denied that she entertained for any ulterior motive.

"I know nothing about politics," she liked to say. "I only love my friends and want them with me."

People smiled at that. Dolly Madison was a born politician—far more so than the shy, scholarly President, who lacked Jefferson's genial nature to attract a large following of political supporters.

As though she did not know there was a coolness between their husbands and hers, Dolly remained on intimate terms with Mrs. Henry Clay and Mrs. John C. Calhoun, wife of the chairman of the powerful House Foreign Affairs Committee. Pretending illness, she asked Mrs. Gallatin to represent her at receptions, after Madison had quarreled with Albert Gallatin, Secretary of the Treasury. She made a close friend of Mrs. William Seaton, when her husband became editor of that influential newspaper, the National Intelligencer.

Finally only one obstacle blocked James Madison's path to re-election. But it was a serious one.

Those "war hawks," Henry Clay and John C. Calhoun of South Carolina—two men in their thirties—came one night to call on the President. They found him in the Oval Parlor with his wife.

"Mr. President, we want war with England," young Clay burst out. "Things can't go on as they are now. Our ships are being raided, their crews and cargoes interned by the British. Our commerce is ruined. There's no hope of a change, until we face the mess out with that bully, England."

Madison held up his hand, as though warding off a blow.

"You know how I've dreaded the thought of war."

"Yes, you've held back, Mr. President." Calhoun shook his shaggy head. "But war with Great Britain is inevitable, whether you want it or not. If war must come, then it must; and our country should arm and prepare to defend itself." He paused. "Mr. President—"

"Yes?"

"We've come to ask you to run for another term—that is, if you'll give us a declaration of war."

Dolly's eyes sought her husband's. James Madison, a pacifist, could not say the words that would give him a second term. He hated war. All his life he had tried to form those principles of government that would make war impossible.

Madison lifted his tired eyes and looked at his tense, hopeful wife. He knew what his dear Dolly wanted. So he said it—and for no other reason.

"I've hoped until now, gentlemen, that there might be some other possible settlement, but war. That an embargo would remedy matters. But if you think there's no other alternative than a declaration of war . . ." and James sighed deeply, "you shall have it."

Dolly rushed over to throw her arms around her husband. Pride and joy shone in her eyes. Mr. Clay and Mr. Calhoun sprang forward to grasp the President's hand.

So the nomination was given to James Madison to succeed himself. On June 1, 1812, he sent the desired message to Congress, urging an immediate declaration of war. On the 18th of the month, war was declared. There was a howl of indignation from Madison's enemies, who claimed the nomination was the price of a change of policy.

And so it was. But Dolly Madison was assured of another four years as First Lady.

THROUGH THE ECHOING HALLS OF THE CASTLE, A GENTLE
little man paced to and fro. Preparations were being frantically made for the defense of the country. Again America
was at war with powerful England. From the depths of his
sensitive soul, James Madison deplored the suffering and
bloodshed that lay ahead.

Dolly walked beside him, her arm in his, her voice firm
and comforting. "Don't grieve so, James," she repeated. "You
did everything possible to keep the nation out of war. Your
embargoes postponed it for years, without loss of prestige
for America. It wasn't your fault that your efforts failed."

"You think so, Dolly?" Madison asked anxiously. "You
think the country believes I avoided war as long as I could?"

The War of 1812 was a less popular conflict than the
Revolution. Because the people felt they had been dragged
into it by the President, it was called contemptuously "Mr.
Madison's War." (There were those, like Henry Clay, who
knew it had better be called "Mrs. Madison's War.")

Throughout the nation, there was some natural indignation
against England. But most Americans thought the war a
stupid mistake. Nor did they feel any confidence in President
Madison; in Richard Cutts, whom Madison had made superintendent of military supplies; or in their old Revolutionary
War generals, Dearborn and Armstrong.

Smarting under years of defeat, the Federalists, now the
anti-war party, called the quarrel with England "unwise,

187

unnecessary, and ill-timed." President Madison should have
stood firm, they said, and not allowed the "war hawks" in
Congress to drag him into the conflict against his will.

Yet on June 18, 1812, America was in for a three years'
struggle, the fierceness of which was to be felt from Canada
to New Orleans.

A few days before war was declared, Aaron Burr slipped
through the British blockade into Boston. So homesick for
Theodosia was he, that Aaron had taken the only passport
the American Embassy in Paris would give him, one that
demanded his arrest on his return home. Disguised in false
whiskers and a wig, and using the name of Peter Arnot, Burr
had landed with but ten dollars in his pocket.

In the eight years since his duel with Hamilton, much of the
bitterness against Aaron Burr had been forgotten. Indeed,
many felt that he had been too harshly judged. Loyal friends
persuaded the New York officials to let Burr stay. His creditors promised they would not arrest him for his debts, if he
remained within the city limits. He opened a small office at
9 Nassau Street, and at fifty-six started a new law practice.

New York had other things to think about than persecuting
Aaron Burr. With frantic efforts, America, totally unpre-
pared, was trying to arm itself against England. The griev-
ances against Colonel Burr faded before more pressing con-
cerns.

A war with Great Britain must be a naval war. And because
of Jefferson's peace policy, the United States had no navy
of any consequence.

Yet during the first months of the war, there were sea
victories. The strongest naval force America could raise, a
squadron of four ships, the *President*, the *Congress*, the
Hornet and *Argus*, put out to sea in search of British cruisers.
When good news came, the nation went wild with joy.

Captain Stewart gave a dinner on board the *Constellation*, lying in the Potomac off Washington. There was dancing under a red, white, and blue awning. And Payne Todd distinguished himself as the most untiring of all the dancers. On the quarter-deck sat his handsome mother, growing plump now, but more vivacious than ever, surrounded by an admiring court of dashing young naval officers.

There were victory balls. In December, 1812, the capture of the *Alert* and the thrilling duel between America's *Constitution* and the British frigate *Guerrière* were celebrated by a dance at Tomlinson's Hotel in Washington. The ballroom was hung with flags, among them those of the conquered *Alert* and *Guerrière*, trophies of our two naval victories.

As the dancers whirled to the strains of soft music, young Lieutenant Hamilton, son of the Secretary of War, strode unexpectedly into the ballroom. Proudly he crossed the polished dance floor, for he was the bearer of a special sign of triumph from Captain Stephen Decatur.

Straight to the radiant Queen Dolly, Hamilton went. Kneeling before her, he presented her with the flag of the British *Macedonian*, newly captured by the gallant captain.

Wild enthusiasm broke out. The room rang with cheers for Stephen Decatur. The flag of the *Macedonian* was just the banner wanted to complete the group of naval trophies on the wall. As the band played *Yankee Doodle*, Dolly Madison stood clasping the conquered flag to her heart. Excitement brought color flaming to her cheeks.

The ladies looked knowingly at each other. They shook their turbaned heads. One question that had troubled Washington, at least, was settled. Mrs. Madison's rosy color "came and went." So it must be natural.

In spite of naval victories, the bitter newspaper attacks against President Madison continued. They belittled American successes and exaggerated the defeats. With General Hull's disgraceful surrender of Detroit without defense in August, 1812, the Federalist press berated, not only Hull's cowardice, but the incompetence of "feebles" like Madison, Eustis and Dearborn.

James Madison had known all along that America was not prepared for war. He had warned those urging him to fight that disaster would follow. But even so—when all that he had prophesied came true, and America's land forces met defeat after defeat—everyone blamed the President.

America was no better prepared to fight in 1812, when Madison suddenly urged war on England, than it had been the five years before. Everyone knew that his desire for a second term had led James Madison to consent to war. It had not helped his reputation. Nor could the people forgive the fact that, with war on his hands, the President knew neither how to lead the fight, nor how to choose men who did. They resented Madison's appointments of Dolly's relatives— the spendthrift Cutts to be superintendent of military affairs; Meigs, a Todd cousin, as Postmaster General.

Perhaps it had not been possible to keep America out of war, when the world was bristling with bayonets, cried the *Federalist Republican* editorially. But what was to be thought of an administration that, when war came, still did not prepare? "After eighteen months of fighting," the editorial asked, "why has not a single ship been launched?"

Dolly Madison flung down the newspaper, hurt tears in her eyes. "Oh, how they hate us!" she raged.

"You'd best not read the papers, my dear." James' voice was even weaker, more discouraged than usual. "They're full of attacks on me. It's not pleasant reading."

But Dolly could not leave the newspapers alone. Not since she had read of the mysterious disappearance at sea of poor Theodosia Burr Alston.

On December 30, 1812, shortly after Aaron Burr's return to New York, his daughter Theodosia, who in June had lost her little boy of the fever, sailed from Charleston to see her father. Mrs. Alston had come north without her husband. He was Governor of South Carolina, and forbidden by law to leave the state.

Theodosia took passage on the privateer *Patriot*, refitting at Charleston. Her armament hidden under deck, the spoils of her raids concealed beneath a cargo of rice, the schooner was bent on making a quick dash for New York.

Early in January, the *Patriot* was known to have met the British fleet off Cape Hatteras. Her captain presented Governor Alston's letter, asking of the Admiral safe passage for his lady. This was courteously granted. That night a terrible storm arose; the *Patriot* was never heard from again.

For months the newspapers speculated as to what had happened. Had the ship been lost in the storm? Captured by the British? Or had she been overhauled by those notorious pirates, Dominique You and the Babe? (Naturally, the departure of so richly-laden a ship was known along that piratical coast.) Rumors came of a wreck, of a crew that had mutinied, plundered and burned the ship, forcing the passengers to walk the plank. . . .

Eagerly Dolly Madison scanned the newspapers for word that Theodosia had been found. She read how Colonel Burr, months later, still walked pathetically along the Battery at New York, waiting for the *Patriot*, or for some rescuing ship.

Dolly also read the bitter attacks against her own husband. Nobody wanted James Madison for president again. But thanks partly to his wife's popularity—and chiefly to the deal

Madison had made with the war party in Congress—he was to have another term. Elbridge Gerry of Massachusetts would be vice president.

The last four years had been hard on President Madison. At his second inaugural in March, 1813, he looked even thinner and paler than when he had first assumed the presidency. He read his speech in such a low, mumbling voice, that no one could hear a word.

After the Capitol ceremonies, "everyone who could pay twenty-five cents for hack hire" hustled to the Castle. The crowd was so great, the babble of voices so loud, it drowned out the music of the Marine Band. People surged through the stately rooms. After offering their congratulations to His Highness, they devoured quantities of ice cream, cake, bonbons and madeira, and departed, leaving the President exhausted by the incessant bowing.

But the First Lady was as handsome, tactful and energetic as ever. She wore a gown of rose satin, trimmed with ermine. Her turban, fastened by a diamond crescent from which towered a white ostrich plume, marked her wherever she walked through the crowd. Her favorite earrings, the letter M carved in amethysts and hung on gold chains, swung gaily as she chatted with friends.

Only a close observer could have noticed how forced was Her Majesty's smile. The criticism of James cut deeply. Dolly, who loved everyone, wanted everyone to love her and her "little Madison."

She could not have smiled at all had she known what lay ahead. That in spite of her courageous efforts, President Madison would grow increasingly unpopular, as disaster followed the armies. That after the battle of Bladensburg, a well-known Federalist lady would drive up to the Castle, rise in her carriage, and, loosening her long hair, pray that she might be allowed to sacrifice it as a halter to hang "Jemmy Madison."

⚜   ⚜   ⚜   ⚜   ⚜

With England busy fighting Napoleon, the war was not going badly. The British had blockaded America's coast. Our larger ships were bottled up in the harbors of Boston, New London and New York. But privateers dodged in and out among the blockading fleet, harassing the enemy.

To everyone's surprise and delight, these "hawks of war" captured five hundred English merchantmen and three frigates. At every victory there were bonfires, the joyous tolling of bells.

"We're going to beat the British—I told you so!" Dolly cried. Kissing her husband, she went off gaily to a "fringe party" at Anna's, where nimble fingers would make white cotton fringe to decorate the epaulets of the workers' husbands, brothers and friends.

As soon as Dolly left him alone, Madison returned to his worries. Probably no man could have made the unpopular War of 1812 a success. But James Madison, unfitted to make a good war president, either by training or temperament, did not even know how to try to make it so.

The nation needed competent military leaders, he knew. Secretary of War Armstrong was too old; the extravagant Richard Cutts, not the person to handle military supplies . . . James sighed, and picked up a copy of the *Spectator*. He had never been interested in military affairs. Without personal enthusiasm for fighting, how could he inspire the nation with an ardent zeal for war?

Often James thought of quiet Montpellier. How wonderful it would be to retire there, through with all this war business!

To be a private citizen, free to write and read and be happy! When he was with Dolly, he was a different man; feverishly alive, as she was. But it was not the quiet Madison's nature. The strain kept him exhausted and ill.

Realizing how her husband changed when she left him, Dolly was frightened. "I must stay at his side, always pushing him ahead to make the best of himself," she thought. "Otherwise this war will never be won."

Ironic it was that Dolly had to bolster James at this time when she needed someone to help her. She was bitterly lonely. Her darling Payne was far away, across the dangerous Atlantic Ocean.

As the war dragged on a year, the British indicated that they might be willing to talk peace. A commission was chosen to go to Ghent, in Belgium, to try to negotiate a treaty.

When Dolly heard of the commission, she had been inspired with an idea. Increasingly, Payne became more self-willed. He refused to go to Princeton; a great disappointment to his mother and stepfather. He was fond of gambling. He drank too much. If only Payne could get away from Washington for a while, his mother thought, he would come home greatly improved. So, much as Dolly hated to part with him, she had persuaded Madison to send his stepson abroad with the peace commission. She knew that two of its members, Henry Clay and Albert Gallatin, would look after the impulsive Payne.

That summer of 1814, while the commissioners discussed the peace treaty at Ghent, young Todd traveled about Europe. As the careless, self-indulgent youth neglected to write home, his mother was forced to ask about him from others. Mrs. Albert Gallatin relieved Mrs. Madison's worry by sending her any news of Payne in the letters she received from her husband. She wrote to Dolly on July 2, 1814,

... Mr. Gallatin says Payne left St. Petersburg before them and took the Sweden route; found the coast frozen, and came by way of Copenhagen, and joined them at Amsterdam the day before they left. He has gone on to Paris, and is to return in three weeks. He will have a very pleasant jaunt, no doubt. I wish you to get the information as soon as possible, for I know you must be anxious. . . .

Payne Todd traveled from capital to capital, sometimes with other Americans, sometimes alone, but always with his aristocratic manner which commanded recognition. He was the stepson of the president of the United States. In Europe they called him the Prince of America, and treated him as royalty.

Meanwhile the war increased in intensity. The British, who had been fighting both the French and the Americans, defeated Napoleon at Waterloo. Now they were able to turn their full forces against the United States.

❦   ❦   ❦   ❦   ❦

Early in the war Madison wrote to Jefferson, "We do not apprehend invasion by land." Within a year from his confident remark, the whole coast was blockaded, from Long Island Sound to the mouth of the Mississippi. And Albert Gallatin, who was in London, worriedly informed the President that the British fleet was to be strengthened for the purpose of sailing into Chesapeake Bay and attacking the city of Washington.

Still Madison did nothing to protect the national capital. Instead, he sent off more troops to join the fighting along the Canadian border.

In August 1814, two months after Gallatin's warning, twenty-one British ships, under Admiral Sir George Cock-

burn, appeared in Chesapeake Bay. With 3,500 veterans freed from service on Napoleon's battlefields, General Robert Ross came to join them.

The people of Washington were frightened. For the first time they realized that they had only 500 regular troops, some untrained militia, and a few gunboats on the Potomac to protect them.

But Secretary of War Armstrong was reassuring. "The Potomac is so full of shoals that no fleet could sail up the river," he explained. "Fort Washington's guns further guard the city. The fort is impregnable."

To everyone's surprise, the English landed at Benedict, forty miles from Washington. Instead of stopping them, the American gunboats were blown up by order of Secretary Armstrong, lest the enemy capture them. Their commander, Joshus Barney, and his sailors fled to General Winder's camp at the Navy Yard, to join the untrained volunteers hurriedly gathering to defend the capital.

On Sunday, August 21, 1814, a messenger galloped to Washington to warn that the enemy had landed. They were marching overland to attack Washington from its unprotected rear, a strategy that no one had foreseen. The town was in a panic.

As president of the United States, Madison was commander in chief of the nation's armed forces. On Monday afternoon, August 22, he left on horseback for General Winder's camp to inspect the militia, volunteers and sailors, lined up to try to stop the British.

Wearing his little round hat with the big cockade, James bade his wife a nervous good-bye. "I don't know that I should leave you, my dear," he said in his uncertain manner. "Have you the courage to stay here without me, if I don't come back until tomorrow?"

"I've enough courage for anything," replied Dolly. Poor Madison, she thought tenderly, he should be the woman, I the man.

In a firm voice, Dolly assured James that the British would never reach Washington. But her husband insisted on leaving a colonel and a hundred men, as a bodyguard for her in his absence.

"If anything happens, look out for the state papers," he said, and kissed his wife good-bye.

As the President rode away with his Cabinet, Dolly smiled and waved. So confident was she of victory that it never occurred to her that harm might befall her husband.

But others, panic-stricken, realized the danger. The road before the executive mansion was jammed with people. They had flung their belongings into wagons, carts and wheel barrows, and, afoot or in carriages, were heading over Rock Creek into Georgetown or toward the Long Bridge that led across the Potomac to Virginia.

George Washington's commission as commander of the Revolutionary Army had already been sent off to safety. But at once Dolly set to work collecting the rest of the official documents belonging to the government. Then there was the boxing of the most valuable of the furnishings purchased by Congress. With such thoroughness did she attend to details, that silver, books, the velvet curtains, and even a small clock, were hidden from the invading soldiers. She did not bother with her personal property. Her handsome gowns and imported turbans were left in the cupboards.

Superintending the servants as they nailed boxes the next morning, Mrs. Madison stopped frequently to strain her ears for the sound of her husband's return. If only James would come! There *was* danger, her pounding heart told her. She sensed it in the ominous quiet that had fallen over the city.

By Tuesday there remained in Washington but a handful of women and children; every able-bodied musket-bearer was at the front. The excited talking of passers-by in the street, the noise of crowded coaches, the galloping horses, the rattle of heavily-loaded carts, the squeaking of heaped-up wagons—all had quieted down.

So unexpected was the enemy's march on Washington, that a dinner for the Cabinet had been planned at the President's for that Tuesday evening. But now, with the enemy advancing through the woods toward the capital, the Cabinet was with President Madison at General Winder's camp, making such haphazard precautions for the city's defense as occurred to them at this late hour.

On the British came by the Bladensburg road, which no one thought to obstruct by felling trees or burning bridges, straight to Washington. So instead of dining at Dolly's, the President and his Secretaries went galloping across country with the motley throng, which made up the American forces, to Bladensburg, where it was hoped the enemy could be stopped.

At Bladensburg, in Maryland, only four miles from Washington, the two armies clashed on Wednesday, August 24th. The Americans, mostly raw militia and untrained volunteers, numbered about 6,000. While the English had 4,000 veterans of Wellington's armies.

By afternoon, straggling lines of disorganized American troops began to stream into Washington through the deserted streets. Worriedly scanning the horizon with a spyglass, Dolly saw no sign of her returning husband. Oh, why didn't he come! Off in the distance she had heard the roar of cannon. Had there been a battle? Each hour added to her mental anguish.

The heat was stifling; but she did not dare take a drink

of water. French John had warned Mrs. Madison the spring might be poisoned. At three o'clock, a servant, Paul Jenning, laid the table for her dinner. Dolly could not eat. The food remained untouched on the table.

An hour later, Daniel Carroll, who had been at Bladensburg with President Madison, galloped up to the door with a scribbled penciled note from him,

Enemy stronger than we heard at first. They may reach the city and destroy it. Be ready to leave at a moment's warning.

Dolly plied Carroll with feverish questions. "Is my husband safe? Has there been a battle?"

"Yes, the President is safe," he answered. "There was a battle at Bladensburg. The base British fired flaming rockets at us." He flushed. "Our men turned and ran. . . ."

Dolly hid her face in her hands. What a disgraceful picture—the American forces running away before the enemy!

President Madison had run, too. But Mr. Carroll did not tell Mrs. Madison that. At the first sign of danger, he had turned to his Secretaries and said, "Come, Armstrong, come, Monroe, let's leave this to the generals." And, with the President in the lead, the gentlemen had ridden off the battlefield.

With the American forces routed, the road to Washington was wide open. Bladensburg was only four miles away. No one knew how soon the enemy could cover that short distance; or how soon the British guns would be turned on the capital.

"You must leave immediately," Carroll warned Dolly Madison.

At that moment James Smith, a groom who had gone with the President, dashed up with a second penciled note from him,

"Our troops are retreating. You had better make all preparations to leave at once and join me in Virginia."

When Dolly turned back into the house, she found herself alone except for a few servants. The colonel and his men, ordered by James to guard her, had fled, leaving the First Lady to look out for herself.

She had started upstairs to put on her bonnet, when she remembered the silver and state papers. They must be sent off, and not a wagon could be found.

"Bring me as many boxes as my carriage will hold," Mrs. Madison told French John. Then she set to work cramming the most important of the documents into smaller packing cases, while the servants gathered around her, their faces worried.

"You must hurry!" Daniel Carroll tugged at Mrs. Madison's arm to get her started. "Please, come. Please . . ." But she shook her head and worked on.

Dolly objected again when French John wanted to spike a cannon at the gate and lay a train of powder that would blow up the English, if they entered the house.

At five o'clock two dusty American officers galloped by.

"Get away quick, or the house'll be burned over your head," they stopped to warn Mrs. Madison. "The enemy are already in the suburbs."

In all the confusion, only Dolly kept her head. Calmly she went again to put on her bonnet and cloak. Then coming downstairs tying her bonnet strings, she allowed Mr. Carroll to send for her carriage. "But I'd rather stay, put a cannon in every window, and shoot it out with the British," she told him.

Perhaps Dolly might have—she had the courage—but Daniel Carroll persuaded her that Admiral Cockburn meant to carry

out his boast to capture the Madisons and take them prisoners
to London.

Mrs. Madison was ready to step into her carriage, piled
with boxes of silver and public documents, when she remembered something. To everyone's horror, she dashed back
into the house.

"Not yet—the portrait of President Washington—it mustn't
fall into the enemy's hands!" she cried.

Gilbert Stuart's full-length portrait of George Washington—a copy of the original one painted for the Marquis of
Landsdowne—was screwed to the wall in the state dining
room. In that frantic hurry, no tools could be found to
remove it.

"Get an axe and break the frame," Dolly Madison ordered.

She watched French John and Magraw, the gardener,
climb ladders, smash the frame and wrench the canvas from
the stretcher. Just then Jacob Barker and Robert DePeyster
drove by. The precious canvas was sent off to safety across
the Potomac in their wagon piled with silver urns and other
valuables.

One more delay. A framed copy of the original Declaration of Independence in the national archives was kept in a
glass case. Deaf to the pleas of her servants to go at once
or her road to escape would be blocked by the enemy, Dolly
ran to break the glass and gather up the valuable document.

"Good-bye, John." She turned to her butler. "Remember
before you leave lock all the doors. Take the key and my
macaw over to the Russian Minister."

Passing through the dining room, Mrs. Madison snatched
some silver spoons from the table and crowded them into her
reticule. Then she ran out and jumped into her open carriage.
With Sukey, her Negro maid, she was driven by Joseph Bolin,
the coachman, off to Georgetown.

Richard and Anna Cutts, their children and servants, had already fled the city, gone Dolly "hardly knew where." But the Federalist papers who laughed at President Madison's flight from the battlefield were equally amused by his wife's hasty departure. The flight of Mahomet, the flight of John Gilpin, and Madison's flight from Bladensburg, all occurred on the 24th of August, they pointed out. In a parody of John Gilpin called "The Bladensburg Races," published in New York, they quoted Dolly as saying to James:

> "Sister Cutts and Cutts and I
> And Cutts' children three
> Will fill the coach, and you must ride
> On horseback after we."

None too soon did Dolly Madison escape. As she left Washington on a road choked with terrified people, the enemy entered the city by another. Her horses galloped to Georgetown and safety, while flames shot up behind her as the British set fire to Washington. After sundown, a red glow lighted the sky over the city.

Queen Dolly spent the first night in a refugee camp, in a tent. Sleep was impossible. She passed the long, miserable hours gazing at the flaming American ships in the Navy Yard, burned by order of Secretary of the Navy Jones to prevent them from being captured by the enemy.

On the next day, Thursday, Dolly crossed the Potomac by the Chain Bridge into Virginia. Following back roads, she hid that night with a Mrs. Richard Love, whose husband was off with the troops. Mrs. Love loaded a musket, and ordered her slaves to bar the doors. But before dawn, fearing the British would capture her, Mrs. Madison hurried on.

On Friday, after two days of terrific heat, a storm broke. Rain fell in such torrents that Dolly was compelled to stop at a tavern crowded with refugees.

Exhausted, wet to the skin, she had no more than reached her room than the tavern mistress discovered her identity.

"I won't have that hussy here," she cried angrily. Mounting the stairs, she screamed, "If that's you, Mrs. Madison, come down and get out. Your husband has mine out fighting; you shan't stay in my house."

Gathering her wet cloak about her, the shivering First Lady fled out into the drenching rain again. Climbing into her carriage with the weeping Sukey, she drove on.

At a Mrs. Minor's house, a few miles down the road, Dolly found refuge. And there on Friday night the President himself turned up with several Cabinet members. So pale and exhausted was he that his wife begged him to lie down and rest. But he had hardly done so before a messenger drove up to the house warning, "The English know where you are, President Madison. Escape while you can."

Dolly insisted that James hide alone in a hut in the woods, where he would be safe. She promised to abandon her carriage, disguise herself with a heavy veil, and hide elsewhere. No one must know that she was Dolly Madison, the wife of the man held responsible for this disaster. The feeling against the President, who had left Washington unprotected, was so bitter that his wife feared the wrath of her own people as much as being captured by the enemy.

In the gray dawn, the Madisons separated. Attended only by one soldier and the nephew of a friend, Judge Duvall, Dolly went off in the storm to hide in the woods while her husband went off in another direction.

On Saturday, word came to them that British had evacuated Washington and gone back to their ships. So the next morning Dolly Madison emerged from the wet woods and hailed a passing farm wagon. She drove in this uncomfortable vehicle the twenty miles to the shore of the Potomac, only to find that the Long Bridge over the river had been burned.

"Will you take me across?" she asked a Colonel Fenwick, who was transporting munitions over the river in the only boat left on the Virginia side.

"No," he answered, "we don't let strange women into the city. How do I know you're not a spy, sent by the British to burn what they left?"

"But I'm Mrs. Madison, the wife of your president." She threw back her thick veil and revealed herself. Then he gladly ferried the First Lady across the Potomac.

A pall of smoke and the smell of burning still hung over the city of Washington. Through debris-filled streets, Dolly Madison made her way to the home of her sister, Anna Cutts. There she waited for James to come to her.

Late Wednesday afternoon, Dolly learned, only a few hours after she had fled Washington, Ross and Cockburn, the British commanders, had entered the city at the head of their troops. After burning the Capitol building, the enemy covered the mile stretch to the other end of Pennsylvania Avenue and broke into the "Yankee Palace."

They were disappointed to find the Madisons had escaped. Also, that retreating Americans had raided the President's cellar and helped themselves to two thousand dollars worth of wines. There was nothing left for the thirsty Redcoats. But they ate the food that Paul Jennings had set out for Mrs. Madison's dinner.

Admiral Cockburn, "who had the manners of a common sailor," made merry over the absent president whom he called "Jemmy."

"Oh, how I'd like to have captured Jemmy and the Mrs.," he mourned. "I'd have taken them back to England, and exhibited them all over the country."

Instead, as a souvenir, the Admiral had to content himself by picking up a seat cushion used by Dolly Madison. He added a joking allusion to her anatomy "too indelicate to repeat."

Ransacking the Castle from cellar to attic, the invaders looked for valuables to carry off. Disappointed at finding very little, they set to work to strip the kitchens, and to destroy everything in sight. General Ross, himself, dragged Mrs. Madison's cherished yellow satin furniture into the center of her Oval Parlor, and stacked it in a heap for a bonfire. Then everything in the mansion—rugs, draperies, bedding, Dolly's imported clothes and turbans—as well as the President's fine library of books, was piled up and set on fire.

After which the soldiers burned the building. As the flames licked up the walls, they fed them by hurling fiery balls of cotton from their bayonets through the windows. Soon the whole house was ablaze.

Seated nearby at the tavern, Ross and Cockburn relished their supper, eaten in the light of the burning "Yankee Palace." They blew out the candles on their table, that they might better enjoy the glow.

Next day the British marched along Pennsylvania Avenue carrying long poles. On the end of the sticks were balls of flaming cotton as big as dinner plates. At each government building the soldiers halted, smashed the upper windows and flung in the burning cotton. Soon the whole structure was afire. In this way the War Office, the Treasury Building, the State and Navy Departments, and the office of the *National Intelligencer*, the editor of which had been bitterly anti-English, were burned to the ground.

Then Ross and Cockburn grew nervous. They could not believe that any government would leave its national capital open to invasion. They decided that the easy conquest of

Washington might be a trick to get the enemy forces inland, then cut off their retreat. Afraid that the Americans were gathering in Virginia or Maryland for such a purpose—or, as legend has it, frightened off by the storm—on Thursday night, after only twenty-four hours of occupation, the British hurried back to their ships.

The American forces, which might have captured the invaders, did not appear, because they did not exist. Not until three days after the enemy had left Washington, did the government return to the Federal City.

On James' return, Dolly drove around with him to see the destruction—the Capitol and Treasury buildings that the English had burned to the ground; the President's house, a heap of smoking ruins. Nothing was left of the Castle but four blackened walls.

Standing beside her husband, Dolly sadly surveyed the mounds of debris that had been her magnificent home. The rooms which she had furnished so lavishly, where she had entertained at such brilliant functions, had been gutted by fire. The ceilings were cracked, the charred and crumbling walls stained by heat and flames; the plaster streaked by Thursday's deluge of rain.

"There's no use in rebuilding Washington, it's too far destroyed," Madison sighed. "I told Monroe we'd best move the government to Philadelphia. The city wants us back."

Leave the site chosen by George Washington for the national capital! Dolly was shocked. "No, James, the government must stay here," she answered, firmly. "We must remain in Washington and rebuild."

Because of Dolly Madison's courage, the government set to work at the task of creating a second Washington. The rubble was shoveled into carts. Carpenters and masons flocked

in. The Capitol was repaired; and within three years a new
executive mansion rose within the blackened walls of the
old.

❦   ❦   ❦   ❦   ❦

Of the many houses offered to the homeless Madisons,
Dolly chose to live temporarily in Colonel John Tayloe's
Octagon House, which the French Minister vacated in their
favor.

It was there, on the night of September 13, 1814, that a
man of about thirty appeared at the door.

"I'm Francis Scott Key. Please may I see the President?" he
begged of Mrs. Madison. "It's important. My friend, Doctor
Beane, has been arrested by the British. He is a prisoner on
Admiral Cockburn's ship, lying off Baltimore. If the Presi-
dent will only give me permission to go there and ask the
Admiral for his release—"

"I'll see that he does!" promised Dolly in her warm,
friendly manner. And she took the worried young man up
to her husband's study.

So Francis Scott Key went to Baltimore, and secured his
friend's freedom. Both men were obliged, however, to remain
on the Admiral's ship overnight, as the British were attacking
Fort McHenry. Through the bombardment, young Key
strained his eyes to see what effect it would have on the fort.
When morning came he was so happy to see that the American flag still waved, Key sat down on the deck of the enemy
ship and wrote the words to "The Star-Spangled Banner,"
which became, in time, the American national anthem.

In the Octagon House the depressed, nerve-shattered
President tried to regain his health and confidence. From all
sides, he was greeted by ugly mutterings. No one could for-

give the fact that Madison and his brother-in-law, Cutts, had left the nation's capital unprotected; that the British had been allowed to land, march forty miles inland, rout an American force nearly twice their number and burn the city—then to escape without a shot being fired at them!

But while the storm raged around her husband, Dolly Madison found herself the most popular person in America. No one had behaved better in the crisis; she had been the best soldier on the American side. Everyone talked of Mrs. Madison's bravery and resourcefulness in saving so much of value from the President's house. Had her husband shown such coolness and good judgment, the disgraceful burning of Washington might never have taken place.

DOLLY MADISON'S DRAWING ROOM AT OCTAGON HOUSE WAS thronged with guests on the evening of February 14, 1815. When a servant announced yet another visitor, the hospitable hostess hurried into the hall to greet him. It was Henry Carroll, a secretary of the American envoys at Ghent. Home from Belgium on the sloop of war, *Favorite*, Carroll bore an important message for President Madison.

"You'll find him upstairs," said Dolly, her eyes anxiously searching Carroll's face.

Without pausing for a reply, the secretary ran up the stairs to the President's office, his diplomatic pouch clutched in his hands.

What tidings it contained no one in America knew. There were no radios or cablegrams to flash the news across the ocean that a peace treaty had been signed. Only now, seven weeks after the signing at Ghent, on Christmas Eve of 1814, would Washington learn that the war was over, although Henry Carroll who brought the document had traveled as fast as he could. In the meantime, fifteen days after the war officially ended, a fierce and unnecessary battle had been fought at New Orleans on January 8th.

"Let's pray this means peace," Dolly murmured to her friends, when she rejoined them. Tensely they waited.

A moment later, Madison's voice, strained with excitement, was heard calling, "Dolly, it's peace! Peace!"

"Oh, thank God! Peace again!" she turned, jubilant, to

her guests. Then, eager for all the household to know the glad tidings, Mrs. Madison rushed out through the hall to call down the basement stairs, "Peace! The President says, it's peace!"

In the servants' quarters French John rang a dinner bell and shouted, "Peace!" Sally Coles, a young cousin of Dolly's who was visiting her, raced out to the slave quarters and shouted, "Peace! Peace!" The Negroes took up the cry.

"Peace! Peace!" The word was on everyone's lips. After nearly three years of war, America and England were to be friends once again.

The news spread like wild-fire. All over Washington, joyful bells rang it from the church steeples. The cannon boomed it from the fort. Candles blazed it out into the night from the windows of mansion and cottage.

In circular room on the second floor of the Octagon House, which served as President Madison's office, James carefully signed the document known to history as the Treaty of Ghent. The war was officially ended.

Then the President and his Cabinet descended the spiral stairs to Queen Dolly's drawing room, which by eight o'clock was crowded with excited diplomats and members of Congress.

Everyone was tired of the war. Federalists and Democrats, their differences forgotton, threw their arms around one another, and united in their thankfulness that the struggle was over. Through the crowd of well-wishers swept the radiant Dolly Madison, then at the height of her regal beauty.

Even the undemonstrative President Madison had lost his sad, solemn look and was smiling. Of all men, he had the most reason to rejoice; the peace treaty rescued him from his blunders. Federalist New England had threatened to secede because of the Madison rule of the last three years. A convention had actually met in Hartford to demand that the President resign and to discuss separation. Peace had come just in time to save Madison's administration and the Union. He was a happy man.

☚ ☚ ☚ ☚ ☚

On February 18th, the Senate ratified the Treaty of Ghent. Peace was publicly proclaimed. A war which had cost America 1,683 ships and the lives of 30,000 men was over. Amid the universal rejoicing, no one stopped to ask whether the terms of the treaty were good or bad.

Past troubles and grief were forgotten. The dock yards rang again with the sound of saw and hammer. President Madison's mistakes as a war president were forgiven; and Dolly Madison reigned as the undisputed queen of the nation. The soldiers, marching home from their long enlistment, stopped to cheer before the Octagon House, where a smiling First Lady waved to them.

During the grim days of the war, young America had found a new strength. And with this feeling of confidence began an era of prosperity, reflected in the social life of Washington. The winter following the treaty of peace—the celebrated Peace Winter of 1815—was a festive season. And the resumption of Dolly Madison's parties was hailed as a sign of a return to normal life.

The First Lady's celebrated smile was never brighter than when she received at the Octagon House. For one thing, Payne was home again. His fond and forgiving mother was completely happy.

In those days when no telegram gave warning, no train arrived according to a time table, young Todd's return was unannounced. One night a tall, dark stranger, whose manly voice spoke with a foreign accent, entered the Octagon House. Mrs. Madison hurried out to clasp him in her arms. After two long years, she had her son again.

Payne's stepfather, the kindly Madison, and his cousin Sally, joined in the welcome. In the parlor, the family sat down to listen to Payne's adventures. While from the hall, French John, Paul Jennings, Sukey and the other servants peeked in to catch a glimpse of the young master.

To the provincial town of Washington, with its 8,000 inhabitants, Payne Todd brought the sophistication of the royal courts of Europe. "The Prince of America"—how young Todd had relished that title! Dolly listened, in rapture, while he told how in Russia such distinguished members of the peace commission as Henry Clay and John Quincy Adams, disbarred because they were not royalty, watched him from the plebian gallery as he danced with the Princesses.

Mrs. Madison was proud to have her aristocratic-looking son back to decorate her drawing room. Payne balanced a graceful teacup. He spoke French with a fluency that fascinated young Sally Coles.

But when the excitement of his homecoming wore off, even Payne's doting mother had to admit that he had changed, but not for the better. More than ever he was the spoiled continental rake, who preferred speaking French to English. This irked Dolly, who knew no foreign languages.

At twenty-three, Payne Todd showed no desire to take up a profession. In Edward Coles' absence, he tried being Madison's secretary. But he was so lazy and indifferent that his stepfather could not rely on him. So the young man returned with enthusiasm to his old life of gambling, drinking and idleness.

Once more Dolly's plans for her son had gone astray.

Young Todd had received more harm than good from his European wanderings. The charm and good looks inherited from his mother were already marred by dissipation. His spendthrift habits foretold for her a long series of anxieties.

Yet even this family trial failed to sour Dolly Madison's sweet disposition. The same serenity and humor that had made her spoil her son, made her suffer less over the consequences. Realistic Dolly knew as well as anyone else that her only child was no credit to her. To forget her disappointment, she threw herself into the gay whirl of society.

All of 1815, she entertained in her inimitable fashion in the temporary quarters of the "Executive Annex." There were dinners, concerts, and a weekly reception during the session of Congress. People came and shook hands "chatting, tea, compliments, ices, a little music (some scandal) and to bed." At the Washington Theater was enacted "Mrs. Madison's Minuets and Allemands," showing her popularity as First Lady.

James endured this life amiably, if not with joy. In contrast to his wife's gay clothes and gayer spirits, Madison looked doubly sober. He never had more than one suit at a time, and that always black. After gentlemen discarded wigs, he continued to wear one on his bald head. Like most of the older men, he clung to the old-fashioned breeches and long stockings.

But once, to everyone's surprise, James appeared in pantaloons, introduced by the radicals of Paris during the French Revolution, and now popular with younger men. Madison was the first president of the United States to wear long trousers.

Dolly's temporary home, the Executive Annex, was better known as the Octagon House because of its peculiar shape. (Actually it has six sides, not eight, and was built to fit the lot.)

This unique Georgian residence of imported brick, still standing at the corner of New York Avenue and 18th Street, was the town house of Colonel John Tayloe of Mount Airy, Virginia. It was built in 1798, by William Thornton, Madison's friend, whose design for the Capitol had just been approved.

Today the Octagon House is hemmed in by buildings. But when Dolly Madison lived there, it stood in bare, open country, surrounded by Lombardy poplars, and had an extensive view of the Potomac.

Friends calling on the Madisons entered the pillared portico that opened into a circular hall, and then into rooms with bay windows and curved walls. On the right of the front door was the dining room; opposite, the drawing room with its crystal chandeliers, Empire sofas and chairs, where Mrs. Madison entertained with the help of Mrs. James Monroe and Mrs. Stephen Decatur. Before the carved mantel, made to order in London, she stood to receive her guests—the gowned Chief Justices, the foreign diplomats gorgeous in court costumes, the naval heroes of the late war, Decatur, Hull, Stewart, and Bainbridge, in high-collared blue uniforms with yards of gold lace and blazing epaulets.

When they came to consult with the President, the Cabinet passed through the round vestibule and up the spiral staircase, which wound past a Palladian window to a circular room on the second floor that Madison used as an office. The walls, hung with maps and engineer's drawings, looked down on the grave-faced meetings of the President and his Cabinet.

The Octagon House was the finest private residence in

Washington, and one of the safest. Colonel Tayloe had thoughtfully prepared an escape from the house in case a mob ran amock in Washington, as one had in Paris during the French Revolution. A sliding panel in the dining room opened onto a secret staircase, that led down to two underground passages. One went to the President's house, so he, too, could escape. The other extended to the Potomac, where a boat was kept hidden.

To make the Octagon doubly romantic, it was said to be haunted—perhaps why the French Minister had vacated the house so willingly to the Madisons! Death had struck there so often that few people liked to live in it. Shortly after the house was built, the Tayloe's son, Charles, died mysteriously. Then his two lovely sisters met tragic deaths on the spiral staircase.

The elder girl became infatuated with an Englishman, to whom her father objected. One night, during a thunderstorm, there was a quarrel. The unfortunate miss ran up the stairs in tears, a candle in her hand. Suddenly her father saw her dive over the banister to her death.

Again Colonel Tayloe disapproved when the younger sister fell in love. The young man was after her money, he claimed. There was another quarrel, this time, at the head of the staircase. As the girl stood before her father, pleading for her sweetheart, he gave her an angry push. She tripped and fell backward down the steps.

On the anniversary of her death the ghost of the poor girl, so it was said, could be heard falling down the stairs. On stormy nights, the apparition of her elder sister wandered through the house, a lighted candle in her hand.

🏵   🏵   🏵   🏵   🏵

One morning Dolly Madison passed under the haunted staircase and out into the garden behind the house. Clad in a blue silk gown and straw bonnet, a watering can in her hand, she walked along the path that led to the slave quarters.

She was bent over, sprinkling her flowers, when a man leaped over the low box hedge that enclosed the garden. Dolly straightened up quickly. It was Aaron Burr.

"Aaron! How you surprised me!" she gasped. Why had he come like this, instead of to the front door?

Colonel Burr, who had once been so suave, so debonair, stood before her, a slight, tense man, decidedly older, in a shabby blue coat. But, at fifty-nine, he was still agile enough to leap over a hedge.

"I had to see you, Dolly," he began humbly—a new tone for Aaron Burr. His hazel eyes lost their piercing look, and became gentle. "I want to ask you about Payne. How is the boy? I often think of him, and wish I could see him."

What subject closer to Dolly's heart could the wily Burr have selected? Touched, Mrs. Madison remembered how Payne, as a child in Philadelphia, had loved the gay Senator from New York who used to jounce him on his knee.

"You'll be glad to know, I've a good law practice in New York again," Aaron rattled on. "My office is filled with an endless stream of clients."

This was more like her old friend! Aaron Burr was boasting of his successes, as he used to boast to Theodosia. But Dolly sensed the terrible loneliness in him, now that he no longer had his daughter's companionship.

"I'm also teaching school . . ." Burr was the actor once more, playing one of his favorite roles, the patron of grateful protégés. "My students are the children of my landlady and two little girls, my wards. A friend died and left me guardian of his children. How I wish my grandson, Gampy, had lived!

Have you forgotten him?"

Dolly knew how Aaron had always loved children. Before the misery in his eyes, she looked away. "No, I haven't forgotten," she replied.

"You haven't forgotten?" His face lighted with satisfaction. "Oh, Dolly, you and Theo were the only people who ever believed in me! I had to see you and tell you about my child. Do you know that she is—dead. The ship bringing her from Charleston to see me was lost in a storm off Cape Hatteras—"

Sobs choked him. Now Dolly knew why Aaron had come. It was not to talk about his grandson, or even to boast of his success. It was because Dolly Madison had been his daughter's friend. She was one of the few people to whom Theodosia's father could show the grief locked in his heart.

"Yes, I know about Theo," Dolly sighed. "Oh, Aaron, my heart aches for you!"

The fate of the privateer *Patriot* still remained one of the mysteries of the sea. It was no longer believed that the ship had been sunk by the British fleet, because she was carrying contraband. Something dreadful was said to have happened on the Carolina beaches, near Cape Hatteras, where lurked the dreaded "wreckers," savage descendants of pirates, who lay in wait for ships to plunder.

Recently, one of the "wreckers" had confessed that on the stormy night when the *Patriot* disappeared, a schooner had come ashore. She was boarded by his men, he said, who found her abandoned. A lady's clothing had been scattered about a cabin.

Dolly hoped that Theodosia's father had not heard another rumor, that the ship had not been abandoned when the wreckers came aboard. . . .

"The *Patriot* went down in the storm," Aaron insisted.

"Let me believe that," he added passionately. "I cannot bear to think of my child in the hands of cruel, murderous pirates."

Dolly's hand went out to him. Burr clung to it—he, who had once been so self-sufficient.

"The world is a blank to me," he cried in despair. "I no longer want to live."

"Poor Aaron," she whispered, consolingly.

Dolly's love for her son, Aaron's love for his daughter, had been a great bond between them. Now having talked of their children, suddenly there was nothing more to say.

Mrs. Madison withdrew her hand. Glancing nervously at the Palladian window on the spiral staircase, she saw a figure behind the pane. She knew who it was.

"I must go, Aaron," Dolly said, picking up her watering can. "It has been nice seeing you again. Good-bye and good luck."

Colonel Burr recoiled, as though she had struck him. Their eyes met; his, once more bland and impassive.

"I understand, Dolly," his scornful smile seemed to say. "You can't ask me in; you don't want to, anymore. All right, my dear, I'll go before your fine husband, or one of your grand friends, sees me and I disgrace you."

Mrs. Madison flushed. Again she saw that slight, wizened figure at the window. "I'm sorry, Aaron, but I really must go . . ." The words died in her throat. She turned and fled back into the house.

❦   ❦   ❦   ❦   ❦

The "haunted" Octagon grew too ghost-ridden, even for Dolly Madison, who had endured it longer than a more imaginative person would have done. She could not help being affected by the many whispered tales of curious rappings on the walls. Of unseen hands that lifted pictures, leaving wire and nail intact, that opened doors and rang bells. On stormy nights there were strange creakings and thuds on the spiral staircase.

"James," Dolly said firmly, "I can't stand this house any more. We're going to move."

And move the Madisons did, in October, 1815—this time to the corner brick house of a row at 19th Street, on the north side of Pennsylvania Avenue, which, like the Octagon House, may still be seen in Washington today. Here, a little further out of town, they remained until the end of Madison's second term, in March, 1817.

It was a less pretentious house than the Octagon, but in it Dolly's gay life went on. She had no fine furniture; most of it was secondhand. On the floor, instead of Oriental rugs, were plain baize carpets. But Dolly Madison did not need the setting of a sumptuous mansion to remain the leader of Washington society. One brilliant affair after another took place in her small second-floor drawing room, with its fringed red silk draperies at the three front windows, its simple carpets, and couches upholstered in "gray patch."

Notable among these functions was the Madisons' dinner for General Andrew Jackson, the hero of the battle of New Orleans, which climaxed a round of balls and theater performances in his honor.

Everyone wanted to meet the famous warrior. That autumn night of 1815 when President and Mrs. Madison entertained for him, eager people surged up the mahogany staircase to their drawing room. It was lighted by oil wicks, flickering in a crystal chandelier hung from the ceiling. About the room Negro servants stood motionless, holding lighted candles.

The First Lady received under the huge chandelier. Beside

her towered the rugged, red-haired soldier, as awkward in
his stiff uniform as Queen Dolly was gorgeous in her Empire
gown of lilac satin, brocaded in silver. The bodice, cut very
low, showed her creamy shoulders.

Once a rough backwoodsman with his queue in an eel's
skin, Andy Jackson was now America's hero. It had been his
victory at New Orleans which brought back, after the burning of Washington, hope to the humiliated nation.

Old Hickory, shy with women, thought Mrs. Madison
charming. She had a way with generals. At one of her parties,
Dolly deplored the absence of General William Henry Harrison of Tippecanoe fame.

"I can't understand it," she mourned. "I commanded the
General to be here this evening. He promised he would."

"Well, Harrison can't come," her husband explained. "I've
ordered him out west to negotiate with the Indians. By now,
he must be thirty miles on his way."

"Still," mused Dolly, "I think he'll appear."

The President had just said, "We'll see, my dear, whose
orders Harrison obeys . . .", when the General strode into
the room. He well knew who was his commander in chief.

🏵   🏵   🏵   🏵   🏵

Social gaieties did not claim all of Dolly's interest that
first winter after the war. She found time to visit Congress,
meeting temporarily, while the Capitol was being rebuilt, in
a brick building on 1st Street. Congress was attracting all
the fashionable world, especially the ladies, to listen to the
debates. They came to hear William Pinckney of Maryland,
who always drew a crowded chamber.

One day Mr. Pinckney had just finished speaking when
the First Lady entered with a group of friends. Catching sight

of her, he rose and repeated his speech for her benefit, "using fewer arguments but scattering more flowers."

Dolly Madison also found time in her busy life for charity. She gathered together a group of women "at eleven A.M. in the Hall of Representatives" the notice said, for the purpose of founding the first orphan asylum in Washington.

Under the leadership of the warm-hearted First Lady and the wealthy Mrs. John Van Ness, plans were made to care for the fatherless children of the city. Mrs. Van Ness donated land for the orphanage. To collect funds, dolls were dressed and bazaars held. Mrs. Madison, the first directress of the institution, took upon herself the arduous task of cutting out hundreds of garments for the city's destitute children. There were no sewing machines in those days. Anna Cutts, Mrs. John C. Calhoun, and Dolly's other friends sewed up the clothing by hand. Mrs. Madison gave money to the orphanage as well, "twenty dollars and a cow."

Observing the welts raised by the heavy shears on Dolly's pretty hands, Eliza Lee asked if she did not find the garment cutting tiresome.

"Oh, no," she replied, "I've never enjoyed anything so much."

Mrs. Van Ness could well afford to give land, and later a building, for Dolly's orphanage. Her father had been David Burns, whose 250 acres took in most of the land on which the Federal City had been built. The old Scotchman had been forced to sell his farm. But, shrewdly, he had held out for a price which made his daughter a great heiress.

Marcia Van Ness was a friend of Dolly's, as was Mrs. John C. Calhoun, wife of the Congressman from South Carolina. But she had few intimates, outside her family. Dolly Madison had all the elements for friendship, but people had to snatch her affection in passing. She was ever the center of shifting throngs. People of all sorts crowded around her. And she had a word, a smile, for them all. "You know, I like the routs all too well," she once wrote Anna Cutts.

James was chronically bored and weary. But never Dolly. The rush of people were the breath of life to her. She wrote to Edward Coles that she had had so much company she was positively "dizzy." But she loved it. The emptiness came when she was cut off from them. Only when Dolly was ill did she grumble a little, "We've had a continual round of company, which has been burdensome."

Dolly's love of children was not limited to orphans. Boys and girls would gather outside her house to watch Mrs. Madison come to the corner bay window to feed her parrot. She always had a wave and a smile for her young admirers. If any child looked ragged and dirty, she called, "Come, sweetheart, let me tidy you up." With her great shears, she cut out a garment for the shabby urchin and gave it to a maid to stitch.

The Cutts children were like Dolly's own. Troubled with a heart ailment, Anna was unwell much of the time. Dolly nursed her sister's Mary and Dolly through measles. She made doll clothes for them, and told them fairy stories. Her parties for the Cutts children, where every child received a present, were made merry by her macaw, always brought in to amuse the young guests. When the parrot chased them to nip at their toes, the children screamed, jumped onto chairs or caught hold of "Aunt Madison." She enjoyed the frolic as much as they did.

The Washington of 1817 was a hustling town compared to the village of a few houses to which James and Dolly had come sixteen years before. There were a few sidewalks and curbings. Shops and homes faced definitely defined streets, instead of being scattered about in pathless meadows.

People were building homes in Washington because it looked, at last, as if the capital of the nation might remain on the Potomac. Congress had voted to reconstruct the government buildings; and thanks to Mrs. Madison, Eliza's husband, Richard Bland Lee, was chairman of the committee in charge. Already the burned Capitol was being rebuilt, this time to be crowned by a dome of burnished beauty.

Often Dolly went with Richard and Eliza Lee to watch the restoration of the President's house. The sad-looking ruin had been remade from the ground up by James Hoban, the original architect.

When the blackened walls were painted white to cover all traces of the fire, people began calling the mansion "The White House," instead of the Palace or Castle. It had always been a white house in a red-brick city. But the repainting job of 1817, needed to cover the marks left by an invading army, gave to the executive mansion its most popular name.

  ❀ ❀ ❀ ❀ ❀

The last two years of Madison's troubled administration were not entirely happy ones. The President's post-war popularity had subsided with the enthusiasm of the nation over the peace. When the treaty of Ghent was made public, it was found that it omitted the chief points over which the United States and England had gone to war. It gave America no increase of territory. It said nothing about impressment, nor did it refer to the rights of neutrals on the sea, the original causes of the quarrel.

"Why did the President sign such a treaty!" the nation grumbled.

The toasts of "Peace and Plenty," drunk at every dinner table in the winter of 1815, grew less frequent. Men talked gravely of taxes and tariff laws. Great Britain was again shutting American ships out of the West Indian trade. American shipyards were idle. American merchants saw ruin ahead.

Of course, it was all President Madison's fault.

Weary of his responsibilities, and deeply hurt since the New England Federalists had demanded his resignation, Madison counted the days until March, 1817, when Monroe would have his turn. He knew the presidency had been an anticlimax to his career. It had hurt, not helped, his prestige.

Queen Dolly's reign ended with a February reception that Washington would long remember. In her short-waisted Empire gown of green satin, and white velvet turban trimmed with white ostrich tips, she outshone all the women guests. Sir Charles Bagot, envoy from America's late enemy, England, said his hostess "looked every inch a queen." But another guest wrote, "Her face and neck were daubed with paint as to fairly glisten." While yet a third thought Mrs. Madison's face "like a flame." Everyone knew by now that she rouged and "pearled" (powdered).

The truth being out, Dolly was generous with her recipe for homemade lip salve:

Take a ½ lb. of hog's lard melted with wax and put in some alkanet root, scented with lemon. Pour into a small box. Apply to the lips.

Dolly's last reception was "an intolerable squeeze," as Washington society called a crowded drawing room, and, in reverse, a "thin" one. Snuff box in hand, Mrs. Madison circulated among her guests to see that everyone had a good time . . . Monsieur de Neuville, the French Minister, and his suite, all in blue velvet coats covered with fleurs-de-lis in gold embroidery . . . Commodore Stephen Decatur, the nation's darling . . . the Portuguese Minister, the witty Abbé

Correa, who spoke seven languages. . . .

But it was on James Monroe and his wife, known in Paris as *"la belle Americaine,"* that all eyes were fixed. The Monroes were to be the next President and First Lady. And Mrs. Samuel Harrison Smith, who admitted she "worshipped the rising sun," began to wonder if she did not prefer Mrs. Monroe's dignity to Mrs. Madison's genial warmth; whether Elizabeth Monroe would not restore to the President's house the stately formality of Martha Washington's day. Some thought it would be a good thing.

But it would be a long time before any First Lady would equal Dolly Madison in popularity. The best wishes of countless friends went with her that spring day of 1817, as she rode out of Washington with her husband and son.

Sad-eyed Mrs. Madison took a last look at Washington. "Oh, how I'm going to miss you!" she sighed, but softly. Without looking at her husband's face, Dolly knew how happy he was to be returning to quiet Montpellier. But how would she fill her empty days?

As for James, he felt only relief. A careworn little man, growing paunchy, his ordeal as president had aged him. He looked far older than his sixty-six years.

To conceal her sadness, Dolly began to tell a funny anecdote. But none of her chatter could get a laugh from Payne, who sat glumly beside her. He, too, did not want to exchange the gaiety of Washington for isolated Montpellier.

"Payne should marry," thought his mother, her anxious eyes on his sullen face. "What he needs is a good wife."

As the carriage bowled south over the post road, Dolly's mind was again busy with plans for her son. She would keep him contented at Montpellier by filling the house with pretty girls. There was Phoebe, Anthony Morris' daughter, whom Mrs. Madison had long thought of as a daughter-in-law.

There was Payne's distant cousin, Sally Coles . . . one reason Sally had been such a frequent visitor. And that Williamsburg belle, Ann Cole, about whom Payne talked so much. . . .

By the time the Madison coach reached the red soil of Virginia, Dolly had her boy safely married. Even a host of adorable grandchildren playing about Montpellier!

The village of Orange, eighty-four miles southwest of Washington, was reached. Then, after a five-mile climb through pine forests, the Madisons came in sight of the white, urn-topped gate posts of their own Montpellier.

The reign of glamorous Queen Dolly was over. But her memory lingered after her in Washington, never to be forgotten.

"Everyone loves Mrs. Madison," Henry Clay once said to her, and he voiced the universal sentiment.

"And Mrs. Madison loves everybody," was Dolly's quick reply.

PACKED AWAY WERE THE PLUMED TURBANS THAT DISTIN-guished Dolly Madison's Washington days, her jewels, and Empire ball gowns. A rural housewife, she resigned herself to the care of her husband and his mother. James was sixty-six; Nelly Madison, eighty-five.

But Dolly was only forty-nine. She was young and felt so. She was full of vitality. Friends said that his wife "looked like Madison's daughter." After sixteen gay Washington seasons, the quiet monotony of Virginia soon palled. "I'm so restless I could scream," she thought those first weeks at home.

James, on the other hand, had never been happier than when trudging through the red clay of the plantation he loved, among the slaves who still called him "Massa Jimmy." Since inheriting Montpellier's 2,500 acres, Madison had enlarged the house to make room for his own friends, without interfering with his mother's household. The architects of the Capitol, Thornton and Latrobe, had changed the original four-roomed house into a long, narrow mansion of simple lines. Two one-story wings, one on either side of the main building, gave the house greater space without destroying Montpellier's perfect proportions. Nearly a century later, after the estate was bought by William du Pont, these extensions would be raised to two stories.

The house was, Dolly admitted, as handsome as any in Virginia. Its architecture was as flawless as Monticello; its situation as sublime as Mount Vernon. But to think of having to remain in this quiet loveliness the rest of her life! Strolling listlessly through the new rooms, Dolly tried hard to be content.

Yet at Montpellier she was to spend the next twenty years cheerfully enough, thanks to her happy disposition. She wrote her sister Anna (and meant it),

. . . I wish, dearest, you had just such a country house as this. I truly believe it is the happiest and most true life, and would be best for you and the children.

James had solved the mother-in-law problem by giving Nelly Madison a separate establishment. A remarkable old lady, she lived in the original house on the right, waited on by slaves who had grown old in her service.

On the left lived James and Dolly. A long hall, connecting the two wings, led into their dining room hung with portraits. Opening off it was Madison's bedroom. His high poster bed, canopied in crimson damask, had been brought by Monroe from the dismantled Tuileries.

Another door led into the Clock Room, so named because of an English clock which regulated the household. Here were grouped some fifty statues and busts, including the marble medallion of James Madison by Ceracchi.

Dolly's square parlor was decorated in the French style, with an Aubusson carpet and her gilt furniture. The walls were almost hidden by mirrors and paintings, six of them by Gilbert Stuart; among them, the framed Declaration of Independence Mrs. Madison had rescued from the White House. Art objects crowded the tables and mantels. "More like a museum than a parlor," one guest described it.

Upstairs were other bedrooms and Madison's library. There James spent most of his time reading, collecting notes for a book on the Constitutional Convention, and answering his correspondence. Books were all about, not only on the shelves, but piled on the tables, chairs, and the floor.

On the long front porch, where four massive white pillars soared upward, Madison exercised by walking his allotted number of miles, even in stormy weather.

A path led west from the house to a summerhouse, where Dolly liked to lie in her lounging chair on hot afternoons, watching the Blue Ridge. Sometimes the mountains seemed to hem her in. "I feel as though I'd never get out," she thought one day. "Oh, if I could see Washington—"

There! She had admitted it, if only to herself. But Dolly's lapse was momentary. Slipping into the house, she bathed her eyes, put on her brightest smile and went to join her husband. Poor darling! He was so content these days. She could not spoil his happiness.

Gaily, she took his arm. Together they strolled across the lawn, past two tulip trees so exactly alike that James called them "the twins." Then down a path they entered Dolly's new garden.

With loving care James had laid out the formal plots of roses, tulips, iris, and oleanders, his wife's favorite flower. He stopped to note with pleasure the trim hedges of box that edged the beds.

"Can't you see this box in ten—twenty years, Dolly?" he asked eagerly. "It will be higher than our heads."

Her heart turned over. Ten years? Twenty? Would they still be at Montpellier? Of course, Dolly knew they would be. There was no public office beyond the presidency of the United States.

Mornings Mrs. Madison walked in her garden; an apron protected her gown, a wide-brimmed hat shielded her eyes from the sun. Beside her, a small Negro boy carried a basket into which Dolly dropped the pink oleander blossoms she liked to pin on her dress.

Here she superintended the work of the French gardener, Beazee, who was paid four hundred dollars a year. Besides tending her flowers, Beazee cultivated the fruits and vegetables so necessary to a household five miles from Orange Court House, the nearest village.

Household duties also claimed part of Dolly Madison's time. Scarcely a meal was served at Montpellier that was not shared with a swarm of visitors. As many as ninety people often sat down to table and remained overnight, with a little "doubling up." Distinguished foreigners, political associates, friends and relatives were always welcome.

Before a meal, Dolly would scan the long, winding drive with a telescope, lest unannounced guests be approaching. She, who loved excitement, never complained of the crowds that milled about her. With plenty of servants, a few dozen extra people were no trouble. "I am less worried here with a hundred visitors than with twenty-five in Washington," she wrote Anna.

The guests, who sometimes stayed for weeks, wearied James far more than his wife. He often cast longing glances in the direction of his "dear library." Yet none were more cordially welcome at Montpellier than Thomas Jefferson and family, or any Washington friends who brought news of the capital.

Mrs. Samuel Harrison Smith, particularly, brought the kind of gossip that Dolly longed to hear. After dinner, when the ladies left the gentlemen to their "segars" and port, Mrs. Smith sat down beside Mrs. Madison to talk about Washington and the new administration.

The reopening of the White House had been eagerly anticipated, Margaret Smith told her interested hostess. People were curious to know whether the lavish hospitality of Dolly

Madison's regime would be resumed.

But to everyone's disappointment, Mrs. James Monroe entertained rarely. She paid no visits, explaining that "Dolly Madison had ruined her health returning calls." She put on royal airs, refusing to allow people to sit in her presence. So the Washington ladies were boycotting Mrs. Monroe. One of her receptions had opened to rows of empty chairs.

"Oh, my dear, how everyone wishes you were back!" Margaret exclaimed.

Dolly beamed. She was pleased that, in spite of Elizabeth Monroe's advantages as the wife of a minister to the court of France, the new president's wife had not outshone her.

On another visit to Montpellier, in 1828, Margaret Smith brought her daughter Anna Maria. Dolly was sixty then, but still as active as a much younger woman.

On the long porch one day, she took the little girl by the hand. "Come, let's run a race, Anna Maria," she suggested. "I don't believe you can beat me. Madison and I often run races here when the weather keeps us from walking."

Mrs. Smith wrote that Mrs. Madison "did run very briskly —it was more than I could do."

On this visit Dolly took her friend in to see Mother Madison. They found her seated, her Bible, her prayer-book and her knitting on the table beside her. At ninety-seven, Nelly Madison's face was not as wrinkled as that of her son's, who was only seventy-seven.

"I'm never at a loss for things to do," Mother Madison told Mrs. Smith. "Except for my hearing, my senses are but little impaired. My eyes are good. I read and knit most of the day. Otherwise I'm helpless, and owe everything to her." She looked gratefully at her daughter-in-law. "She is my mother now, and takes care of me in my old age."

The care and affection she gave the feeble old woman,

Dolly felt, was less than adequate return for all James did for Payne.

Instead of settling down at Montpellier, Payne Todd idled away his days, first in one city, then in another. He constantly asked and finally demanded money from his tender-hearted mother. Meanwhile, he piled up debts which were paid by his stepfather. But Dolly knew with what scorn the thrifty James regarded her son.

Payne had tried various occupations, and in all he had failed. His present foolish venture was a silk farm. He had brought back with him from Europe experienced silk factory workers, and intended to plant mulberries and raise silk worms at Toddsbirth, a plantation near Montpellier, which he had bought. Always impractical, he imported workmen to manufacture the silk before he planted the trees.

Dolly wanted Phoebe Morris for a daughter-in-law, and had Anthony Morris' daughter often at Montpellier. Perhaps too much. Payne grew resentful at being managed. The affair had drifted into indifference long before Phoebe's death in 1825. And to Dolly's disappointment, Sally Coles became Mrs. Andrew Stevenson.

Besides, Payne was in love with Ann Cole of Williamsburg, who was hard-hearted or farsighted enough to refuse to have anything to do with him. Resenting this, Mrs. Madison reminded her son that there were other girls in the world besides Ann. But Payne preferred to drown his sorrow—if his nature was capable of real grief—in drink.

A great part of the time Dolly hardly knew where he was. Anna Cutts' daughters, Mary and Dolly, wrote that Payne was in Washington. His mother hastened to write him, ". . . had I known where to direct I should have written you before this; not that there is anything particular to communicate, but for the pleasure of repeating how much I love you."

She was constantly thinking of gifts to send him, although in the same letter she admitted "our last tobacco was a failure."

> Yours, dearest, promising to write me again, came safely . . . you did not tell me whether you had been successful with your (geology) collections. If not, you will want supplies proportioned to your detention; I am anxious you should have them. You know the little I have in my power is at your command, though but a drop in the bucket. . . .

It was well that Dolly had distractions, even at Montpellier, so she could not brood too much over Payne.

In August, 1824, Madison invited General Lafayette, then in America for the 50th Anniversary of the Battle of Bunker Hill, to visit him at Montpellier. The charming Frenchman arrived on November 11th, with his son, George Washington Lafayette, and his secretary, M. Le Vasseur.

George Washington's "boy," now grown stout and elderly, was delighted to be back in Virginia, the state he had defended as a youthful commander. As the Madisons and their guests talked together, they often spoke of Thomas Jefferson, whom Lafayette had found at Monticello in failing health and reduced to poverty by selfish people who came in hordes to visit him.

Madison sighed and looked thoughtful. Would the same misfortune overtake Montpellier?

Lafayette enjoyed going with Dolly to Walnut Grove, the plantation slave quarter, to call at the cabins. He was amused by the Negroes' efforts to speak the French they had learned from Beazee, the gardener. He was charmed by their quaint stories and the singing of their spirituals.

After inspecting Dolly's garden, Lafayette drew plans for its enlargement into the shape of a horseshoe. Against the hillside, he laid out the descending terraces to suggest the

House of Representatives; the flat stretch of ground below, the floor of the House; a formal vase, the Speaker's chair. He taught Beazee how to groom the geometrical flower beds between the box-bordered paths.

"I'll send you some tiger lilies," Lafayette promised Mrs. Madison, the morning of his departure.

When the bulbs arrived from France, Dolly planted Lafayette's lilies. Also the Scotch thistle seed he sent, marked "very rare"—that is how the hated thistle was first propagated in Virginia.

During the infrequent intervals when they were alone, Dolly tried to spare James' weak eyes by writing his letters and reading to him. Since Edward Coles had resigned as Madison's secretary, and Payne failed at the job, Dolly had served as her husband's "eyes and right hand," although her own eyesight was far from strong.

When she spelled were as "ware" and changed ie to ei, people laughed at what they supposed to be the ex-President's spelling. Dolly wrote with a flowing hand, almost too self-committing. Had she written less distinctly, people might not have discovered how poorly she spelled.

Answering the letters that came to James Madison from all over the world took much of Dolly's time. Almost daily, he wrote Jefferson about his crops, the health of his merino sheep, or to confer with him on farm problems. Dolly learned to share James' rural interests. She wrote to Payne of the disappointments which came to "us farmers," when the frost killed the spring planting; or when the tobacco was a failure and "sold for seven" when seventeen was expected.

Dolly was worried about her sister's heart condition. Through weekly letters, she kept in touch with Anna Cutts and her two daughters. Dolly's own eyes were troubling her;

she endured frequent attacks of rheumatism, but she managed to write her young nieces "a great deal of nonsense."

"My love for you makes me wish to trace your every word and deed throughout the year," Dolly wrote her namesake, Dolly Cutts. "In my quiet retreat I like to hear of what is going on, and hope, my dear, you will not be timid in telling me . . . you will soon be going to parties, give me a detailed account of what is going forward amongst the various characters in Washington . . . We are very old-fashioned here. Can you send me a paper pattern of the present sleeve, and describe the width of dress and waist; also how turbans are pinned up, bonnets worn, as well as how to behave in the fashion?"

Dolly had not lost her interest in clothes. But when the girls wrote their "Aunt Madison" of the new dance, the polka—where a man took you in his arms—she was shocked and replied primly, "I have no idea of the new dance you speak of, or its motions, but approve of your declining to learn it, if disapproved of by society. Our sex are ever losers, when they stem the torrent of public opinion. . . ."

Mrs. Madison asked Anna's daughters to send her some clever new novel. She had bought "Cooper's last, but did not care for it because the story was so full of horrors." She thought of reading the *Romance of History*, but there is no evidence that she ever got around to it. Dolly did little reading for her own pleasure.

Much of her time was taken up with writing to Payne tender, pathetic letters. In every one the refrain is "Come home!" On December 2, 1824, she wrote to him in Philadelphia,

My dear son, it seems to be the wonder of all that you should stay away so long from us. Now I am ashamed to tell when asked how long my only child has been absent from the home of his mother. Your father and myself entreat you to come to us . . . Your father thinks as I do that it would be best for your reputation and happiness as well as ours that you should have the appearance of consulting your parents on subjects of deep account to you, and that you would find it so on returning to Philadelphia, which shall be whenever you wish it. I have said in my late letters, all that I thought sufficient to influence you. I must now put my trust in God alone . . . If the young lady you have followed so long (Ann Cole) has not yet been won, I fear she declines the chance, Son, to favor your happiness. . . .

Meanwhile Anthony Morris was writing to Anna Cutts about Payne,

. . . whose long stay in Philadelphia you no doubt know of, and who is now anxious to return to Montpellier, only he has gambled away all the money his mother has sent him. To enable him to go home, two hundred dollars in cash, and the assumption of four hundred dollars payable at any convenient future day, are said to be required. . . .

Dolly learned of her son's debts through Anna. Again they were paid, and he came home. But Payne was so bored and restless at Montpellier that his mother was rather relieved when he again took his departure, this time for New York.

Mrs. Madison's Washington friends still remembered her, and wrote her about their good times. She read their letters wistfully, these echoes from the gay world she had loved. "How I would like to visit Washington!" Dolly thought. But how could she, with James happily chained to his desk each day, writing his book on the Constitutional Convention?

. . . not a mile can I go from home [she wrote Sally Stevenson]. This is the third winter in which my husband has been engaged in the arrangement of papers, and the business seems to accumulate as he proceeds, so that it outlasts my patience. Yet I cannot press him to forsake a duty so important, or find it in my heart to leave him. . . .

🏵   🏵   🏵   🏵   🏵

On February 9, 1825, John Quincy Adams became president. His wife, Louisa, loved music and books, read Plato in the original Greek, and entertained very little. People thought Louisa Adams "cold and haughty." She was too retiring and scholarly to be a popular First Lady.

. . . my beloved Dolly, your absence from this city is more and more lamented [Eliza Lee wrote Mrs. Madison]. The cheerfulness diffused through the circles over which you presided will long be sought in vain.

Dolly smiled over Eliza's letter. Another First Lady, who had lived in Europe while her husband was minister, had not eclipsed the untraveled Dolly Madison.

Such assurances now meant a great deal to her. Around the Madisons, old friends were passing away. On July 4, 1826, Thomas Jefferson died—as great a loss to Dolly as to James. Their grief was deepened when Monticello was sold to pay Jefferson's debts, and Martha Randolph and her children left.

Death struck close to home, too, during these years. In 1829, at the age of ninety-seven, Mother Madison died. Dolly sincerely mourned her mother-in-law, with whom she had lived in peace and affection for thirty-five years.

James was so depressed by the death of his mother and his best friend, that Dolly greeted with relief an invitation to attend the convention for the revision of the Virginia Constitution in Richmond. It was the first time the Madisons had been far from home in seventeen years. With the change of scene, Dolly's good spirits came back. But on their return to Montpellier, James was so exhausted by the journey that his wife doubted he would ever leave home again. He rallied, however, and outlived Dorothea Henry Winston, who died in February, 1831.

The following year Anna Cutts grew worse. Dolly longed to rush to Washington to her sister's bedside, but at Montpellier was her ailing husband who had first claim on her.

Beloved Sister Anna—Mrs. Mason has just written me to say you are a little better, and those dear daughters of yours, Mary and Dolly, whom I shall ever feel are my own children, have often consoled me by their letters since you were unable to write. . . .

Dolly's last letter to Anna was dated August 2, 1832. Two days later, her loved "sister-child" died of dropsy of the heart, after a deceptive improvement had led Dolly to believe she was recovering.

So crushed was Dolly by Anna's death that she seemed to age in a week. At once she wrote Richard Cutts, "Come to us as soon as you can, and bring your dear children with you. I am as deeply interested in them as if they were my own. . . ."

Mary and Dolly Cutts stayed on at Montpellier as Mrs. Madison's adopted daughters. Their fun brightened the house, for there were few guests now. As rheumatism and old age crippled James more and more, his wife became not only his nurse and companion, his "eyes and right hand," but as she herself said, "the shadow of my husband." Dolly even took on herself the task of dressing her husband's scanty locks and powdering them. His valet, Paul Jennings, she complained, did not do it properly.

The Madisons' only recreation was a short drive each day behind their four gray horses. On pleasant Sundays they drove in to the Episcopal church at Orange Court House.

One morning Dolly received a letter from Payne in New York. Aaron Burr had suffered a stroke of paralysis, he wrote, but had regained the use of his limbs. Payne had met him on the Battery, wearing shabby clothes and a fur cap pulled down over his high forehead. People turned to point out Burr on the street . . . a queer old fellow, a little mad . . . but still the man who killed Alexander Hamilton—still a traitor to his country.

Aaron, old and sick! "We're all of us getting on," Dolly thought.

But the next news from Colonel Burr seemed to belie his years. Dolly was astonished to hear that he had married Eliza Jumel, the rich widow of Stephen Jumel, a French wine merchant.

Madame Jumel lived in the Roger Morris mansion, near the upper tip of Manhattan Island; a house still standing. Longing for social recognition, but snubbed because of her notorious past, Eliza Jumel, a woman in her fifties, had set her cap for the well-born Colonel Burr. Under the pretense of seeking legal aid, she pestered him into marriage.

Madame Jumel became Mrs. Aaron Burr at the Jumel Mansion on July 1, 1833—and Burr, the laughing stock of New York. After which, the elderly bridal pair went on their honeymoon to Connecticut in Eliza's gaudy, yellow carriage behind a pair of high-stepping horses.

"She married him for position; he married her for her money. One good turn deserves another," said a guest at the Madisons'. "At any rate, she's wealthy enough to take care of the old man."

"Oh, Burr will go through her money!" predicted James.

He did. He spent it as fast as he could, even selling Eliza's new yellow carriage and horses. In four months, Madame Jumel, not receiving the social recognition she craved, accused Burr of squandering her fortune. The quarrel brought on Colonel Burr another stroke. When he was able to walk, his wife threw him out of her house and sued for divorce.

Aaron returned to his boarding house on Bowling Green, and there Payne went to see him. (There had always been a warm bond between those two spendthrifts.) He found Burr propped up in bed—a paralyzed, embittered, pathetic old man, who had had his last adventure.

"The old goat, what folly to marry at seventy-seven!" wrote Payne, who at forty-one was still a bachelor.

"Aaron is seventy-seven?" Dolly murmured in amazement, on reading Payne's letter. It seldom occurred to her that she was sixty-five herself.

❁　　❁　　❁　　❁　　❁

As his eyesight and strength failed, one by one James Madison's customary activities—his daily drive, his walk on the porch—slipped from him, until his time was spent entirely in his bedroom off the dining room. Rheumatism had crippled his fingers so he could not manage a knife. He ate his meals at a small table, placed near the door of the dining room, so he could chat with his guests.

When J. Madison Cutts, Anna's son, was married in 1834, the wedding journey was made to Montpellier. Although James was too feeble to join the family at dinner, he asked that the door of his bedroom remain open so he could hear the talk at the table.

During the meal, Dolly looked up with surprise to see the invalid standing in the doorway, in his white nightcap and black silk dressing gown, a wine glass in his crippled hand. Gallantly he raised it and drank to the health of Ellen, the bride.

Fearful lest he should fall, Dolly rushed to her husband's side. As she guided his tottering feet back to his chair, a sense of belonging to James swept over her—a terrible responsibility for his well-being. The years had developed in her a sincere affection for this quiet little man of eighty-three, nearly twenty years her senior. They had taught her that he was indeed "the Great Little Madison."

James loved his wife, as he loved his home, with a surprising warmth for so precise, so austere, a nature. Looking at her, he saw the devotion for him shining in her eyes. And he was satisfied.

🌿　　🌿　　🌿　　🌿　　🌿

Knowing Dolly's depression over Anna's death, the unselfish Madison insisted that she go to Washington and visit her Cutts nieces for the social season of 1835-6. Dolly feared leaving him, even in the care of a faithful maid, Becky. But James seemed so much better, that at last she went.

After an absence of eighteen years, Dolly Madison returned to the scene of her triumphs on October 19, 1835. She saw many changes. Pennsylvania Avenue was partly macadamized. The first train with a steam locomotive had been run between Baltimore and Washington. Clay, Calhoun and Webster were the leading statesmen in the fine new Capitol, finished by Charles Bulfinch.

Andrew Jackson, that wild Irishman from Tennessee, had succeeded the cultured John Quincy Adams as president. Mrs. Madison heard with disgust of Jackson's bad grammar, his quarrels, his duels. How he relaxed by stretching himself under the trees on the White House lawn, a corncob pipe in his mouth. Especially she resented Jackson's removal of Richard Cutts as superintendent of military supplies, a lucrative job to which Madison had appointed his wife's brother-in-law.

With some dismay, Dolly Madison realized that the elegant Virginia regime was over. Tennessee and the frontier West had rolled in with Andrew Jackson and taken over Washington. The "People's President" kept open house. Anyone could come to his receptions, in muddy boots and overalls. In derision of its fallen dignity, Mrs. John C. Calhoun and Mrs. Henry Clay said that the former Castle was indeed the White House—a mere house and a whitewashed one!

Dolly Madison wiped away a tear. She, who had entertained at the Castle with such elegance, could not bear to hear of this sacrilege.

When Emily Donelson Wilcox, Jackson's grandniece, gave a children's Christmas party at the White House, Mrs. Madison at first refused to attend. But she could never resist a young people's frolic—besides, Dolly was curious to see her old home—so she went, taking with her J. Madison Cutts' little daughter, Addie.

Hoban had rebuilt the President's house. Latrobe had added the tall porticoes in front and rear, so the mansion did not look so long and stark as in Dolly Madison's day. And it was miraculously piped for running water. Mrs. Wilcox, Emily's mother, showed Mrs. Madison the shower baths, the faucets for water in the kitchen and pantries. Then the shrill laughter of youngsters drew them toward the East Room, where Jackson's grandchildren—seven in number—and their playmates, under the watchful eye of an old mammy, were enjoying ice cream and cake.

Dolly Madison sat chatting with Mrs. Wilcox when a tall

man, with bristling white hair, entered the room. It was
President Jackson. Remembering the brusque, uncouth hero
of New Orleans she had entertained, and the stories she had
heard about him since, Dolly was surprised at his courtly
manners. But there was another side to Andrew Jackson.
Loyal to his friends, unforgiving with his enemies, he was
always courteous to the ladies.

The President, who loved children, had come to watch the
fun. Dolly liked him for that. But she found it hard to forgive Jackson for dismissing Richard Cutts.

❧   ❧   ❧   ❧   ❧

When Dolly returned to Montpellier, she was shocked to
see how James had failed. The doctor advised Warm Springs.
But the invalid was too weak to leave his bed. A great suf-
ferer, he rarely complained.

Dolly no longer left the plantation, even to go as far as
Orange Court House. "It would be an event for me to go
there, five miles from home," she wrote Payne. As her husband's strength ebbed, she was seldom absent from the sick
room for more than a few minutes.

I have been so long confined by the side of my dear
sick husband, never seeing or hearing anything outside of his
room, that I make a dull correspondent [she wrote her
nieces]. Your uncle's poor hands are so swollen as to be almost useless, so I lend him mine . . . Take care of yourselves
this weather; I wish I could cover you with furs. . . .

It was mainly due to Dolly's tender care that James Madison, delicate all his life, lived to be eighty-five. Becky helped
his wife nurse him. Together they watched the dear face
grow whiter. . . .

The doctor urged Madison to take a stimulant, hoping to prolong his life until the glorious Fourth, and thus be the fourth president to die on the birthday of the republic. But James refused.

When on the morning of June 28, 1836, Sukey brought his breakfast, James turned his head away. He could not swallow.

"What's the matter, Uncle?" asked his niece, Eliza Willis, who sat beside his bed.

"Nothing more than a change of mind, my dear."

His head dropped. Mrs. Willis ran to her uncle's side and bent over him anxiously. As quickly as the snuff of a candle, he had ceased to breathe.

Sukey's scream brought Dolly on a run into the room. Throwing herself on her knees beside the still form, she called her husband's name. Then she bowed her head in that terrible, first recognition of loss.

When Dolly could control her grief, they told her how James Madison had died. He had passed away, as he had lived, with a quiet jest and a kindly smile on his lips.

*T*HE FIRST SAD DAYS OF DOLLY'S WIDOWHOOD WERE COM-
forted by the letters of sympathy that poured in from all
over the nation.

But after the excitement of Madison's death had died away,
Dolly found herself very much alone. Silently she paced the
empty rooms at Montpellier. Red-eyed, she sat for hours staring at the blue hills that James had loved.

After forty-two years of marriage, her "best friend" was
gone. Dolly realized for the first time how she, as well as
Thomas Jefferson, had relied on James' advice. Payne she
could not lean upon. Lost and forlorn, the Widow Madison
knew that now she would have to stand upon her own feet.

John Payne had hurried to his sister's side from his home
in Kentucky, bringing with him his daughter, Anna. Richard
Cutts and his children had come from Washington. Anthony
Morris, Dolly's friend for forty-six years, also arrived to
comfort her, accompanied by his granddaughter, Mary
Nourse.

Cheered by the presence of these dear ones, Dolly sat down
to answer the letters of condolence that flooded her desk.
One of the first came from President Jackson.

As Mrs. Madison read the President's praise of her husband,
tears blinded her eyes. She took up her pen to reply,

The high and just estimation of my husband by my countrymen and friends and their participation in the sorrow occasioned by our irretrievable loss, expressed through its su-

preme authorities and otherwise, is the only solace of which my heart is susceptible on the departure of him, who had never lost sight of that consistency, symmetry, and beauty of character in all its parts, which secured to him the love and admiration of his country.

The best return I can make for the sympathy of my country is to fulfill the trust his confidence reposed in me, that of placing before Congress and the world what his pen has prepared for their use, and with the importance of this legacy, I am deeply impressed.

Dolly referred to the notes on the Constitutional Convention at Philadelphia in 1787, kept daily by the patient Madison. These notes James was still arranging for a book at the time of his death. The task now fell to Dolly.

As she worked over her husband's journal, she began to realize its historic value. Madison had known intimately the men who met to frame the Constitution, their hopes and aims. He had taken a leading part in the debates. Who could better tell of those stirring days? There were no reporters then to write up the speeches. James Madison—her James—had been the only person to take down notes. In the future the world would have to rely on his written word for what went on, what men said and what they did.

So Dolly labored on, when she should have rested her weak eyes. Until finally she collapsed with a nervous breakdown. The old trouble with her eyes increased. Through the fall and winter of 1836, she was forced to lie in bed, the curtains drawn to shut out every ray of light.

As Dolly lay ill in late September, Anna Payne, the daughter of her brother John, came to tell her that Aaron Burr had died on the 14th of the month. In a shabby inn on Staten Island, New York, he had passed away, his eyes on Theo's portrait.

"Colonel Burr was an old friend of yours, Aunty," Anna said softly. "We all know how badly you must feel."

Feel? To her own surprise, Dolly felt very little, beyond the wonder that both James and Aaron had left her, and that she lived on alone.

Besides ill health, Dolly Madison was harassed by financial worries. Montpellier was an expensive bit of "gentlemen farming," that had never paid for itself. Due to too-generous hospitality, Madison had died, like Jefferson, almost bankrupt. Nor had Dolly been a great force for thrift.

"Nothing is too good for one's friends," she would say. With her, it was always give—give time, give food, give great bunches of flowers. "She is too generous with herself," people said of Dolly Madison. Now there was little more to give. A few retrenchments had been made after James' death. The horses sold, all but one pair. But these economies had come too late.

So long before she was well again, Mrs. Madison was up, at work finishing the Constitution papers for Congress to buy. James had valued his manuscript at fifty thousand dollars. In his will, he bequeathed to his wife the net proceeds from it, after legacies amounting to fifteen thousand dollars were paid.

Dolly should have rested. By the spring of 1837, she was so run down that her doctor ordered her to White Sulphur Springs. Returning to Montpellier at the end of August in better health, she wrote Anthony Morris,

I passed four days at the Warm Springs, and two weeks at the White Sulphur, drinking moderately of the waters, and bathing my poor eyes a dozen times a day. The effect was excellent. My health was strengthened to its former standing, and my eyes grew white again; but in my drive home of six days in the dust they took the fancy to relapse a little.

I met with many friends on "my grand tour" and had every reason to be gratified, but for my own sad impatient spirit, which continually dwelt on my duties at home yet unfinished. In truth, my five weeks' absence from Montpellier made me feel as if I had deserted my duties, and was not entitled to the kindness everywhere shown me, and so I am at home at work again.

Back at her desk, Dolly began assembling her husband's letters and scholarly speeches, which she also hoped to sell. She was engaged in this task in October, 1837, when she was notified that Congress would purchase Madison's Record of the Debates of the Constitutional Convention during the years 1782-7 for thirty thousand dollars.

Dolly, who had expected fifty thousand dollars, took to her bed again from disappointment. How she missed James' judgment in financial affairs! Accustomed to the most lavish hospitality, she was, she admitted "too old to change my habits." With an expensive plantation to maintain, and an idle son to support, Dolly realized that she would have to sell off slaves and land. That autumn she sold the greater part of Montpellier, keeping only the house and a few hundred acres.

As winter approached, Mrs. Madison's spirits ebbed. The prospect of long, lonely months in the country depressed her. John Payne had returned to Kentucky, leaving his daughter Anna as her aunt's new adopted daughter. But even with Anna Payne's bright companionship, a dreary winter at Montpellier seemed intolerable.

"Return to Washington!" Dolly thought. Why not? There was nothing now to prevent her. And the Cutts house—her own, in fact, for Madison had willed it to her—stood empty and waiting on Lafayette Square.

The President's Square on L'Enfant's plan of the city had

been rechristened Lafayette Square, after the visit of that famous Frenchman in 1824. On the bare, ugly common, once the public market, Andrew Downing of Newburgh, New York, had laid out a little park.

On the northeast corner of the square and H Street stands an unpretentious, two-story house with dormer windows, still known as the Dolly Madison House. With only a few alterations, it remains as in her lifetime.

Built by Richard Cutts during Madison's presidency, the house was occupied for many years by Dolly's sister Anna and her family. But the extravagant Richard Cutts had made bad investments; further, lost his sinecure as superintendent of military supplies. On paying off Cutts' debts, James Madison took his Washington home in exchange.

It was to this house, rich in family associations, that Dolly came in December, 1837, the year that Victoria was crowned Queen of England. Here, within sight of the White House, where she had known her happiest days, Mrs. Madison spent the last twelve years of her life.

Provincial as Washington still seemed to foreign eyes, to Dolly it presented a bewildering scene of fashion and gaiety. Inventions had wrought great changes. Gas for illumination was being tried out; coal used to heat houses. Mrs. Madison heard with wonder of the use of ether to deaden pain; and in a whisper—for it wasn't a topic mentioned before ladies— of the new bathtub, a huge wooden affair lined with zinc, the use of which the doctors were fighting as unhealthy.

But it was the same friendly Washington, that had never forgotten its most popular First Lady. Almost at once, the little gray house facing the park was filled with friends. John Sioussat, Mrs. Madison's "French John," came to look after her "little establishment." There the Widow Madison held court as she had in the Castle. On New Year's Day and the

Fourth of July she kept open house. The throngs of people, who made a short call on the President, hurried over for a longer visit with a famous lady—the still fascinating Dolly Madison.

The widowed Martin Van Buren was president. Abraham, the eldest of the President's four sons, assisted him at social functions. But Dolly saw the White House needed a First Lady. Angelica Singleton of South Carolina, a cousin of Dolly's, had gone with her to a White House reception. Cleverly Mrs. Madison left the pretty Angelica with Abraham and went off to inspect her beloved Oval Parlor, that President Van Buren had done over in blue. Shaking her turbaned head, Dolly wandered through the rooms, trying to accustom herself to new manners, new names, new faces.

But it did not take Mrs. Madison long to adjust herself. Angelica Singleton was married to Major Abraham Van Buren in November, 1838. And so frequently did the young bride turn to her cousin for advice that Dolly Madison became known as the First Lady, by proxy, of the Van Buren regime.

So, at seventy, Dolly Madison became once more the leader of Washington society. She did not need the White House residence to entrench her social position. In her shabby little house she held court as graciously as though she were still First Lady.

Among the interesting people who passed in and out of her door were three elderly, respected widows of famous men— Mrs. Decatur, Mrs. Lear, and Mrs. Hamilton.

Since her husband had been killed in the famous duel of 1820, Mrs. Decatur no longer lived in the fine brick house opposite Mrs. Madison on Lafayette Square. The only time poor Susan Decatur left her cottage in Georgetown was to come and call on Dolly Madison.

Mrs. Tobias Lear, Martha Washington's niece, was an old friend. A beautiful old lady, whom Dolly's nieces and nephews called Aunt Fanny, Mrs. Lear had given Dolly Madison a ring containing George Washington's hair.

The sight of Mrs. Alexander Hamilton, the widow of the man whom Aaron Burr had slain, brought back the old romantic days to Dolly Madison. An energetic little woman of eighty, Elizabeth Hamilton lived around the corner on H Street. She was Dolly's neighbor, but not a friendly one. When the Widow Madison came to call, Mrs. Hamilton faced the woman who had befriended her husband's "murderer" with angry eyes.

"Don't be bitter, my dear," Dolly wooed her with her soft southern voice. "We must be friends. In this new Washington, we're all that is left of the old."

It took every ounce of Mrs. Madison's famous charm to win Elizabeth Hamilton sufficiently to bring about a return call. But, eventually, the widows became friends.

Mrs. Alexander Hamilton, too, was frantically appealing to Congress to publish her husband's letters, but without success—Hamilton and the Federalists were a thing of the past. Nor was Mrs. Stephen Decatur having any better luck collecting the prize money owed her husband for his exploits at Tripoli, back in 1804.

Mrs. Madison knew of Mrs. Hamilton's pitiful appeals to Congress. She knew of the loans Mrs. Decatur was forced to arrange with the banks. And the kind-hearted Mrs. Madison lavished on these two sad widows the little she had, if only some plums from the tree in her yard. Just as she still managed to send money to Payne.

The thirty thousand dollars paid by Congress for Madison's Reports on the Constitutional Convention, and the money left Dolly by her husband, would have enabled her to live

comfortably had it not been for the constant demands of her
gambler son. Part of Montpellier had already gone to pay his
debts. Now Dolly was forced to sell the mansion and the
remainder of the land. Payne found a purchaser, Henry W.
Moncure of Richmond, Virginia.

"I can never go to Montpellier again," thought Dolly,
sadly.

When Mr. Moncure heard of Mrs. Madison's grief at parting with her old home, he offered to cancel the sale. But
Dolly proudly declined to break the arrangements Henry
Moncure had made with her son. She told him she only
wanted a few of the Negroes, some of the furniture, and the
family burial plot.

A mortgage of three thousand dollars to John Jacob Astor
on her Washington house, the sale of Montpellier and most
of her slaves; all these sacrifices were not enough to lift
Dolly Madison's burden of debt. Yet none dared criticize in
her hearing the son whose extravagances had forced her into
dependency on what Congress might do for her, and reduced
her to want within sight of the White House where she had
once entertained so magnificently.

After the sale of Montpellier, Payne brought further sorrow to his mother by carting off her furniture and precious
souvenirs to Toddsbirth. Repeatedly she begged him to return
her possessions,

My Dearest—it has been too long since I was cheered with
a line from you. What are you about that prevents your
communicating with your mother? You are taking special
care of our mutual property of every sort, I trust, & my
confidence in you to restore it to me is not diminished by the
sad & tedious time in which I have been deprived of its use.
A part of the furniture I wish to divide with you, & a part

of it desire to sell. But I wish to be with you & together choose what best to dispose of—Anxious Mother!

None of Dolly's treasures were returned to her. Later, when the house at Toddsbirth burned down, she lost everything she had there.

Payne vanished from Toddsbirth, without explanation, for long periods of time. When a score of letters failed to bring a reply, Dolly would write to the postmaster to make sure they had been delivered.

Her son resented what he called the "apron strings." He drank to excess; he ate to excess. While his mother and Cousin Anna were struggling for the bare necessities of life, and dependent on the charity of friends, Payne was sending to Europe for rare cheese and other table luxuries. As a result of his gluttony and self-indulgence, he grew fat and bloated. Few would have recognized in him the graceful, laughing-eyed "Prince of America."

But for the affection of her nieces and nephews, Dolly Madison would have led a forlorn home life in her old age. Always she had some young relative living with her. Now it was Anna, the daughter of Dolly's brother John and his wife, Clara W. Payne, a Canadian by birth. Anna was Mrs. Madison's adopted daughter and secretary. She was not pretty, but she was devoted and lively, and a great comfort to her aunt.

Another generation of Cutts children was growing up. Little Rose Adele Cutts, the daughter of the J. Madison Cutts, had been born in the Dolly Madison House on Lafayette Square. A pretty, brown-haired child, Addie gave promise of becoming the famous beauty who married Stephen A. Douglas, whom Lincoln defeated in 1860 for president. Dolly was proud of Addie and her sturdy young brother,

Madison Cutts, Junior, whom she called "my little Madison."

Living also in Washington were those dear friends of Dolly's youth, Eliza Lee, a widow now, and Anthony Morris. At seventy-four, Mr. Morris was as sprightly as ever. Dolly spent many happy hours at his home, the Highlands.

The Daniel Websters, on Lafayette Square, also kept a watchful eye on their neighbor in the little gray house. It might be a gift of some West Indian preserves, received from Mrs. Webster's nephew in Cuba; a crate of oranges or some strawberries. Frequently Mrs. Madison and Anna were asked to the Websters for a hearty meal.

Daniel Webster's magnificent head was a familiar sight in the Washington market, where he liked to pick out his own provisions. These he brought home in a basket, carried by his Negro servant, Paul Jennings.

Paul, who had bought his freedom from Mrs. Madison, was now living with the Websters. From French John, Paul discovered that his former mistress was in need. It was he who told Mr. Webster that Mrs. Madison's "table was scant and her pantry almost bare." It was Paul who brought Mr. Webster's groceries to her. Paul even shared with her his own basket.

Smiling Dolly Madison suffered to herself and complained to no one. Mr. Moncure was slow in paying for Montpellier. Desperately poor, obliged to accept aid even from a former slave, Dolly wrote to her son, who neglected her business affairs, addressing him with unwonted formality as "My dear sir."

I have hope & expectation of your writing me all about yourself & my affairs. Will you tell me whether or not Mr. Moncure will pay me the remnant due (on Montpellier)? I shall say nothing to him at this instant of the sufferings he now causes by his delay . . . But one short note from you

since we parted. I'm not well or should say more. Mr. Simms
has sent me a Bill for nearly fifty dollars—Again—burn my
letters of business.

John Quincy Adams was trying to get Congress to purchase Madison's letters and state papers, but there was no
certainty of a sale. The nation was in the midst of another
presidential campaign. Congress had more important things
to think about than aid to destitute widows.

To the shouts of "Tippecanoe and Tyler too!" Dolly
Madison's old friend, General William Henry Harrison, became president. But after one short month, "Old Tippecanoe" died of pneumonia—the first president to die in office.
Vice President John Tyler became chief executive.

Mrs. Madison knew the Virginian, John Tyler, well. His
wife was an invalid. His hostesses were his two daughters and
his daughter-in-law, lovely Mrs. Robert Tyler. Appealing to
Dolly Madison, a fellow Virginian, to guide them, young
Mrs. Tyler wrote:

There was a doubt at first whether I must visit a person or
send cards. I asked Mrs. Madison's advice upon the subject,
and she says, return all my visits by all means. So three days
in the week I am to spend three hours a day driving from one
street to another in this city of magnificent distances. . . .

As social mentor to the Tyler family, the Widow Madison
enjoyed the concerts of the Marine Band on the White House
lawn. Many were the invitations carried by servants between
the big white house on Pennsylvania Avenue and the little
gray house on Lafayette Square. Dolly attended a reception
to Charles Dickens; a dinner for the Minister to Spain, Mrs.
Madison's old friend, Washington Irving; the quiet family
wedding in the East Room of Elizabeth Tyler and William
Waller; also a children's party given by the President's

granddaughter, Mary Tyler, who received her guests dressed as a fairy princess. The elderly Dolly Madison, seated at the supper table opposite her three-year-old hostess, entered into the children's fun.

Mrs. Madison, who had posed for many portraits, now had one of the new pictures called a daguerreotype taken for Mrs. John C. Spencer, a close friend. The photographer wrote to make the arrangements,

It is a fine day for having your likeness taken, the sun is not so bright as to affect your eyes, & yet sufficiently so for the purpose. I should like to have you wear one of your pretty white turbans, & your neck dressed as it was at Mrs. Tayloe's the other evening. . . .

Dolly Madison's head had never been turned by admiration. Widowed and poor, she was still Queen Dolly—the same good natured, kindly person that she had been in the heyday of her fortunes. Dignified and smiling, she reigned over the capital, giving help to others when she could—and with brave serenity, receiving aid. During a severe winter, she became patroness of a charity ball to raise money for the needy of Washington. Money she could no longer give. But she gave generously of her time and happy self.

Loyally her friends rallied around her. They asked her to dine and always made her the guest of honor. They kept a vacant place in their carriages for her. Understanding of the spirit of these gifts kept her, who in days of fortune had been lavish with others, from refusal when friends gave her shawls, gloves and trinkets.

On the days when the Widow Madison received, her little house was crowded. Years later, Addie Cutts, wrote her childhood impressions,

The earliest recollection I have of Aunt Madison is associated with a lovely day in June, when arrayed in our best my brother and I accompanied our mother across the little square opposite the White House. We were ushered in by Ralph, the young Negro who had succeeded Paul . . . We were announced as "Young Master and Miss." My mother was "Miss Ellen." This was called Mrs. Madison Levee Day, and everybody came to make a short visit, gossip a little, then give place to newcomers. Aunt stood near the window. I was a curious little girl only eight years of age, and my wide-open eyes saw a sweet-looking lady, tall and erect. She greeted us affectionately and told us to go with Cousin Anna (Anna Payne), who would amuse the young people. I clung to my mother's hand and took observations after the manner of children in general.

Aunt Madison wore a purple velvet dress, cut low and filled in with tulle. Her pretty white throat was encircled by a lace cravat, such as the old-fashioned gentlemen used to wear, tied twice around and fastened with an amethyst pin (which I remember as Aunt afterwards gave my mother the earrings to correspond, and I was sometimes allowed to wear them). Thrown over her shoulders was a lace shawl as in her portrait. I thought her turban was wonderful, as I never saw anyone else wear such a headdress. It was made of some soft silky material and became her.

There were two little bunches of very black curls on either side of the smooth white brow (gray hair was unfashionable); her eyes were blue and laughed when she smiled and greeted the friends who seemed so glad to see her. I wondered at her smooth soft skin, as I was told she was over seventy, which at that time was a great age to me.

The levee was over at four o'clock, when only we of the family remained with Aunt, who was still fresh and smiling . . . she disliked nothing so much as loud talking and laughing.

Her "little Madison" often stood by Dolly's side at her receptions, holding her hand. One day she told the boy that the statue of Jefferson, then in front of the White House, went to dinner whenever it heard the bell ring. "I would sit for hours watching the statue to see it move," Madison Cutts told when he grew older, "until I realized it never heard the bell ring, so Jefferson's statue never went to dinner."

As a younger woman, Dolly Madison had loved to wear the most elaborate gowns, turbans and jewels. Now she repeatedly appeared in the same black velvet dress in which she was painted by Wood. Yet the most popular hostess in Washington was a handsome old lady in a shabby, high-waisted gown, unchanged from the fashion of her days of glory. No one laughed at Mrs. Madison for wearing that dated white satin turban; that velvet dress, old-fashioned in cut, its dinginess brightened by a scarf of gay Roman stripes and a white tulle ruff at her throat.

The yards of tulle around her neck gave softness to her face. Dolly explained gaily, "After seventy the throat becomes a little scraggy." Rouge and powder covered her wrinkles. A row of black curls sewed to her turban hid her gray hair.

In her faded and worn costume, Mrs. Madison went everywhere and was admired by everyone. Two evenings a week she played whist with John Quincy Adams, the British Minister Lord Ashburton, and Senator William Campbell Preston.

Dolly Madison was always charmingly vague about her age. Even the banker, William Corcoran, who helped her with loans, could never get the truth from her.

Knowing how sensitive she was about the matter, Dolly's family celebrated her birthday without commenting on the number of years it marked.

Once her "little Madison" rashly exclaimed, "Why, Aunty, you're no older today than on your last birthday!"

The family was aghast. But his aunt only smiled and said, "So you remember, dear?"

🏵   🏵   🏵   🏵   🏵

Dolly Madison was seventy-four in April, 1842, when she made her first trip to New York City. For one so little traveled, the journey was a great undertaking. But Congress had done nothing about the Madison papers. Dolly was going to New York to offer them to Harper's, the publishing house.

Anna Payne accompanied her aunt on this important mission. On the way they stopped at an inn on 13th Street in Philadelphia for a few weeks. And Dolly's Quaker friends vied with each other in entertaining her.

In New York, a satisfactory business arrangement between Mrs. Madison and Harper's was concluded. One volume of letters, concerning constitutional questions since 1829, was to be published. Exhausted, Dolly returned to Washington.

But on November 21, 1843, Payne wrote of disputes in the settlement with Harper's—the invariable result of all business affairs which the querulous, suspicious man managed for his mother. And again Dolly's financial worries mounted.

There was still the chance that Payne might make a good marriage. During the winter of 1844, Maria S. L'Egare, a sister of Hugh, the Secretary of State, visited Dolly Madison. Both Dolly and her sister, Lucy, hoped "the Colonel" (Payne's military title) would win the popular and musical Maria. But nothing came of it. Perhaps even his mother knew by now that no intelligent woman would accept the man Payne Todd had become.

On February 28, 1844, Mrs. Madison went with President Tyler on a cruise down the Potomac on the warship *Princeton*. To entertain his guests, one of the big guns, ironically called the Peacemaker, was fired. It exploded and killed two Cabinet members, an ex-senator and many others.

Dolly Madison escaped injury. Characteristically, the seventy-six-year-old guest was down in the cabin, listening to the singing of the young people who had gathered around the piano. When the explosion came, Mrs. Madison hurried on deck to help care for the forty dead and wounded. Later, when the boat docked and Dolly reached her home, she found it crowded with anxious friends who had rushed to find out if she was safe.

Her heart full of the suffering she had seen, the Widow Madison could not trust herself for weeks to speak of that terrible afternoon. She felt keenly the injustice that in the newspaper accounts of the disaster not a sailor's name was mentioned as having died or been injured. Quietly she continued out of her meager funds to look after the needs of the seamen and their families, upon whom the catastrophe had brought hardships.

Mourning settled upon Washington, as four men prominent in the government were buried from the White House. The President's sympathy for young Julia Gardiner, whose father, an ex-senator from New York, was one of the *Princeton* victims, resulted in a second marriage for the widowed, fifty-four-year-old Tyler.

The second Mrs. Tyler, a girl of twenty, enjoyed the position of First Lady during the last eight months of Tyler's term. While it lasted, Julia Tyler put on regal trimmings. She received her guests seated on a throne, with her maids of honor beside her. Guests were presented, their names called out in the European fashion.

"What are we coming to?" Dolly Madison sniffed. Julia Tyler was a Northerner and that was against her.

Champagne flowed freely now at the Tyler receptions. And guests danced the polka of which Dolly's shocked nieces had written her. The venerable Widow Madison watched these antics with flushed cheeks. To whirl and hop and glide in the arms of a man like that was scandalous. Such a hilarious dance, she thought, should only be indulged in by man and wife.

At last, in 1844, Congress got around to voting funds for Professor Sam Morse's new invention, the telegraph. On May 24th, Dolly Madison, with a number of important people, gathered in the office of the clerk of the House of Representatives to witness the sending of the first message by telegraph from city to city. The words "What hath God wrought!" sent by Annie Ellsworth, the daughter of the Commissioner of Patents, were received in Baltimore—all of forty miles away—and repeated back to Professor Morse in Washington.

The inventor turned to the elderly lady beside him and asked, "Would you like to send the next telegram, Mrs. Madison? The second ever sent."

Of course, she would! Flushed and excited, Dolly composed a message to the wife of a congressman living in Baltimore. In a few minutes it flashed over the wires, "Message from Mrs. Madison. She sends her love to Mrs. Wethered."

"I'm living in an age of marvels," Dolly thought. "There will never be another one like it."

There was use for Morse's invention the following year. The telegraph spelled out in dots and dashes on a strip of paper the name of James K. Polk as the Democratic nominee to run against the Whig, Henry Clay.

Polk was the first dark-horse candidate for president to

gain that office—a frail, uninspired little man from Tennessee. At his inaugural ball on March 4, 1845, a great crowd thronged the National Theater; and in the midst of the crush, a pick-pocket stole Commodore Elliott's wallet.

"Of all its contents," mourned the Commodore, "I most regret losing a letter from Dolly Madison and a lock of her husband's hair."

The First Lady with whom Mrs. Madison was to be the most intimate was the wife of President Polk, whom she had known since 1835, when Polk became Speaker of the House. Sarah Polk was prim. There was no more dancing at the White House, no more card playing or alcoholic drinks. Mrs. Madison was glad to see the last of the frivolities that had marked the end of the Tyler regime.

❦   ❦   ❦   ❦   ❦

Richard Cutts died on April 7, 1845. The following December, his son, Richard D. Cutts, Junior, and Martha Jefferson Hackley were married in Norfolk, Virginia. On their return to Washington, it was to Aunt Madison's house the young couple came to spend six months.

Everyone of importance came to Dolly's reception for them, the largest of the year in Washington. The bride was a namesake of Martha Randolph; the groom, popular in Maryland and Virginia society. The friends of the two families taxed Mrs. Madison's tiny house to capacity.

Few of the guests realized that the charming and affable hostess was crushed by new sorrows brought upon her by her dissipated son. Payne was growing more and more eccentric. Now he was planning a new home for Dolly at Toddsbirth, spending large sums of money on what he claimed would give her comfort.

The house was to be a towerlike building with a ballroom and state dining room. Around it, Payne Todd intended to erect a strange conglomeration of cottages, including one for his mother. The plan for her cottage had no door. Was the aged occupant supposed to climb in through a window?

Dolly did not live to see the completion of this odd home. Lack of money, fortunately, stopped its construction, as it had the carrying out of Payne's previous scheme of a silk farm.

Dolly's son did other strange things. He made a will and freed, in a grand gesture, the slaves he had long ago gambled away. He tried to run for Congress, but his would-be constituents ignored Todd's campaign. No doubt they realized he was no longer quite sane.

Grown as fat and gross as Falstaff, Payne was despised by his cousins, who had once admired him. He was even feared. Anna Payne wrote, "My childish memories of him do not bear repeating. I was always a little afraid of him . . . don't ask me why."

Later Anna was to learn the basis of her fear of Payne Todd. After Dolly Madison's death, Payne tried to break his mother's will in order to secure the money she had left to her "dear daughter," Anna Payne. But the jury turned down the shameful request. Payne was forced to content himself with half of Dolly's estate and the money realized from the sale of her household effects.

Payne Todd outlived his mother by two years, and then died of typhoid fever in a Washington hotel. Only one friend followed his body to an unmourned grave in the Congressional Cemetery.

During her lifetime, Dolly Madison would never listen to a word of criticism against her son. Courage as well as loyalty was in the apology she once made for him, "Oh, my poor boy! Forgive his eccentricities; his heart is all right."

Only once did Dolly reveal her heartbreak. "Little Anna, don't trouble about it," she soothed her niece, whom she found weeping over some trifle. "There's nothing in this world really worth caring for. . . .

Was Dolly remembering Mammy Amy's words, when as a child she ran to her nurse weeping over the loss of her first piece of jewelry?

"Yes," Mrs. Madison repeated, looking intently out of the window, "believe me, I who have lived so long repeat to you—there's nothing *in this world* really worth caring for."

Since returning to Washington, Dolly Madison had attended the Episcopal Church of St. John on Lafayette Square (known today as the President's Church, because a pew is set apart for the president of the United States). At services she sat with Mrs. Alexander Hamilton, Mrs. William Thornton and Mrs. Tobias Lear.

But Quaker-born Dolly felt the need of a closer association with the church. She spoke to the rector of St. John's, the Reverend Mr. Hawley, of her wish to become a communicant. Anna Payne and her aunt were baptized. Then on July 15, 1845, at seventy-seven, Mrs. Madison was confirmed by Bishop Whittingham of Maryland, with Mrs. John Quincy Adams and her daughters.

❦   ❦   ❦   ❦   ❦

On February 19, 1848, Dolly's only living sister, Lucy Todd, died of apoplexy. How strange that she, the eldest daughter, had survived all the others, Dolly mused. Now she was indeed alone.

One troublesome event followed another. The Widow Madison had a narrow escape from a fire started by incendi-

aries, who placed some of the new Lucifer matches between
the shutters of the hall window and the staircase of her house.
At four o'clock in the morning, as the flames crept towards
her room, a neighbor saw them and awakened Mrs. Madison's
servant, Ralph. He ran upstairs through the smoke to his mistress' room, broke down the door, and found her quietly
sleeping in clouds of smoke.

Ralph seized the aged woman in his arms. He rushed down
the burning staircase, out a side door, and placed her in safety
in a far corner of the garden.

"The trunk!" Dolly cried. "My husband's letters!"

Back into the burning house bounded Ralph. With the fire
crackling around him, he rescued the trunk with its thirty
thousand dollars' worth of treasure—the valuable papers that
were more precious to Madison's widow than her own life.

Ralph had barely placed the little trunk beside her when
the neighbors arrived with buckets of water to put out the
fire. Although extensive damage was done, Dolly, attired in
a black velvet wrapper and nightcap, with feet bare, went
back into the house laughing. Her trunk was safe—the papers
that represented a substantial money value she sorely needed;
but more than money, the memory of her husband's glory.

❦   ❦   ❦   ❦   ❦

By May 31, 1848, Dolly Madison faced what she had
dreaded—an auction of her personal effects. Her old-fashioned
gowns, her famous turbans must be raffled off to raise money
for the bare necessities of living. On the day of the sale, she
calmly made arrangements with the auctioneer.

"You've wealthy friends, Mrs. Madison," the glib, oily-
mannered fellow told her. "The Daniel Websters . . . Lord

Ashburton . . . President Polk . . . . they'll gladly come and buy."

Dolly covered her face with her hands. "No, I won't notify my friends of the sale . . . I refuse . . ." she sobbed. She could take money from Corcoran, the banker, and from John Jacob Astor. But charity from her friends—never!

"Aunty! Aunty!" rang out a joyous voice. Her "little Madison" came bounding into the house and clasped his aunt in his arms.

Young Cutts had run all the way from the Senate chamber to tell her the good news. Congress had voted to purchase the remainder of the Madison letters and state papers, also those of Jefferson and Hamilton, paying twenty-five thousand dollars in each case.

"Oh, thank God!" cried Dolly, kissing her nephew through her tears. She had hoped for thirty thousand dollars. But no matter! She almost pushed the auctioneer out of the house.

Of the twenty-five thousand dollars, five thousand dollars went to pay Dolly's obligations, among them the mortgage to John Jacob Astor. Her debts included these pathetic items: seventy dollars to redeem some silver forks and gravy spoons; twenty dollars to get back a gold chain; two dollars to pay a young nephew for postage on his letters to her (she had asked that an account be kept). Other amounts were for food. Some of the larger loans, such as those to the banker Corcoran, were from rich people "not disposed to crowd."

Relieved of the burden of debt, Dolly Madison went on a little jollification. On July 20, 1848, she took Mrs. Alexander Hamilton, Eliza Lee, and Anthony Morris for a boat ride on the Potomac to Piney Point.

Since Payne Todd had squandered all the money paid Mrs. Madison for her husband's notes on the Constitutional Convention, Congress now protected her by putting the money from their second purchase in trust. Twenty thousand dollars was invested in securities for her. She could dispose of the trust fund in her will. But during her lifetime it was safe from her worthless son.

Payne was furious. He had not written to his mother in a year. But at once he deluged her with threatening letters; swore he would attach the trust, and further harass her. His conduct embittered the last years of Dolly's life and no doubt shortened it.

Congress not only saved Mrs. Madison from poverty, it granted her honors. As the widow of an ex-president, but also for her own sake, it voted her the franking privilege and a seat on the floor of the Senate and in the House, an honor never before granted to a woman.

Coming out of the Senate, she was besieged by autograph seekers, for this was the heyday of the autograph album. Important people were constantly being asked to write a piece of signed verse.

Dolly Madison's autograph was in great demand. The verse signed by her was usually a quotation, as in the album of Mrs. James J. Roosevelt, whose husband was Congressman from New York in 1843. Dolly copied a sonnet to Lafayette, with the added thought: *"The memory of departed virtue is inscribed upon the soul like writing upon adamant."*

"I've a new autograph album, Mrs. Madison," said a friend of Anna's. "I want you to be the first to write in it."

Dolly hugged her. "You little flatterer, if you'll get me a good quill, I'll do it. I can't write with those new steel pens."

Writing of any sort had become increasingly difficult on account of Dolly's failing eyesight. Anna added to her many duties that of answering her aunt's letters. She copied Mrs. Madison's handwriting so closely that a note from her niece satisfied her friends.

In public life Dolly Madison continued to wield great influence. With Mrs. Alexander Hamilton and Mrs. John Quincy Adams, she headed the woman's committee to raise funds for the Washington Monument. James Madison had been the second president of the society organized to build a memorial to George Washington. So it was fitting that his widow should be a guest of honor at the laying of the cornerstone, on the Fourth of July, 1848. Escorted to the platform by General Walter Jones, the dignified, upright figure in black was seated between Mrs. John Quincy Adams and the ninety-one-year-old Mrs. Alexander Hamilton.

That hot July day, as Dolly Madison faced a crowd of some 15,000 people, she only half heard Robert Winthrop's oration, "Lay the cornerstone of a monument which shall adequately bespeak the gratitude of the whole American people. . . ."

It was to have been a 600-foot shaft, rising from a classical temple, containing over the portico a colossal statute of George Washington in a chariot drawn by six horses and driven by Victory. But the contributions had only dribbled in. Would James have been disappointed at the simple white marble obelisk? Dolly wondered.

". . . the illustrious Father of his Country. Build it to the skies; you cannot outreach the loftiness of Washington's principles . . ." Winthrop's voice droned on.

Washington, Adams, Jefferson, Madison, Monroe, John Quincy Adams, Jackson, Van Buren, Harrison, Tyler, Polk . . . how many presidents she had known; how many First Ladies. But whoever was mistress of the White House, Dolly Madison had reigned over the national capital for nearly fifty years—as the wife of the Secretary of State, as Lady President, and as the Dowager Queen. Even in her poverty and old age, she was still a power.

Dreaming over the past, Dolly found it hard to believe. An unknown Quaker maid, she had moved into a world of fantasy and beauty, riches and gaiety. She had met the great and famous of her day—presidents, authors, politicians and generals. She, who was suppressed and poor, had become admired, respected, envied, talked about. That girl isolated on a lonely Virginia plantation, who wondered if anything would ever happen to her, had become Dolly Madison.

It had not been all luck either. She had not had a wealthy, powerful father to help her, as had Mrs. Alexander Hamilton, seated beside her. Dolly Madison had achieved success largely by her own effort. She had once written to her niece, Mary Cutts, "May your fortunes, dearest Mary, be even better than the sybil's prediction. There is one secret, however, she didn't tell you, that is the power we all have in forming our own destinies."

Sitting on the platform that hot July day the Washington monument was dedicated, Dolly thought over a life she had loved. The lock of Washington's hair in her ring reminded her of George Washington and the Revolution.

Then her eyes rested on a tall, gaunt fellow slouched in his seat, listening to Winthrop's speech. As she studied the rugged, homely face of an obscure western congressman named Abraham Lincoln, Dolly Madison did not know that she was looking on down the long years into more American history.

✿ ✿ ✿ ✿ ✿

For James K. Polk's last reception, on February 7, 1849, the White House was ablaze with lights. Hundreds of people, including foreign ministers, judges, senators and congressmen, flocked up the stairs and into the Oval Parlor, now called the Circle Room, to pay their respects to President Polk.

Receiving with him was Sarah Polk, a handsome woman of the Spanish donna type, in her favorite purple velvet, dark ringlets covering her ears. Beside Mrs. Polk stood an elderly lady in white, the venerable Mrs. James Madison.

The music from the Marine Band played in the hall. The great East Room was lighted by hundreds of candles. But there was no dancing, no card playing, and no refreshments at a Polk reception—the proper Sarah Polk saw to that! Couples strolled sedately around the huge room, bowing to the other guests and admiring themselves in the mirrors.

At midnight the Marine Band broke into the President's March. Everyone stopped promenading and turned expectantly toward the door. In came small, long-haired James Polk with Mrs. Madison on his arm.

Slowly, majestically, the President made a tour of the crowded East Room. Dolly wore white satin and a remarkable turban bedecked with white fringe. She was eighty-one, but in her low-cut gown her shoulders were still firm and white. As she passed before the bowing throng on the arm of the president of the United States, her manner was that of a gracious queen. For those brief moments she was young again . . . this was James Madison beside her . . . that was Aaron Burr smiling at her from the crowd . . . and she was back in her old home as the First Lady, the toast of Washington—Queen Dolly.

Did those White House guests suspect as they bowed her out later that night, that it was for the last time? This triumphant procession marked Dolly's final public appearance and appropriately brought her life to a close. Six months later, at ten-thirty at night, on July 12, 1849, as Anna read to her from the Gospel of St. John, Mrs. Madison fell into a coma. Two days later, she died and was laid to rest beside

James Madison at Montpellier.

But to her friends, the memory of Dolly Madison was mirrored in her regal appearance on that last White House night. She had entered Washington society on the arm of Jefferson; she was leaving it on the arm of Polk. Her reign spanned nearly half a century and covered the terms of eleven presidents.

At the White House door that evening, Dolly met Mrs. Lee, also over eighty. "Dear Eliza . . ." The Widow Madison linked her arm through that of her old friend, who had been bridesmaid when Dolly married John Todd. Eliza had also been present that night when Aaron Burr first brought shy James Madison to call. From Harewood, Dolly had written to Eliza for the last time as the Widow Todd and for the first time as Mrs. James Madison.

Anthony Morris, a serene old gentleman, his flaxen hair white, but his blue eyes still sparkling behind his spectacles, joined Eliza and Dolly as they were leaving.

"May I take you young girls home?" he asked gaily.

Dolly Madison smiled at her "early and most faithful friend." Anthony, too, had been part of the Todd wedding party. He had loved the bride and watched over her tenderly for nearly sixty years.

On Anthony Morris' arm, Dolly started out to his carriage. She lifted her turbaned head with the proud gesture of old. Her tired body was very erect. "Come, Eliza," she said.

Behind her the chatter of voices grew fainter. But the Marine Band broke into a stirring martial strain as Dolly Madison walked down the stairs and out into the night.

To the President of the United States

I received, Sir in due time the communication from Congress, made more grateful to me by the kind expression of your sympathy, which accompanied it)

The high and just estimation of my Husband by my countrymen and friends, and their generous participation in the sorrow, occasioned by our irretrievable loss, expressed through its supreme authority and otherwise is the only solace of which my heart is susceptible, on the departure of him who had never lost sight of that consistency, symmetry and beauty of character in all its parts which rendered his transcendant as a whole, and worthy of the best aspirations

I am now preparing to execute the trust his confidence reposed in me — that of placing before Congress and the world, what his pen had prepared for their use, and with the importance of this Legacy, I am deeply impressed

With great respect &c
D. P. Madison

Bibliography

Among the books used for research were:

Bradford, Gamaliel. Wives. New York and London, Harper & Brothers, 1925.

Clark, Allen Culling. Life and Letters of Dolly Madison. Washington, D. C., W. F. Roberts Co., 1914.

Cutts, Lucia Beverly (Mrs. Madison's grandniece) edited by. Memoirs and Letters of Dolly Madison, wife of James Madison, President of the United States. Boston, Houghton Mifflin & Company, 1886.

Dean, Elizabeth Lippincott. Dolly Madison, the Nation's Hostess. Boston, Lothrop, Lee & Shepard Co., 1928.

Goodwin, Maud Wilder. Dolly Madison. New York and London, Charles Scribner's Sons, 1896.

Minnigerode, Meade. Some American Ladies. New York and London, G. P. Putnam's Sons, 1926.

Prindiville, Kathleen. First Ladies. New York and London, The Macmillan Company, 1940.

Smith, Margaret Bayard. The First Forty Years of Washington Society, edited by Gaillard Hunt. New York and London, Charles Scribner's Sons, 1906.

Adams, James Truslow. The Living Jefferson. New York and London, Charles Scribner's Sons, 1941.

Rives, William C. Life and Times of James Madison. Boston, Little, Brown, 1868.

Carroll, Mary Tarver. The Man Who Would Not Wait—The Story of Aaron Burr. New York and Toronto, Longmans, Green & Company, 1941.

Fox, Frances Margaret. Quakers Courageous. Boston, Lothrop, Lee & Shepard, 1941.

Lewis, Ethel. The White House. New York, Dodd, Mead and Company, 1937.

Hunt, Gaillard. Life in America One Hundred Years Ago. New York and London, Harper & Brothers, 1914.

Humphrey, Grace. Women in American History. Dolly Madison. Indianapolis and New York, Bobbs-Merrill Company, 1919.

Gay, Sydney Howard. James Madison. American Statesmen Series. Boston and New York, Houghton Mifflin & Company, 1899.

Colver, Anne. Theodosia: Daughter of Aaron Burr. New York and Toronto, Farrar & Rinehart, Inc., 1941.

Stevens, William O. Washington: The Cinderella City. New York, Dodd, Mead and Company, 1943.

Brant, Irving. James Madison: The Virginia Revolutionist, 1751-1780. Indianapolis and New York, Bobbs-Merrill Company, 1941.

Wandell, Samuel H., and Minnigerode, Meade. Aaron Burr. 2 volumes. New York and London, G. P. Putnam's Sons, 1927.

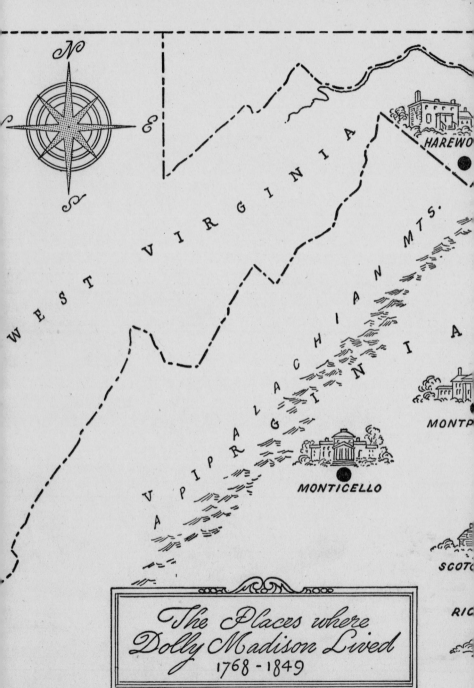

PENN

N
E
S

WEST VIRGINIA

APPALACHIAN MTS.

VIRGINIA

HAREWO

MONTP

MONTICELLO

SCOTO

RIC

The Places where
Dolly Madison Lived
1768 - 1849